Ayrshire Folk

Ayrshire Folk

Glimpses of Bygone Lives

John Kellie

carn

© John Kellie, 2015.
First Published in Great Britain, 2015.

ISBN - 978 0 9567550 8 7

Published by Carn Publishing,
Lochnoran House,
Auchinleck,
Ayrshire, KA18 3JW.

www.carnpublishing.com

Printed by Bell & Bain Ltd,
Glasgow, G46 7UQ.

JOHN KELLIE

John Kellie was born in Ayrshire and educated at Pinmore, Kilmarnock and Glasgow. An enthusiastic outdoorsman and freelance writer, over the years his work has found its way into a variety of magazines on both sides of the Atlantic, as well as broadsheet and tabloid newspapers. He taught secondary school English for the best part of three decades, both in Scotland and Canada, until a brush with malaria in the jungles of New Guinea prompted a rethink and he is now writing and travelling full-time. His first book, *Ayrshire Echoes,* was published by Carn in 2013.

To the memory of my maternal grandparents,
John and Elizabeth Bryson of Orchard Street, Galston.

Contents

Illustrations

Illustrations by the author, unless otherwise credited

Introduction

Close to the summit of the wild hill-road linking the village of Straiton with Bargrennan in Galloway, there stands a little-known, mysterious monument. Besieged by peaty pools and mossy hummocks, a square, grey stone protrudes from the moor whose eastern face is engraved with the following simple message: *Agnes Hannah Died Here*. No explanation. No details. No date.

A good many years ago, when I first learned of the memorial's existence, I automatically assumed that discovering who Agnes Hannah was and finding out what circumstances had led to her death would be a relatively straightforward matter. It turned out that I was wrong. Despite exhaustive searching, all I was able to unearth in print was a few brief references to the tragedy and this, coupled with snippets of information that I managed to glean from local people, provided me with the barest of outlines of the dead woman's story. Agnes Hannah, it emerged, had been a midwife - perhaps a district nurse - who found herself caught in a snowstorm on an exposed section of the hill-road while making for the shepherd's house at Black Row to attend a confinement. She attempted to take shelter in the lee of a shooting-butt but perished nonetheless. And that was the point where the trail went cold. No-one, it seemed, could tell me any more - not, crucially, the date of Agnes's death nor any clue as to where she might be buried. The present memorial, I learned, had been put in place during the 1960s or '70s as a replacement for an older stone, seen in living memory but which had inexplicably vanished and whose inscription is believed - tantalisingly - to have recorded the date when Agnes lost her life in the snow.

How easily we forget! The case of Agnes Hannah may be an extreme one but, so saying, while carrying out my research for this book I was repeatedly struck by just how much of Ayrshire's past has been forgotten, or is in grave danger of being forgotten. Granted, the county's most illustrious figures are relatively well catered for with books relating to the life and works of Robert Burns occupying a considerable expanse of library shelf-space, with William Wallace and Robert the Bruce following on behind, each with a respectable number of column-inches to his credit. But of the lives of ordinary people a good deal less is to be found - how they lived and how they died; their successes and shortcomings, their triumphs and tragedies; those defining moments when some rose up to greatness while others turned aside from the straight and narrow to follow a less creditable path. Poet or ploughman, tinker or pedlar, man of the cloth or man of the road - ordinary people's lives meant just as much to them as our own do to us and through the stories that they left behind they enable us to connect with the past.

With this in mind, my aim in *Ayrshire Folk* has been to focus principally on men and women of modest means, the ups and downs of whose lives are no less valid than the experiences of the privileged few - and probably a good deal more interesting. For the most part their stories are verifiably true but where I have had to fall back on oral history and legend I have endeavoured to acknowledge this in the text. I am, however, in a position to vouch personally for the truth of the final chapter since (as in my previous collection of stories, *Ayrshire Echoes*) I have taken the liberty of concluding the book with a tale passed down through my own family.

During the course of my research I have been fortunate in receiving a great deal of encouragement and assistance but the following people's individual contributions merit particular mention - Munro Clark, Smyrton; Brenda Clarkson, Kilmarnock; Alisdair Cochrane, Prestwick; Neil Dickson, Troon; Bobby Grierson, Cumnock; Robin Heaney, Coylton; John McFedries, Kilmarnock; Glenys McMillan, Prestwick; Tom Murray, Newmilns; Ken Wood, Mauchline; and Dougie & Jean Wyllie, Pinmore. I would also wish to thank the staff of the Burns Monument Centre, Kilmarnock; North Ayrshire Heritage Centre, Saltcoats; Stewartry Museum,

Kirkcudbright; and, especially, the Scottish and Local History Department of the Carnegie Library, Ayr.

Finally, I would like to express my enormous debt of gratitude to my friends, Hugh Sloan of Girvan for his unfailing generosity in imparting a lifetime of country wisdom and Frances Smith of Cumnock without whose keen eye and unflagging interest this book would undoubtedly have been much the poorer.

As for the story behind Agnes Hannah's memorial stone, well, I haven't given up the search just yet…

LIFE AS IT WAS

1 The Barr Castle Ball Game

Situated on a rocky knoll above the Burn Anne, Galston's oldest building, the Barr Castle, has withstood the rigours of a tempestuous climate for more than four centuries now, probably on the self-same spot that an ancient predecessor once occupied. Locally the story is told of how William Wallace was once forced to take refuge within this older building, successfully eluding his pursuers only when he exited via an upstairs window and clambered down the branches of a conveniently-located tree. Regrettably the tree in question is no longer *in situ*, and the fact that not a shred of evidence exists for Wallace's leafy escapade has done little to diminish the story's appeal.

A second legend connects Scotland's hero with the Barr Castle, sadly no easier to verify than the first, but which tells of how his men were in the habit of playing a fairly rumbustious form of handball against the castle walls as a means, it is said, of maintaining their fitness for battle. On the face of it the story might seem a little fanciful perhaps, but the possibility, however remote, that a game played by medieval soldiery might have triggered a sporting tradition which continued unbroken until well into the twentieth century is undoubtedly a tantalising one.

Other theories have, of course, been proposed. One suggestion is that handball was introduced into Ayrshire by Irish migrant workers, with evidence cited that a similar game was prevalent in the men's home country, albeit played under different rules. Certainly the sport appears to have grown in popularity just at the time when the Irvine valley weaving industry was absorbing a large number of incomers, and by the time that a local poet, John Wright, was writing in the 1820s handball was apparently firmly embedded in Galston's sporting calendar. In a footnote to one of his poems, Wright observed that 'handball is, and has long been, a favourite amusement with the villagers of Galston.' The poet himself was a noted competitor.

A popular form of recreation on fine summer evenings, handball matches traditionally took place at the 'Baur Ailley' - a narrow passageway adjacent to the Barr Castle's north-facing wall where today a small, well-tended garden occupies the space. The width of the playing-area was defined by vertical lines, chalked on the castle wall, but the extent of the court to the rear remained undefined. To mark the minimum height for an admissible shot a horizontal board was secured to the wall two feet or so above ground-level. For many years 'the Barr Tree' stood at a strategic corner of the court - a descendant perhaps of Wallace's supposed saviour - and was regularly used by the home-side to tactical effect. Eventually, however, the old tree was removed - felled, so it is said, during the 1880s.

The rules for handball were clearly laid out. A team would normally consist of three players, though doubles and singles matches also took place on occasion. Self-evidently, in a team of three, the player on the right (known as 'the foot player') required to be skilled in the use of his right hand; while his counterpart on the left ('the head player') would by preference be a left-hander. It was, of course, crucial that the centre player be equally proficient with both hands. Certain standards had to be adhered to. Prominently-displayed on the castle wall, a notice gave players a categorical warning - 'If Swearing, No Playing' - and responsibility for upholding this and other rules was assigned to an umpire, often a veteran handball player himself, whose job it was also to keep tabs on the score.

Before a match could get off the ground, a coin was tossed in order to decide on which team would be placed closest to the castle wall - the position known as 'hauns in' - and thereby gain the advantage of serving first. The team's middle player would then serve by striking the ball against the castle wall and it was up to opposing team members (who were 'hauns oot') to attempt to return the rebounding ball with no more than a single bounce permitted. A point was awarded to whichever team succeeded in playing an unreturnable shot, known as a 'clocker'. Service changed hands whenever the team currently serving dropped a point at which time the competing teams would reverse their respective positions on the court. The first team to amass a score of 35 points was declared the victor.

The great majority of handball players were men of modest means and, though in time the practice grew up for teams to distinguish themselves by colour, no expensive, specialised clothing for the sport was required, simply loose-fitting garments which allowed maximum freedom of movement. In the early days the majority of players risked a stubbed toe by competing barefoot, and bruising on the hands remained an ever-present hazard. The actual ball was custom-made locally from rubber, enclosed within an outer casing of pigskin (sourced from a nearby piggery) and containing at its core a small pebble. As the name of the sport implies, no racquet was needed, the cupped palm of the hand being sufficient to propel the ball.

As the sport grew in popularity a number of regular fixtures became established. During the first half of the nineteenth century an annual match took place between Galston and its near neighbour, Newmilns, whose players trained for the occasion on a practice-court of their own. For whatever reason, this clash of local rivals petered out during the 1860s, a minor setback to handball locally perhaps but by no means sufficient to jeopardise the sport's continued success. Following the 1888 season, when slippery underfoot conditions had threatened to disrupt play, the base of the court at the Barr Castle was coated the following year with a smooth concrete base and the adjacent castle wall similarly rendered part-way up. Wooden stands were erected for the convenience of spectators. Such was the sport's popularity by the early years of the twentieth century that it was said that in summertime handballers could be found practising at virtually any vacant gable-end in Galston. If sufficiently talented, it was perfectly feasible for an aspiring young player to rise from the juvenile to the junior division, then ultimately through the ranks to senior level.

Like other sports, handball built up a considerable fan base with the result that certain local competitors developed what amounted to minor celebrity status. One such was James Sharpe - nicknamed 'Clockie' - a virtuoso of the game whose speciality was to direct the ball into the angle formed between the Barr Tree and an adjacent wall - a spot which in time became known as 'Clockie's Corner' - thus making the rebound extremely hard to predict. An instance is on record, however, when Clockie appeared rather less in control of the situation. Charged with responsibility for soliciting a contribution to club funds from local luminary, the Earl of Loudoun, he was advised that it was customary to address the noble peer as 'My Lord'. But when the two men came face to face, the occasion, it seems, proved too much for him. 'Yer Lord God Almightyship,' Clockie was heard to blurt out, 'I'm here to ask for a donation to the Handball Club.'

Barr Castle, Galston

Such artless civility must surely have made a refusal well-nigh impossible.

The Earl of Loudoun wasn't the only local bigwig to support the sport. Though still predominantly a working-class pastime, a number of wealthier local citizens chipped in, for the first time putting up prizes for local players. An army man, William McGill, donated two sets of belts, to be competed for annually by juniors and seniors respectively, each winner's belt finished with an engraved silver plate which read as follows: 'Presented by Lieut. William McGill, 70th Regt., to the Juvenile/Senior Handball players of Galston, to be competed for annually - August, 1859.' For the first time in 1880, teams competed for The Barr Castle Handball Challenge Cup, an elegant silver trophy that proved to be much sought after by handballers over the next half-century. It was not until 1921 that winners' badges made their first appearance, provided by a local coal-owner and kirk elder, John Littlejohn, who in another philanthropic gesture also bequeathed to Galston Parish Church stained-glass windows to commemorate those members who had fallen during the First World War. James Hendrie, a local solicitor, put up a silver medal to be awarded to the best singles player.

The high point in the handballing calendar each year was Glasgow Fair Saturday when excited crowds of spectators would converge on the Barr Castle from far and wide to watch teams compete for the coveted Challenge Cup, as well as for the Mull Cup, a trophy for local factory workers. After defeating Paisley in 1921 and seeing off a challenge from Carfin in Lanarkshire sometime later, members of the Galston Club felt justified in claiming for themselves the title, 'Handball Champions of the World.' Sadly, with the benefit of hindsight, it looks ominously like a case of pride before a fall. Following on from these glory days of handball during which the sport was at its pinnacle, things could only go downhill.

It seemed that destiny had decreed that within a few short years the sport of handball would slip into an irreversible decline. The Glasgow Fair Saturday of 1939 was the last occasion when teams lined up to compete for the Challenge Cup. So, what went wrong? How could such a popular, thriving institution vanish virtually overnight from the local sporting calendar? Well, even prior to 1939 the rise in popularity of an alternative ball-game had been noted, this sport played with the feet rather than the hands and conducted nationwide on a far more commercial basis. Around the same time improvements in the public transport system had made travel a good deal easier than in the past, and the inhabitants of the Irvine valley were no longer restricted to what their immediate area had to offer. But probably the final straw for handball was the outbreak in 1939 of the Second World War when a significant proportion of the community's young men - every one a potential handball player - were conscripted into the armed forces, by no means all of whom would return to the valley once hostilities ceased. On summer evenings the streets of post-war Galston no longer rang with the eager cries of handballers, and the time would come - sooner, perhaps, than anyone might reasonably have predicted - when their traditions and sporting achievements were erased almost entirely from local memory.

2 The Colm's Day Fair

The annual Colm's Day festivities at Largs are believed to have a very ancient origin, dating back perhaps as far as the time of St Columba. Arriving in western Scotland from his native Donegal in the sixth century AD, Columba established his religious community on the isle of Iona before spreading his acolytes far and wide in an effort to convert the people of the land to Christianity. Today, fourteen centuries on, any connection that the wandering saint might have had with the Ayrshire coast is uncertain but it is entirely feasible that, sailing from Iona in their currachs, his followers might well have put ashore at Largs in the capacity of missionaries. It certainly isn't too great a leap to get from *Columba* to *Colm*.

Colm's Day fell each year on the first Tuesday after 12 June, a curious arrangement which is likely to have resulted from a change in the dating system whereby eleven days were excised from the old Celtic calendar. Perhaps the first Tuesday of the month was the original - more logical - date for the fair, though an alternative theory holds that the celebration formerly took place on the occasion of St Columba's birthday. Spanning three days, if the event was sacred in its early origins, then clearly somewhere down the line it took a distinctly more worldly turn when it developed into a lively forum for commerce, dedicated in large measure to the buying and selling of livestock in addition to acting as a hiring fair for those in search of new employment.

In a watercolour painting of the Colm's Day sales a little-known nineteenth-century artist, Samuel Parbler, depicts a genteel assemblage of well-dressed prospective buyers who are gathered around a show-ring in which plump, red-and-white cattle are being rather listlessly exhibited, the entire scene set against a stylised rural backcloth of tidy fields, gentle hills and prosperous-looking dwellings. The reality, we might suspect, was probably a good deal more boisterous as a motley ragbag of visitors converged on the douce seaside town 'frae a' the airts' and took up residence for the duration of the fair. The Colm's Day sales were noted in particular as an opportunity for the local populace to trade with their Highland neighbours and it is on record that at one time the people of Largs might have seen their bay thronging with more than 100 Highland vessels, newly arrived from the sea-lochs of Argyll and each bearing a cargo of livestock that was destined for the sales. Once within reach of the shore, however, the visitors' cattle were unceremoniously tipped overboard and expected to swim for their lives, though horses were treated a little more decorously, it is said, when they were afforded the luxury of a gangway. An array of Highland tents mushroomed along the shoreline and the sound of Gaelic voices was commonplace in the town streets at this time. In Samuel Parbler's alternative vision of the sales, a rather stiff calmness reigns and there is no-one to be seen who might readily be identifiable as a visitor from the Highlands.

The Colm's Day sales continued throughout the nineteenth century and in 1890 the local newspaper, *The Largs and Millport Weekly News*, reported the highest turnout of livestock for a good many years as some 40 or so bawling cattle and upwards of 200 skittish horses were lined up along Gallowgate Street to be viewed by dealers from as far afield as Glasgow and Paisley in the north and Maybole and Girvan in the south. Trading in lambs was reported to be lively, the creatures in question not being present but instead bought 'blind' by dealers who used their knowledge of the breed and local conditions to agree on a price. Of the animals brought forward for sale, calving cows fetched from £12 to £18, bull stirks from £4 to £8, but the best price of the day - £70 - was obtained for a particularly fine horse.

But, for all its apparent success, the fact was the Colm's Day sales had been in decline for many years - perhaps, it has even been suggested, since as far back as the late eighteenth century. The number of animals put up for sale had steadily dwindled and, by the time of the 1937 fair, the *Weekly News* reported that a mere six horses and two cows had changed hands, these latter the first cattle to be brought to the fair for more than a decade. For a time now, the newspaper added, only one single horse-trader had continued to attend the event: John Crawford of Beith, a farmer who was effectively the last of his breed. The blunt truth was that the Colm's Day Fair had outlived its usefulness. Up and down the land improved communications had largely done away with the need for large-scale, showpiece fairs and regular markets had become established which were accessible to the majority of the Scottish population. Manufactured goods had for some considerable time been ferried into the most remote Highland communities, doing away with the need for an annual pilgrimage to the south. By the early part of the twentieth century, the pageantry and colour of the Colm's Day sales had all but vanished.

But that was only part of the story. Colm's Day had always had more than one string to its bow and, as time went on, people flocked increasingly to the fair for amusement and recreation. On the evening beforehand, show-folk would routinely turn up in their caravans and, working through the night, have their stalls in place by the following morning. In June 1890 the *Weekly News* reported that, in addition to normal passenger services, a special train had operated on fair-day specifically to transport day-trippers to Largs from Kilbirnie, Beith, Dalry and Ardrossan while a small armada of steamers made repeated runs throughout the day, ferrying passengers from Millport, Rothesay and Wemyss Bay.

Arriving visitors found the principal streets of the town transformed into a funfair, lined on both sides with tents, booths and barrows which tempted them to part with a few coins in exchange for sweets, nuts, ice-cream and all manner of gewgaws. Shooting-galleries, swings and merry-go-rounds had sprung into action, operating to the jolly musical accompaniment of hand-cranked barrel organs. Vying for your attention, a lady juggler competed with a man whose unusual talent was an ability to cut out paper shapes behind his back. Magicians performed sleight-of-hand card-tricks while, in a dramatic scene, a fire eater followed up his main act by apparently consuming a full-length bayonet. 'Italian-looking' women worked the crowds whose pet birds would - for a fee - select from a pack the precise card whose written message, you were assured, was the key to unlocking your future. A considerable expanse of the pavement had been covered with the chalked drawings of a street artist.

In exchange for a few coppers, you might choose between seeing a miniature circus, operating with a handful of performers and a single pony, and a much-vaunted exhibition of 'mesmerism' - a practice akin to hypnotism, highly fashionable in Victorian times. Hailing all comers, the operator of a boxing-booth was keen for your attention, the man's appearance distinctly battle-weary, or you might be tempted by the more gentle prospect of a miniature yacht race, due to take place imminently in a large water-tank. All around, music was provided by buskers 'from various corners of Europe and beyond', some of them sporting an exotic pet monkey to catch the eye of passers-by. Native bagpipers found themselves in competition with virtuosi of the accordion, clarinet, dulcimer, harp, organ, whistle and even an instrument described as the Italian bagpipes. To the accompaniment of a hurdy-gurdy, an operatic singer offered up a falsetto rendition of a Verdi aria while, at the other end of the spectrum, an infirm man - an old soldier perhaps - performed his modest repertoire of hymn-tunes. Every time he received a donation, the man's dog was trained to express its appreciation by spinning around twice in a circle. On a similar spiritual theme, a band of 'Faith Pilgrims' from Rothesay staged a series of musical services which proved popular with visitors and locals alike. A fun-filled kaleidoscope, you might imagine that the Colm's Day Fair offered something for everyone, its chaotic array of sights and sounds a much-needed antidote to the humdrum routines of everyday life.

Well, not quite everyone. *The Weekly News'* correspondent, for one, found ample opportunity to scoff, sneering repeatedly about 'unwashed' show-folk who were 'as ill-looking, and as dirty as ever [he] saw at the Fair'. He continued in a similar vein, offering the opinion that 'many foreigners have a rooted aversion to soap' but - lest we detect a trace of prejudice -

Largs Main Street (Dane Love Collection)

24

immediately added that 'the home-bred show-folk don't find much use for that article either'. (What sanitary facilities might have been on hand, he fails to mention.) Relentlessly negative, he accused the Scottish bagpipers of being 'about the most disreputable people in the whole Fair' before rounding on 'the worst class of showmen' who were, he claimed, too drunk to continue working after 10 p.m. Based on 'those evidences of drunkenness and other vices' which he claimed to have witnessed on the streets, he argued unilaterally that it was 'desirable that our annual fair should be abolished'.

Strangely, the Police Court records for that week painted a rather different picture. John Young, of no fixed abode, pled guilty to a charge of breach of the peace and was fined ten shillings and sixpence (just over 50p) with the alternative of seven days' imprisonment. Apprehended at Beith, Jane and James McGhee faced the prospect of a week in jail when they were convicted of making off with a sum of money and various other items from their lodgings in New Street, Largs. It was noted that both James and Jane appeared relieved at the leniency of their sentence. All in all, a fair-minded observer might conclude that neither of the two cases was perhaps of the utmost gravity.

As it happened, the proposal made by our crusty late-Victorian reporter was not acted upon, the fair was permitted to continue, and almost half a century later, in the years leading up to the Second World War, visitors were still flocking in considerable numbers to join in the festivities. But much of the fair's distinctiveness had been lost. The old trade in livestock had dwindled to virtually nothing and it wasn't long before the funfair itself showed signs of buckling in the face of more up-to-date competition. Inescapably, the glory days of the Colm's Day Fair had slipped into the past and the sight of shaggy Highland cattle, emerging dripping from the waves, was a spectacle never likely to be repeated.

3 Dingin' Doon the Doo

The roots of Kilwinning's annual archery contest date back to a more barbarous age when the victim of various bloodthirsty pastimes was a defenceless living bird. By no means confined to Ayrshire, variations on the sport of 'cock throwing' were once fairly widespread and frequently formed part of the revelries associated with Shrove Tuesday when an unfortunate fowl would be secured, often on top of a pole, before an array of contestants who proceeded to pelt the hapless creature with whatever missiles came to hand. The hero of the day was he who finally hurled the object that brought the cock's suffering to an end. Thankfully the senseless cruelty of the practice came in time to be recognised and the earliest records of the Ancient Society of Kilwinning Archers indicate that, by the latter part of the seventeenth century, carved wooden replicas had taken the place of live birds.

Believed to be rooted in training for siege warfare, Kilwinning's archery tradition dates back to the late fifteenth century when local bowmen are known to have competed for the title, 'Captain of the Papingo'. Deriving from Old French, the term papingo referred to the figure of a parrot, familiar in heraldry, but also came to be applied to the decorated wooden models, complete with detachable outstretched wings, which replaced the living birds of former times. In the opening chapters of his novel, *Old Mortality*, Sir Walter Scott gives a highly-romanticised account of a papingo shoot - or 'popinjay', as he chooses to call it - which he places in Clydesdale in 1679. Though the sport was traditionally practised using bow and arrow, Scott's seventeenth-century protagonists had by then adopted firearms with which they shot at 'the figure of a bird, decked with party-coloured feathers, so as to resemble a popinjay or parrot.' In what the novelist admits to be another 'innovation on the established practice', the gallant Henry Morton scooped first prize by dramatically striking the wooden bird while thundering by on the back of a galloping horse. Proclaimed 'Captain of the Popinjay', Morton was expected to foot the bill for the rest of the day's entertainment and refreshments.

In fact Scott's romantic vision doesn't diverge too widely from historical reality though the archers of Kilwinning retained their loyalty to the bow much longer than the characters in *Old Mortality*. Normally preparations for the town's annual Papingo Shoot got underway some months in advance of the contest itself, generally in early March, when the town beadle took to the streets to the accompaniment of fife and drum. Bearing aloft a tall Lochaber axe - a species of halberd - on which the papingo was conspicuously placed, he halted at intervals throughout the town to announce that the archery season was now open. Continuing to the abbey tower, he climbed to its airy summit in order to affix the wooden papingo to a twelve-foot pole which he then placed so as to project horizontally outwards from a specially-placed slot in the parapet, 120 feet up. Up until the day of the official Papingo Shoot, this wooden bird would remain *in situ*, enabling would-be competitors to undertake practice at any time they chose - with the exception of Sundays. Sometimes, we are told, small groups of friends might meet in the shadow of the abbey tower to compete for a small prize, perhaps a joint of veal or mutton, and retire once the honours were settled to an evening of socialising with their wives, friends and families.

Procedures for the actual contest were well established. With one foot placed on the bottom step of the tower, competitors took turns at shooting upwards from the front of the building - an act which several headstones in the surrounding burial ground can attest to, having been pitted in bygone days by the steel tips of descending arrows. The archer who first succeeded in *dingin' doon the doo* - that is, knocking the 'pigeon' off its perch - was adjudged the winner and accorded the title 'Captain of the Papingo' for the forthcoming year. Traditionally the victor's spoils consisted of a colourful sash of Persian taffeta, known as a *benn*, which he wore over the shoulder and was entitled to keep on condition that he came up with a suitable replacement for his successor in twelve months' time. Thus the Papingo Shoot continued for two centuries or more until 1688 when, concerned about a recent dip in interest, the laird of Blair Castle, William Blair, sought to reinvigorate the old tradition by heading a committee which drew up rules and regulations for Kilwinning's Society of Archers and persuading new and influential members to join. His efforts met with some success, it seems, and from that year on an unbroken record of the Society's activities was maintained.

A significant event in the Archers' history took place in 1724 when David Muir, a local merchant and factor to the 9th Earl of Eglinton, presented as a prize an elegant silver arrow, a version of which forms to this day the centrepiece of the Captain's trophy. As it turned out, Muir himself took first prize that year, leaving him little option but to donate a second arrow to be competed for the following year. A decision was taken that in future each prize-winner would be entitled to retain the coveted Silver Arrow for one year only before attaching to it a medal inscribed with his name and the date of his victory and returning it to the Society. It was, however, agreed that the trophy would become the property of any archer who succeeded in winning the competition six years in a row, provided that he pay to the Society the sum of £5 - a feat which has still to be accomplished. It has been suggested that some of David Muir's business dealings may have been a little shady but his final act on this earth was unquestionably philanthropic. Dying in his seventies in 1741, Muir intimated in the terms of his will that his farm of Woodgreen, immediately north of Kilwinning, and the income deriving therefrom should be put to use for the benefit of the poor.

Things took a bit of a downturn during the opening years of the nineteenth century when the Society of Archers experienced a number of setbacks. The tower used for the Papingo Shoot, one of two surviving from Kilwinning's medieval abbey, was struck by lightning in 1805 and went on to suffer a partial collapse four years later - the sole fatality believed to have been an unfortunate pig - but the last straw came in 1814 when the entire structure had to be demolished. With surprising rapidity, however, a replacement tower was designed, commissioned and erected, all within a timescale of little more than two years. Over 100 feet in height and complete with four clock-faces and two bells, the replacement tower was funded by public subscription and completed for what, by today's standards, sounds like the remarkably modest sum of £1,590, eleven shillings and tenpence precisely.

The decades that followed saw the Society of Archers move distinctly upmarket when, in addition to developing an extensive bureaucracy of grandly-titled office-bearers, it adopted as its patron no less a personage than Prince Albert of Saxe-Coburg, Prince Consort and the husband of Queen Victoria. In line with its recently drawn-up dress code, members

Kilwinning Abbey, location of Papingo shoot

were expected to wear 'a double-breasted green long-coat, lined with white silk', secured by 'a broad black morocco belt with brass buckle'. In place of gloves, 'gauntlets of white leather' were the garments of choice. It is hardly likely that the considerable costs involved would have caused many worries for the Society's Lieutenant-General in 1844 - Archibald Montgomerie, 13th Earl of Eglinton - whose medieval-styled extravaganza at Eglinton Castle five years earlier had set him back a cool £40,000. The Earl's London-based step-brother, Charles Lamb (for the purposes of the infamous tournament, the 'Knight of the White Rose') held the position of Major-General and, among the Society's honorary members, no fewer than 27 were ladies. In another clear departure from tradition, a resolution was passed to the effect that the Papingo Shoot should henceforth take place on 26 August which, by no coincidence whatsoever, happened to be the birthday of HRH Prince Albert. Astonishingly, contenders for the Captain's trophy were granted the right to compete by proxy, nominating - and presumably paying - a highly-skilled representative to shoot on their behalf. Increasingly socially stratified, membership of the Society was divided into three discrete groupings - Boys, Tradesmen and Gentlemen - each of which had its own exclusive competition. Evidently the Ancient Society had moved some considerable distance from its early warlike origins.

An evocative memoir of the Boys' Papingo was penned in the late 1850s by a Kilwinning man, James Manson. The son of a local tailor, Manson had followed in his father's footsteps until the age of nineteen when, in a dramatic change of direction, he made the switch to journalism when he was appointed sub-editor and music critic of the *Glasgow Herald*. Nothing if not versatile, during Manson's lifetime he published a body of original verse as well as editing a comprehensive two-volume anthology of international melodies which included, as it happened, a strathspey by James Boick entitled The *Kilwinning Archers*, as well as showcasing Manson's own tune, *The Kilwinning Papingo Waltz*. In his account of the archery contest and its associated ceremonial, the author looks back to the event as he remembers it more than thirty years previously.

The specific Boys' Papingo recalled by Manson took place at a time when the reigning Captain was Alexander McGown of Smithstone House, immediately north of Kilwinning. The author sets the scene on a late-May morning as, shortly after daybreak, troupes of barefoot servant girls converged on the house, bearing gifts of food from farmers throughout the district who, according to Manson, 'like[d] to see the festival kept up.' The farmers' offerings of curds and cream, cakes, oatmeal and cheese were laid out on 'snow-white covered tables' which had been set out on the front lawn in anticipation of the arrival of the boy archers. While preparations for breakfast were underway, the sound of a band became audible, growing steadily louder as it drew near. Presently the town beadle strode into view, fronting a long procession of adults and children and carrying on the point of his Lochaber axe a freshly-painted papingo, decorated with a festive array of colourful ribbons. Behind him came the band, followed in turn by the boy archers themselves who marched three abreast and were attended by a train of young girls, dressed up for the occasion and decked in flowers and ribbons.

It is not hard to imagine the chatter, excitement and laughter as the entire company, adults and children alike, settled down to a 'hearty and merry' breakfast on the lawn. Once the meal was over, the tables and benches were drawn to one side and country dancing quickly ensued with music courtesy of the town band as well as a smaller, three-man operation on fiddles and bass whom Manson refers to as 'the Wylies of Kilwinning'. Jigs, strathspeys and reels followed quickly one after another until the jollifications were interrupted in the early afternoon by the sonorous beat of a drum, signalling to the company that the next stage of proceedings was due to get underway. With Alexander McGown to the fore, flanked on either side by the two previous years' Captains, the time had come for the competitors, their friends and families to depart from Smithstone House and process to Kilwinning Abbey where the Boys' Papingo would be held.

The competition comprised two parts. At the beginning of the initial session the beadle read aloud from a list of names, indicating the order in which the boys were due to compete, based most likely on a drawing of lots. At this stage the papingo had already been positioned at what was judged a suitable height for junior archers with its detachable wings only loosely secured. For each arrow fired, the boys were expected to pay the sum of one penny. Any marksman who succeeded in striking the target would be awarded a small, coloured ribbon known as a 'point', but for the greater feat of dislodging a wing a competitor would be presented with one of the larger ribbons from the morning procession. Shooting continued until mid-afternoon or until no more ribbons remained to be won, at which point the first part of the contest was complete and participants adjourned to the adjacent freemasons' lodge where, at a cost of sixpence per head, a hearty dinner was served up.

After the meal, the boys reconvened at the abbey tower for the final stage of the competition which began with the enactment of a rather curious ritual. Standing with his back to the tower and facing the group of onlookers, the current year's Captain raised his bow and, drawing back the string, loosed off a single arrow high into the sky. Theoretically this 'roving arrow' was the very one which had won the contest a year before. Invested with a near-mythical status, the fact that it was held to be irrecoverable did nothing to prevent a host of small boys from scampering off in its pursuit.

The ceremonies duly attended to, the beadle then read out the names of those boys who had their parents' permission to compete for the captaincy. For this part of the shoot, Manson indicates that the papingo was set 'so loose that a very slight touch would bring it down'. Competition, he insists, was good-natured and continued until a victor emerged who was duly accorded warm congratulations from all of his fellow-competitors. Thus the question of the boys' captaincy was settled for another year but the day's events were not yet at an end with target-shooting continuing until perhaps 8 p.m. when the boys left off their sport to convoy their new Captain through the town streets to where a lively ball took place, a genuine community event in which all ages danced together without distinction.

In his account of the papingo, James Manson also gives details of the Tradesmen's and Gentlemen's competitions but his comments this time are briefer and lack the colour and vitality that characterise his treatment of the Boys' event. (Having left Kilwinning for Glasgow at the age of nineteen, his first-hand experience of the adult competitions was likely to have been more limited.) The men's papingos, as he describes them, followed a broadly similar format to that of the boys but with a number of procedural differences. When the Tradesmen gathered for breakfast at the Captain's residence, in addition to homely local fare they were permitted a small extra in the form of a dram or a tot of rum. As in the boys' event, the company proceeded after breakfast to the abbey tower where the rules of the contest were read aloud - no nicknames to be used; no swearing or bad language; the judge's decision to be final; entrants to be charged the sum of sixpence for each arrow fired. A spare bow was made available for any competitor without one and arrows thus fired - or 'common arrows' - would always be retrieved for re-use. With the papingo in place, projecting from the topmost battlement of the tower, shooting for ribbons got underway. An official of the Society who was posted on the rooftop to recover any stray arrows must surely have kept his wits about him. Sometime later a break was taken for dinner, then, the ritual of the 'roving arrow' having been duly attended to, the papingo was set up once again, more loosely now, and candidates stepped forward one by one to compete for the captaincy. When a winner emerged, he was congratulated by a 'laying on of hands' and adorned in the Captain's 'bonnet and bands'. James Manson refers in passing to an old tradition whereby the victorious archer was accorded the dubious honour of having two arrows snapped crosswise over his head but suggested that, by his own time, this curious custom had fallen into abeyance. The Tradesmen's Papingo concluded with a dance beginning at 10 p.m. which ended only when musicians and dancers alike were equally weary.

Presumably well used to generous breakfasts, the Gentlemen received no curds and cream at their papingo in August, though the chances are that this minor deficiency was more than made up for by the fact that they and they alone were eligible to compete for the Silver Arrow. As the beadle marched through the town, the century-old trophy hung suspended from his Lochaber axe along with a piece of silver plate to be awarded to the victor at butts-shooting. The contest went along similar lines to the Tradesmen's and the Boys' Papingos and once a winner had emerged, the Gentlemen then moved on to the cross where they toasted the health of their new Captain-General with 'a large bowl of negus' - a hot concoction based on port, sugar, lemon and spice - though Manson mentions that in former times wine had been drunk in such quantities that 'a small barrel' had been required. It is hard to avoid gaining the impression that a good deal less fun was to be had at the Gentlemen's Papingo than at the equivalent Boys' and Tradesmen's events, and Manson concludes his remarks by saying that the festival was 'much changed' but 'continue[d] to be maintained with some faint traces of its former jollity'. If it all sounds a little half-hearted, it is probably because in the late 1850s James Manson knew full well that time for the papingo was running out.

The event's decline can probably be put down to a number of factors. In recent decades Kilwinning had undergone rapid industrialisation, a process which had had the effect of disrupting the life of a traditional, stable community. At a time when pressure for parliamentary reform was intense, the rigid class divisions of the papingo had become increasingly out of sync with the times and the blatant elitism of the Gentlemen's event must surely have stuck in many working-class throats. Participation even in the Tradesmen's Papingo was limited to artisans and farmers and the town's population of colliers, mill-workers, labourers and ironworkers found themselves excluded. There was no papingo for the likes of them. With what in retrospect looks like a weary inevitability, the contest and its associated ceremonial steadily wound down until finally, on a pleasant, sunny day in July 1870, it shuddered to a halt. During the afternoon shooting at the butts and for ribbons had gone ahead as per usual, the standard of archery reportedly high, but when the competitors broke off for refreshments, their chairman, William Brown's, remarks to the assembled company were telling. While acknowledging that the Society had 'suffered adversity' in recent times, he concluded his speech by expressing the hope that 'a bright day' might be imminent. Sadly, his optimism was misplaced. When the party returned to the abbey tower after dinner, not one single contender came forward to compete for the Captain's title. No contest took place the following year. And so, after a proud history of some 400 years, the Kilwinning Papingo had come to an end.

At least for the time being. Twelve years later, in May 1882, efforts were made to revive the old tradition when nearly fifty archers competed at the Kilwinning butts. When the contest was over, the men processed briefly through the town streets to the accompaniment of a marching band but then they simply melted away. A mere shadow of its former self, no attempt was made to re-run the event the following year. After the false dawn of 1882, it was to be another seven decades before a renewed interest in local history and heritage resulted in the setting up of an archery tournament between the Ancient Society of Kilwinning Archers and the Royal Company of Archers, based at Edinburgh, which took place in due course in the town's McGavin Park in June 1951. As part of the event, the Silver Arrow was ceremonially returned to Kilwinning from the Royal Company, in whose safekeeping it had been kept in recent times, and the next logical step, of course, was the revival of the historic Papingo Shoot. This time the attempt to revitalise the old tradition proved successful and the Ancient Society of Kilwinning Archers continues to flourish to this day. Its members can claim with justification that they belong to the oldest archery association in existence.

4 The Cadgers' Races

The sport of kings has a long and distinguished history in Ayr with horseracing in the town dating back more than 400 years. The first formally organised event took place over a two-day period in 1771 and the celebrated Ayr Gold Cup followed some three decades later in 1804. Well-heeled local bigwigs, such as Lord Eglinton and the Duke of Portland, threw their weight behind the races and by 1838 prize money at the Western Meeting had climbed to a total of £2,000, a considerable sum at the time. In spite of its wealthy backers, however, it wasn't the only show in town. A mile or two down the road, a parallel event took place which catered for an altogether different strand of society and coexisted with its more illustrious neighbour for a period of well over a century.

In contrast to race meetings attended by lords and ladies, this rival fixture was held on the north side of the River Ayr where the burgh of Newton-upon-Ayr had grown over time from a small settlement of salmon fishermen into a wider community that included other groups of workers, principally weavers and coalminers. In spite of the area's growing diversity, the burgh continued to mark the close of the salmon fishing season each summer with a festival known as the Kipper Fair, held on the first Friday after 12 August and believed to date back as far perhaps as the seventeenth century. The event derived its name from the kippered salmon, and at a later date mackerel, that was fed throughout the day to hungry revellers in local hostelries. It can hardly have been a coincidence, then, that in 1747 Newton-upon-Ayr's 'cadgers' (or carters) fixed their first race-day to correspond with the existing August holiday.

It quickly became an annual fixture. From 1830 onwards the newly-formed Whipmen's Society of Newton and St Quivox (a benevolent organisation for carters and their families) was closely involved and it was usual for the race-day preparations to get underway a couple of weeks beforehand. Local cadgers would gather to elect their Captain for the year who, once chosen, was accorded the dubious honour of being carried shoulder-high through the streets and 'jagged wi' peens' by his roguish peers. In preparation for the main event, the streets of Newton-upon-Ayr received their one and only clean-up of the year.

In the forenoon of the day of the races the cadgers would arrive on horseback at the Captain's house where traditionally a flag was hoisted before the men tucked into a breakfast of bread and cheese, served by their host's wife and washed down with a tot of whisky. Preceded by a selection of bridles, saddles and spurs which had been donated as prizes and mounted on top of tall poles, they then embarked on their annual parade through the streets, their numbers swelled along the way by townsfolk, young and old, who had dressed up for the event in their best clothes. Particularly keen to make an impression, young women and girls had been carefully coiffured by friends and neighbours the evening beforehand and their hair then scented with oil or pomade. The cadgers themselves by contrast wore their standard workaday clothing though, in a nod to the importance of the occasion, their trademark Kilmarnock bonnets had been decked with fluttering royal blue ribbons. Following in the wake of a marching band, they proceeded along the streets of the burgh, making frequent halts at various public houses where they fortified themselves with kippered salmon and a dram while their gaily-decorated horses waited patiently outside. By the time the cadgers reached their destination on the Newton sands, it seems likely that a majority would already be quite merry.

In preparation for the race-day festivities, an assemblage of stalls and barrows had mushroomed alongside the Newton shore where anyone still peckish after his feed of kippered salmon might sample such tasty treats as dates, treacle candy and 'hairy grozets' (or gooseberries). One *weil kent* nineteenth-century hawker was 'Straven Jock' who turned up each year to sell gingerbread men from a tray supported by a strap around his neck. If trade proved slack, the wily Jock had been known to launch the odd free sample into the crowd, a gimmick that he knew from experience would more than pay for itself by the additional custom it attracted. But if gingerbread didn't take your fancy, then you were free to try your hand at the crossbow shooting gallery where the prize on offer was 'a nievefu' o' nits' (fistful of nuts). No competitor, we are told, left empty-handed.

Only once the tide had sufficiently receded could the day's main event get underway. The cadgers' races were not an occasion for fancy thoroughbreds. Rather the horses entered were heavy draught animals, released from their daily labours in order to compete. When the order was given to go, the riders urged their mounts across the sands until, reaching a given marker, they wheeled around and returned to their original starting-point, the entire process to be repeated a second time. The total distance covered amounted to approximately two miles and the outcome of most races was decided on the basis of three such contests. In the early - more barbarous - days of the sport a victorious jockey was expected not only to be first in reaching the winning-post but also, when he got there, to snatch the head from an ill-fated live goose, suspended by the feet from a crossbar. Not every race went to plan. To the delight of the crowd, many a noble steed would hurtle off in the wrong direction entirely while others simply lay down in the sea and refused to cooperate further. Always inclined to be chaotic, the cadgers' races had no rulebook to govern their conduct and disputes were commonplace. When bystanders added their tuppenceworth, fisticuffs frequently ensued. But for most of the working folk of Newton-upon-Ayr the race-day was a cheerful and good-natured escape from the humdrum routine of their everyday lives. Although organised principally with local people in mind, a special train was run in 1852 to allow visitors from other areas to enjoy the spectacle of the races, and the sight of heavy Clydesdales pounding their way through the surf must surely have been a dramatic one. Such was the draw of the event during the middle years of the nineteenth century that as many as 40 or 50 riders signed up to compete and several hundred spectators spent their day upon the sands.

Carthorse races weren't the only form of entertainment on offer. Foot races were also held, often won by 'a nimble collier' or 'a supple tailor' rather than one of the cadgers, and on at least one occasion there was a wheelbarrow race in which competitors were required to run blindfold. Riders in the donkey derby sat back-to-front, facing the animals' tails, and the object of the exercise was to complete the course in last place. In at least one recorded instance one of the four-legged participants had to be carried bodily over the finishing-line. Satirical broadsheets were distributed (by the intriguingly-named local printer, 'Treacle Doup' Connell) whose object was to lampoon well-known community figures, and the local newspaper, the *Ayr Advertiser*, got in on the act, whimsically speculating on the form of such promising runners as *Ee-aw, Skeleton* and *Rickle-o'-banes*. It seems certain that a contest in which only lame horses were entitled to compete would find little favour today, and some might entertain similar reservations about a foot race run exclusively by 'auld wives', the prize on offer being a pound of tea. Notions of dignity and humanity, we might conclude, were rather different from today's. It appears, however, that a fleet-footed Irishwoman by the name of Connaught Kate felt no such qualms about taking part since it is recorded that she took first prize on more than one occasion.

An ever-popular feature of the fair was a greasy pole, somewhere between fifteen and twenty feet tall, which had been rubbed all over with soap so as to make it as slippery as possible. The prize, a leg of mutton, was perched on top. Over the years two competitors became known for their success in the event, one the son of Connaught Kate and the other a blind man by the name of Willie Blood (or Anderson) who was assisted in his efforts by being thrust upwards from beneath by boys using wooden rods. If it all sounds a little uncomfortable, then clearly the prospect of a succulent roast was sufficient to distract poor Willie from his short-term tribulations.

Once all of the races had been run and the honours of the day decided, the scene of the action moved back into the town where the cadgers and their mounts paraded once again along Main Street before crossing the New Brig and processing along the principal thoroughfares of Ayr, finally dispersing when they made their way back to the Captain's house. One of his last official duties, however, remained to be discharged. In front of large, cheering crowds, the Captain was expected to perform a sword-dance in front of the Newton steeple prior to the start of a lively evening ball where fiddlers scraped out jigs and reels and dancers hooched and leaped and, by all accounts, downed whisky by the pailful. It was customary for the festivities to continue unabated until 5.30 a.m. when jaded revellers would peel away and disperse towards their homes. It seems reasonable to assume that there would be no scarcity of sore heads in the vicinity that day.

Sadly, the colourful spectacle of the cadgers' races didn't go on for ever and the festivities associated with the event gradually petered out during the 1880s. A number of factors contributed to their demise. Although the races survived the construction of a railway line running north from Ayr harbour as well a newly-completed sea wall, both of which had the effect of isolating the Newton sands, warnings were given at the time that such developments might place the future of the event in jeopardy. These changes happened to coincide with a time when the cadgers themselves were under pressure, their trade steadily undermined by the expansion of the rail network. To cap it all, the mid-Victorian period was a time of changing attitudes and the growth of temperance movements had heightened disapproval of the drunken antics with which the cadgers' races were closely associated.

The last race meeting to be held on the sands took place in 1879 and coincided with the cadgers' final procession through the streets of Newton-upon-Ayr. The following August the event was relocated to an area of fields to the north-east of Tam's Brig where attempts were made for a number of years to run the races along more orderly lines. It was to prove a spectacular failure. What had apparently gone unnoticed was the fact that the thrills and spills of the cadgers' race-day were an essential part of its popular appeal and the new, more regulated proceedings came across as insipid by comparison. Crucially, with the parade no longer being held the link had been severed between the races and the local community and, without that connection, the event was effectively doomed. The last cadgers' races were run in 1887.

Of course, formal horseracing as we know it today continued at Ayr, its heavily-ordered proceedings a far cry from the chaotic merriment of the old-time fairs. Today the Newton sands are bleak and largely deserted, and the colourful spectacle of the cadgers' races is all but forgotten.

5 The Trade in Arran Water

At first glance, Troon might seem a surprising location for a band of eighteenth-century smugglers to base their operations. Surrounded on three sides by salt-water, the Point of Troon would have presented few options to men surprised from the landward side by the forces of the law. The broad, sandy beaches immediately to the north and south afforded little by way of cover. And if that wasn't bad enough, the Troon smugglers had, not one, but two customs stations in their backyard, with troops posted to back up local officers both at Ayr and Irvine. As of the early part of the nineteenth century, customs officials were stationed at Troon itself.

Yet, for all that, in the late eighteenth and early nineteenth centuries the parish of Dundonald - which included the Troon area - was a veritable hornets' nest of smuggling, one of the most notorious perhaps in the whole of Scotland. In order to control the shoreline, those with smuggling interests leased a considerable stretch of coastal land from local landowners, the Fullartons, who appeared tacitly to condone their tenants' illicit activities. When revenue officials approached the family matriarch, Mrs Fullarton, in 1767 regarding the possibility of leasing land near the Point, they found that redoubtable lady quite immoveable.

Highly-taxed items such as whisky, brandy, silk and tobacco routinely arrived at 'the Troon' from Arran, Kintyre, the Isle of Man and beyond, to be shouldered ashore for onward transportation on pack-horses or in carts. The entire operation was made possible by the sheer number of local people involved, the suggestion being made that practically every family living in Dundonald parish during the late eighteenth century had at least one member who was involved in smuggling. When a shipment of goods was thought imminent, mounted men would keep watch along the shoreline, their numbers boosted during daylight hours by children, posted among the dunes and charged with responsibility for raising the alarm if troops or excisemen were to make an appearance. Close to the Point itself, a hut was provided for a 'shepherd' who busied himself with the needs of his flock while simultaneously keeping a close eye on what might appear over the western horizon. It was said that, within an hour of a likely vessel being sighted, as many as five hundred horses, some drawing carts, would have converged along the shoreline, ready to uplift the ship's illicit cargo.

Not everyone, of course, was minded to collude with the illegal trade. Though married to the sister of a known smuggler, John Whyte of Craigend was a regular informer who was ultimately driven from his home for his pains. Relocating to Ayr, Whyte found employment with the customs service there, spying and reporting back on any smuggling activity he might catch wind of. The son of a local farmer, Peter McNeight was given a watching brief by the authorities to patrol the coastline on horseback and such was his success in seizing contraband goods, it was said, that he became hated and feared by the smuggling fraternity in equal measure.

Clearly things didn't always go the smugglers' way and customs officials scored some notable successes. In September 1765 John Whyte reported a boat behaving suspiciously, loitering until darkness fell, he suspected, prior to disgorging her illicit cargo. Backed by a group of soldiers, customs men Charles Mitchell and Peter McNeight attended the scene where they were successful in seizing 47 casks of spirits as well as a number of horses and carts. In 1773 officers based at Irvine confiscated a quantity of tobacco and eleven casks of rum at Troon. The years that followed saw no let-up in the battle between smugglers and the authorities as the struggle spilled over into a new century. In 1814 a haul of 120 gallons of whisky - widely referred to as 'Arran water' - was made near Troon, a substantial total which was exceeded some three years later when excisemen confiscated no fewer than 130 gallons in a single operation.

The stakes, of course, were high. Anyone caught in the act of smuggling risked being given 'a berth in the fleet for life' - in other words, pressganged into naval service - and it was not uncommon for encounters between smugglers and revenue officers to be accompanied by violence. While witnessing the unloading of smuggled goods at Troon in October 1766, Peter McNeight was assaulted, dragged from his horse and, in an attack that lasted some half an hour, was beaten to within an inch of his life by two men armed with sticks. Plainly revenue officers and their informers were reviled individuals, and it was undoubtedly this that led in March 1767 to an attempt on the life of Alexander Gordon, a senior customs official based at Ayr.

Irvine Harbour

Having served previously at Leith and Kirkcudbright, Gordon was promoted in 1765 to surveyor of customs at Ayr. His clear determination to eradicate smuggling quickly became apparent, making him rather less than popular in certain quarters - as subsequent events would demonstrate. Early in 1767 Gordon issued subpoenas to thirteen alleged smugglers and a similar number of Ayr merchants who were suspected of receiving contraband goods, summoning them to appear in court at Edinburgh. To say that he ruffled local feathers would be an understatement, so when he set out on horseback one morning from Ayr to Irvine with a single travelling-companion, fellow customs officer John McMurtrie, Gordon's enemies leapt at the opportunity for revenge.

Once their business in Irvine was complete, the two officials were returning that evening in the company of an Ayr merchant, William Harris, when their small party came under attack. A gunshot rang out through the darkness and, though none of the three men was struck, Harris's horse was shot out from under him and killed, thus leaving him at the mercy of his attackers. While the customs men showed a clear pair of heels, poor William Harris had his work cut out in convincing his assailants that he was not their intended target. Eventually released, the merchant managed to borrow a horse from nearby Fullarton House and thus complete his journey, presumably badly shaken but at least with his life intact. For the most part, those identified as responsible for the ambush were servants of known local smugglers but before they could be apprehended the suspects fled the country, either to Ireland, as it was thought, or possibly even France. Also implicated in the crime were a local farmer, Matthew Hay, and an Ayr merchant, John McClure, and the two men were locked up pending trial in the tolbooth of Ayr. The case against them collapsed, however, when it emerged that a vital witness, John McMurtrie, had disappeared from the local area - very possibly following intimidation. The two men on remand were duly released.

During face-offs with the smugglers, it was by no means unknown for the revenue authorities to come off second best. Just such a case cropped up around the New Year of 1813 when officers from Kilmarnock descended on the Dundonald premises of a publican, John Orr. Said to have been tipped off by one of Orr's neighbours, the excisemen quickly located ten casks of Highland whisky which they duly seized and loaded on to a horse-drawn cart which they commandeered on the spot. As they set out to return their haul to base, there is no reason to doubt that the officers believed their day's work complete.

Understandably Dundonald's visiting Highlandmen were much aggrieved at their loss and quickly they resolved to recover their property by force - egged on, it was said, by a villager by the name of Rab Brown. Guided by a raucous band of locals, they crossed the fields to Gulliland, arriving in time to intercept the revenue men who, mistaking the mob's brandished sticks for firearms, performed a rapid turnabout and retraced their steps towards Dundonald. Somewhere along the way, most of the confiscated whisky casks rumbled out of the cart, the rope which secured them having been severed by one of the Highlanders using an axe supplied by the rabble-rousing Rab Brown. By the time the excisemen reached the manse of Dr Duncan, where they planned to seek refuge, there remained in their possession a single, solitary cask. Not for long. As the last of the excisemen backed through the door of the manse, he was disarmed at the last minute by a one-armed Highlander named Neil Stewart and the final cask liberated as a result. As the exciseman's cutlass flew from his hand, knocked high in the air by a Highland cudgel, it is said that a spontaneous cheer arose from the crowd.

For at least one of those present, however, the merriment proved short-lived. Sometime after the New Year fiasco, the consequences caught up with the innkeeper, John Orr, who found himself escorted to prison in Ayr, having been identified by one of the excisemen as an enthusiastic participant in the 'deforcement' - or repossession - of the whisky casks from the authorities. The unfortunate publican was not freed until some twenty months later following intercessions on his behalf by such august personages as Colonel Kelso of Dankeith and the Duke of Portland. Even after his release, the belief proved persistent that the Dundonald innkeeper had been the victim of a miscarriage of justice, having spent most of the day of the riot lying drunk in a closet.

No lives were lost during the Dundonald debacle, but a situation arose some eleven years later which concluded rather less happily. It began in the early hours of Wednesday 18 August 1824 when a Monkton farmer, John Dow's, sleep was disturbed by a rapping at the door of his home at Fairfield Mains. Dow's farmhouse was positioned close to the junction between two fairly widely-used pathways: the first, a track running west from Monkton, down through the dunes and on towards the shore where it encountered the north/south route followed by those crossing the sands between Troon and Prestwick. The two trails would have intersected close to the mouth of the Pow Burn, just west of Fairfield Mains.

When John Dow opened up to his night-time callers, he was faced with a group of angry men - exactly how many is not on record - who urgently requested his assistance. The story that emerged was as follows. Dow's visitors, it transpired, had been handling a consignment of illicit whisky on the shore when they were approached by a number of seamen who interrupted their journey across the sands from Troon to Ayr to demand payment in exchange for their silence. One version of the tale asserts that the sailors had been drinking heavily; another that they pressed their case by impersonating excisemen who were known on occasion to be willing to turn a blind eye if sufficiently bribed. Not satisfied, however, with the sum of money offered - some say a guinea, others £1 - the importunate seamen demanded in addition a share of the Arran water, promptly appropriating one of the barrels by force. This was the point when the smugglers retreated to Fairfield Mains and roused John Dow from his sleep. The farmer's decision to become involved was one that would prove fateful.

Dow was praised at the time as 'a respectable man, and of peaceable habits' with no hint in the local press that he had any previous connection with smuggling. We might question, however, whether the smugglers would have sought help from a man of unknown sympathies. There is an alternative version of the story which suggests that the Fairfield farmer, like many another apparently upstanding citizen, was a regular friend to the smugglers who had been involved in the night's illicit activities from the very start. What we do know for sure is that John Dow was present during the smugglers' attempt to recover their lost whisky and it was then that tragedy struck.

One or two discrepancies exist in accounts of what transpired. Some state that a scuffle broke out during which Dow, a powerful man, threw one of the sailors to the ground, while another version of the story suggests that the farmer approached his man rather more peaceably, in a effort perhaps to negotiate. Matters quickly escalated and the upshot was that at some point during proceedings violence erupted and John Dow sustained a grievous knife-wound, either to the groin or lower abdomen. Too badly wounded to walk, the farmer had to be carried home from the beach and died of his injury within 48 hours. The seaman responsible, it is said, fled the scene.

The man under suspicion of murder was John Johnston, a sailor on board the sailing-ship, *Avon*, of Ayr, and a reward of twenty guineas (£21) was offered for his arrest. Roughly 27 years of age, Johnston was a local man, said have grown up either in Crosshill or Maybole, the son of a Scots woman who made her living by selling textiles door to door, and a father described variously as 'African' or 'mulatto' - the latter a term used to denote a person of mixed race. Growing up in what must have been a fairly uniformly white society, perhaps inevitably the boy came to be known as 'Black Johnston', though his ethnicity appears to have done nothing to hold him back. Although Dow's death was much regretted locally, a degree of sympathy was also felt for the plight of John Johnston who was a highly popular figure, it seems, among the seafaring community of Ayr.

Crosbie Kirk, near Troon

A search of the house which Johnston occupied with his wife and small children in Garden Street, Ayr, revealed nothing, though it would later be suggested - perhaps a little improbably - that the wanted man had been concealed beneath a bed at the very time that the search was being carried out. Placards posted for his apprehension proved no more successful. It was rumoured that, after leaving Garden Street, Johnston took refuge in a cellar of the King's Arms Hotel where friends provided him with the necessities of life until he could be slipped quietly aboard a Liverpool-bound vessel, the *Three Sisters*, under cover of darkness and allegedly disguised as a woman. What, we might wonder, was the fate of the fugitive seaman's wife and children, abandoned through no fault of their own in Ayr? Their story is not known.

No further sighting of Johnston was ever reported in his native land, though an Ayr man was reputed have encountered him some three years after his disappearance in South America, on board a ship at Demerara in what was then British Guyana. Johnston's sense of guilt, the man reported, did not appear to stretch as far as the possibility of his returning to Scotland to face trial. Raising a glass of brandy, he was said to have uttered the words - 'Here's to Auld Ayr: I would not care to go back and die for the man yet!'

Matters did not end there, however, and the story of John Johnston had a final bizarre twist. A decade or so after the seaman's flight aboard the Three Sisters, a soldier from Ayr was said to have been on parade with his regiment on the Caribbean island of Saint Vincent, then a British colony, when he spotted among the crowd of spectators a man whom he instantly recognised as John Johnston. The individual identified was arrested on the spot and duly escorted half-way round the world to Ayr where his first public appearance was eagerly awaited by an excitable crowd of onlookers. Faces fell, however, when it quickly became clear that a terrible mistake had occurred and the man apprehended was a victim of mistaken identity. Whether the Caribbean gentleman thus incommoded was compensated for his inconvenience is not on record, nor indeed how he made the 5,000 mile journey back to his sunny island home. In the aftermath of the debacle, John Johnston and his story seem finally to have faded from public consciousness and what the sailor's ultimate fate might have been has never come to light. By contrast, his alleged victim, John Dow, was laid to rest in the quiet turf of Crosbie kirkyard, a short walk across the fields from the spot where he had breathed his last.

The truth was that, by the time of John Dow's murder, the halcyon days of the Troon smugglers were already retreating into the past. For decades the enforcement agencies had struggled to hold the line against smuggling, routinely outcompeted in their operations by the smugglers' superior vessels and floundering in the face of sullen non-cooperation from the population at large. What finally swung the odds in the authorities' favour was a change in government policy whereby duties were steadily reduced, thus undermining the smugglers' potential for profit and culminating during the 1840s when Prime Minister, Sir Robert Peel, abolished tariffs entirely on some 600 items and reduced them on many more. So, at the end of the day, the smuggler's trade - dashingly romantic or a base criminal activity, depending on your viewpoint - was brought under control neither by derring-do on the high seas nor moonlit operations along windy shorelines, but rather by a few scratched lines from the nib of a politician's pen.

6 Old-Time Men of the Road

Political correctness hadn't yet entered Scottish consciousness in the days of Daft Wull Speirs. It was quite possible two centuries ago for an individual's quirks and foibles to be smiled over while he or she remained firmly embraced at the heart of the local community. Just such a character was Daft Wull Speirs, about whom a number of anecdotes have come down to us.

Reputed to have been a weak-witted son of the Laird of Camphill, Wull took to the road as a 'gaberlunzie-man', or tramp, whose routine stamping-ground stretched from Beith and Dalry in the north to Kilwinning and Irvine in the south. Once a nimble-minded youth, Wull's disorder was allegedly traceable to a traumatic experience that he underwent on an occasion when an enraged (and unidentified) person dangled him by the ankles from the parapet of the bridge at Dalry when the River Garnock below was in full flood. Such was the boy's terror, so we are told, that he never fully regained his wits and, unable to settle to a normal existence, took thereafter to a life on the road. That, at least, is how the story goes, though you might imagine that there had to be a little more to it than that. What a modern-day analyst might make of Wull's case, I am not in a position to say.

During his subsequent peregrinations, Wull was said to have been made welcome throughout the area in dwellings that ranged from cottages to castles. Tramping the country roads (whiles alone, other times in the company of two associates, Soople Sanny and Rab Paik) Wull was known for his empathy for dumb animals, an affinity that may ultimately have led to tragic consequences. One of his regular haunts appears to have been the area around Eglinton Castle and a number of the stories that survive relate to Wull's encounters there with the 12th Earl of Eglinton, Hugh Montgomerie, with whom he was clearly on the best of friendly terms.

Evidently Wull was conscious that a degree of deference was expected in his dealings with the gentry, but it was equally apparent that he had no intention of allowing matters to be taken too far. On an occasion when Wull

Eglinton Castle today

was engaged in manufacturing a broom, the 12th Earl amused himself by concealing Wull's knife at a point when his back was turned. 'Hae ye lost ocht?' the Earl is supposed to have asked with studied nonchalance while Wull rooted around in search of the lost item. Wull's suspicions being obvious, the Earl feigned outrage, demanding to know whether he was believed to be guilty of theft. 'Na, na, my lord,' Wull replied coolly. 'I dinnae say ye stole it, but I will say this - if ye hadnae been there, my knife wouldnae hae gane awa'.'

For all his perceived limitations, certain anecdotes give the impression that Wull was nobody's fool and at times he showed himself to be a wily operator, fit to bandy words with anyone. On crossing Earl Hugh's path one particular morning, Wull recounted a premonition which had come to him in a dream during the course of which the noble lord had made him the gift of a pound of sugar while his wife, the countess, had presented him with a similar quantity of tea. Warned by the Earl of the contrary nature of dreams, Wull scarcely paused for breath before replying. 'In that case,' he suggested, 'it'll be you that's gaun tae gie me the tea and her Ladyship that'll gie me the sugar.' Wull brought the conversation to a close with every appearance of humility, lamenting the fact of his deteriorating memory. On another occasion when invited to choose between two coins - a large copper penny and a small silver sixpence - Wull was heard to declare - 'I'll no' be greedy. I'll juist tak' the wee white yin.'

Meeting the Earl one day in Kilwinning, Wull's hopes of a refreshment were dashed when he learned that the laird had no money about his person. His spirits quickly revived, however, on hearing the suggestion that he continue to Leezie Wylie's hostelry and wait there until the Earl returned with the price of a bottle of ale. Sometime later, when the pair were companionably ensconced in the public-house - an odd couple to be sure! - the laird suggested that Wull must be a proud man to be seen drinking in the company of an Earl. 'Ay,' scoffed the irreverent Wull. 'An Earl that hasnae a fardin' [farthing] in his pooch!' On another occasion, taking a short-cut through a plantation within the policies of Eglinton Castle, Wull was intercepted by Earl Hugh who pointed out rather firmly that that wasn't the road. 'Dae ye ken whaur I'm gaun?' quizzed Wull. The Earl replied the he did not. 'Then hoo the deil dae you ken whether it's the road or no'?' retorted Wull with what can only be described as unarguable logic.

Dumfries House today

Sadly Wull's life is believed to have ended as the result of a tragic accident. When his broken body was discovered at the bottom of a mine-shaft at Corsehillmuir, near Kilwinning, a collie-dog was found to be lying by his side, and the assumption was that he had perished in an attempt to rescue the stranded animal. Tragically, it seems likely that Wull's deeply-held affection for his fellow-creatures was what had led to his untimely demise.

For all his widely-used nickname, Wull Speirs wasn't so daft. His series of encounters with the Earl of Eglinton make that crystal clear when during their exchanges it is invariably the noble lord who comes off second-best. He wasn't, however, the only 'wise fool' to outwit the aristocracy of late eighteenth-century Ayrshire and a number of the stories told about Willie Brown, a native of the Cumnock district, bear a striking similarity to those involving Daft Wull Speirs.

It appears that Willie Brown (or more likely 'Wullie Broon'!) was on friendly terms with the cook at Dumfries House and, during a visit to the kitchens one January day, Willie was tempted to detach the leg of a newly-roasted chicken which he proceeded then to consume with undisguised relish. When the time came for his lordship's dinner to be served, the missing drumstick did not go unnoticed and Willie, being prime suspect, was duly summoned and invited to explain himself. During the course of the discussion, Willie claimed with perfect suavity that it was quite normal for 'hens [to] hae but yae leg this time o' year.' He then invited the bemused Earl of Dumfries to accompany him to the poultry-yard where the nobleman's birds were observed, without exception, to be standing on one leg - the other, of course, tucked up beneath them for warmth. Seeing this, the Earl cried out and waved his hat in the hens' direction, prompting them to scatter two-legged in all directions. He turned to face his companion with a look of triumph but Willie was not beaten yet. 'Ye should hae cried "whish!" to the yin on the table,' he told the incredulous Earl, 'an' I wouldnae wunner to hae seen it slip doon its ither leg tae!'

On a similarly chilly winter's day some ladies of the Earl's household had made a trip to a frozen pond on the estate where they planned to form a skating-party but, concerned about the safety of the ice, they asked Willie to try its strength on their behalf. Put thus on the spot, Willie found it convenient to defer to the ladies' superior social status, informing them that he had spent enough time among gentlefolk not to know better manners than that. 'I mak a pint never to step afore gentry - an' leddies especial,' he told them with every appearance of sincerity, before concluding with an accompanying flourish - 'Eftir you, leddies, gif ye please - eftir you!'

A couple of generations later Jock Aird was believed to have been born in 1812. Cutting a highly-distinctive figure in the Kirkmichael district, he was in the habit of wearing a long, trailing coat and sporting in addition a tall, tile hat made of silk which doubled up when required as a receptacle for such comestibles as might come his way during the course of his rambles. By habit studiously polite, Jock was nonetheless inclined to lose his temper if sufficiently goaded by local youths though he was said always to have calmed down instantly if presented with a conciliatory handshake. On overhearing the minister of Coylton observe one day that the time was twenty minutes past three precisely, Jock checked his own ancient pocket-watch before remarking a little too loudly - 'I think it's nearer the hauf 'oor, but it wadnae dae tae contradict the meenister.'

The middle years of the twentieth century saw a sharp decline in the number of 'gaun-bodies' to be found on Ayrshire's backroads and byways, though a last, determined few clung on for a time to the old ways. Alec

Colquhoun and his wife, Maggie, were a familiar sight on the streets of Newton-upon-Ayr, Prestwick and the surrounding districts with their donkey-cart and trademark cry of 'Cley, brey and stookie!' A 'candyman' of an earlier age might have traded toffee or sweets in exchange for unwanted items such as rags - hence the name - but by Alec's time it was more normal to offer items such as clay ornaments and cheap household goods. He had followed in the family tradition, his father and uncle, Jamie and John Colquhoun, having both been rag-and-bone men before him who proudly claimed aristocratic extraction and wore formal frock-coats and top-hats to back up the assertion. Another of John and Jamie's quirks apparently was that, though they announced their wares in homely broad Scots, in conversation they switched immediately to flawless standard English. For their part, Alec and Maggie were said to have been unassuming souls who treated their donkey with great kindness during the course of their rounds. The couple's only weakness, apparently, was beer and it was rumoured that even their 'cuddy' developed a taste for alcohol. The beast was said to have been stabled indoors at their residence in Prestwick Road, Ayr.

It may have been in the role of tattie-howker that Joe Cran first arrived in Scotland but, though ever-identifiable by his marked Irish brogue, he was never to return to his homeland. In the course of his ramblings, Joe beat a regular path between three familiar farms, situated at Straiton, Bargrennan and in the Stinchar valley, where he was confident of picking up casual employment. During his spells at Pinclanty, near Barr, Joe would turn up unannounced, settle into the bothy, then move on sometime later without so much as a goodbye. A small, stoutish figure with a beard and moustache, Joe's somewhat dishevelled appearance was probably the result of bothy-living. Though his meals were supplied from the farm kitchen, modern washing facilities were absent and he was in the habit of performing his ablutions at the 'spout' of a horse-trough. A feisty character, when Joe's sleep was interrupted one summer morning by the crowing of an early cock, he opted for a quick and decisive solution. Seizing hold of the offending creature, he promptly silenced it by thrawing its neck.

Joe's weekly pleasure was to pad the three miles or so to Jimmy Johnstone's establishment, the King's Arms at Barr, where he would sit awhile and dispose of a few shillings, though it is reported that he was never

Jock Aird at the Kirkton Inn, Dalrymple

more than a moderate drinker and was always fit to see himself home. Never under any circumstances would Joe travel by car and if a motor vehicle were even to approach - still a fairly notable event in the upper Stinchar valley during the 1940s - he would invariably scramble up the roadside banking in order to keep well clear. In his farm-work Joe was an individualist. Whether hay-making, skailing dung or bringing in the oats harvest, he declined to follow tried and tested methods, preferring instead to follow his own whim. When asked to report on the progress of his work, he had a standard, perhaps rather Irish, response - 'Another start will finish it!' In the end, Joe gave no greater notice of his ultimate departure than he had of any others when he was found dead one morning in the bothy at Pinclanty, not yet an old man. With no known relatives or friends, the cost of his burial at Girvan was met by the farmer of Pinclanty, Anthony Sloan. It would not be quite accurate to say that Joe was the last of his breed, but neither was he far from it. Of Annbank Annie, who tramped the Stinchar valley backroads some years after his death, little appears to be known other than her unusual status as a female wanderer and her legendary ill-nature.

As the twentieth century marched on, increasing mechanisation of traditional farming practices steadily eroded the need for manual and seasonal labour and, as if to prove the Irishman, Joe Cran's, fears well-founded, space on roads once occupied by wayfarers, cuddies and carts, was increasingly encroached upon by motor vehicles. The trend towards globalisation was well on the way to diluting local colour while expanded welfare systems had the effect of removing certain notable individuals from the agricultural labour pool. Undoubtedly the onward march of progress brought valuable and wide-ranging benefits in its wake, but it is equally clear that they came at a cost. The passing of our old-time men of the road is part of the price we have paid.

7 The Rowantree School

It should come as no real surprise that in former times Ayrshire's most isolated rural schools were to be found in the sparsely-populated uplands of south Carrick. But as transport links improved during the early part of the twentieth century and increased mechanisation of agriculture cut a swathe through the landward population, south Ayrshire's wee schools found themselves living increasingly on borrowed time.

First to close was Loch Doon School, situated on a sheltered bay on the south-western shore of the loch. Some time previously reports had circulated that the school had a mere three pupils on its roll, two of whom were rowed across the loch by their father twice daily. In stormy weather, therefore, there was never more than one pupil in class. It probably came as no surprise, then, when the end for Loch Doon School came in 1931. Next in line were Ballochdowan and Glenapp Schools, their small numbers of pupils to be bussed thenceforward to Ballantrae. The closure of Clashgulloch School followed in February 1938, its handful of pupils to travel down the Stinchar valley in future to be educated at Barr. With only two pupils on the roll, the moorland school of Corwar closed its doors in September 1942, its premises subsequently leased to the SYHA as a youth hostel. Down on the Main Water of Luce, Barnvannoch School held out until 1947 when its four remaining pupils had their education transferred to neighbouring Wigtownshire at a cost to Ayrshire ratepayers of 35 shillings (£1.75) per pupil per day.

But what was probably Ayrshire's most remote country school outlived these others, protected perhaps by its intense isolation and the absence of any feasible alternative. Located at nearly 900 feet above sea-level on the wild hill-road that runs between Barr and Bargrennan, the Rowantree Public School came into existence in the aftermath of the 1872 Education Act which had, for the first time, made schooling compulsory for all Scottish children between the ages of five and thirteen. The property of Archibald Kennedy, 3rd Marquess of Ailsa, it is likely that the school building had previously served as accommodation for some of his lordship's estate workers but, following the 1872 Act, he made the premises available to the newly-convened School Board for the parish of Barr - though he was canny enough to reserve the right to resume possession if he so desired.

The school's catchment area straddled the lonely frontiers of two counties, its pupils drawn both from the southern extremity of the Ayrshire parish of Barr and also from the hill-farms and shepherds' cottages over the border in Bargrennan parish, Kirkcudbrightshire. Distant from any significant centre of population, it was (and, to a lesser extent, still is) a rough patch of country, difficult of access and subject to the vagaries of wild, upland weather. Hardly surprisingly, it was a tough educational billet and there is little doubt that the school's challenging topography, coupled with the demanding lives of local people, contributed to the difficulties faced by those staff who undertook to teach there.

It was one thing for the 1872 Act to have made education compulsory, another matter entirely to ensure that children were consistently in class. Updated weekly, the Rowantree School's early logbooks highlight the never-ceasing problem of poor attendance. Given the school's exposed and elevated location, of course, the elements played a significant part and references to problems associated with bad weather are commonplace. 'A storm, accompanied with showers of snow, began to blow on Wednesday and raged without intermission till today,' wrote the Rowantree School's first (uncertificated) teacher, John McSkimming in February 1875.

The winter of 1878-9 appears to have been a particularly severe one and in early November the teacher currently in post, John McFadzean, noted that snowy weather was adversely affecting pupils' attendance. A few weeks later, he observed that the snow was still 'blocking up the road' and, two months on, at the beginning of the new year, 'frost and snow still continue to impede the roads'. By February attendance was still being hampered by days which were 'entirely a snowstorm throughout'. In order to get to school, of course, the majority of Rowantree pupils were obliged to travel considerable distances on foot and in harsh winter weather their journey was potentially a hazardous one. On one extreme occasion a female pupil was released early from classes 'as she had to cross the river and the ice was beginning to break up'. In February 1881, McFadzean noted with palpable relief that 'the weather seems to be changed from winter to spring'. It subsequently emerged that he had spoken too soon. Several weeks later the school logbook records the fact that 'snow fell every day since Monday, nearly the whole of the week'.

Snow wasn't the only weather-related problem. In October 1875 attendance was down as a result of 'waters [...] in full flood which rendered the roads impassable'. Two months later John McSkimming recorded that 'today was so wet and stormy that none of the scholars at all were present'. Given that it was Hogmanay, mind you, we might be a shade sceptical. Even during spells of settled winter weather, the absences persisted. Towards the end of January 1876 McSkimming observed that 'attendance was irregular this week although the weather was favourable for the season, the short day being the excuse'. If the local people lacked enthusiasm for education, then perhaps we oughtn't to be too surprised. To an unlettered generation, accustomed to subsisting by the sweat of their brow alone, book learning must have seemed at best tenuously relevant.

Of course, winter couldn't go on for ever and, when the weather did finally pick up, surely attendance would be bound to improve? Not a bit of it. Between spring and autumn the explanations for absences noted in the Rowantree School logbook paint a fascinating picture of seasonal agricultural activities that took place in the local area. When the ground dried up sufficiently in late March and early April, children stayed away from school to assist in planting seed-potatoes. 'Attendance this week not so good,' wrote John McFadzean on the last day of March 1879, 'owing to the planting of potatoes.' A fortnight later he recorded that 'Scholars [were] taken up with the lambing' - a crucial time in the shepherds' calendar and liable to occupy the best part of the next month.

Once the lambing season was over, May was the time for peat-cutting and McSkimming noted in 1875 that 'children [were] being kept at home to help at the peats'. John McFadzean echoed his predecessor's observation in May 1881 when he recorded that 'the weather is so propitious for the peats [that] every one of the pupils is taken off that can do anything at them'. In the long days of June, lambs had to be marked and their mothers shorn of their fleeces and clipping would commonly extend until mid-July. 'Sheep shearing is still going on in this locality,' wrote McFadzean in 1877 - 'A number of pupils are taken up in opening and shutting gates.' The dog days of July were occupied with hay-making until, towards the end of the month, school broke up for a six-week summer holiday. When classes resumed in mid-September, a number of pupils were still engaged in grouse-beating for surrounding shoots and it would only be a matter of weeks before they were withdrawn from school once again to assist in digging the very potatoes that they had planted six months earlier. By the time that they returned from the potato harvest, winter was just around the corner with the first significant snowfalls frequently arriving in early November.

In addition to work- and weather-related absences, children were subject to routine ailments, such as colds, measles, boils, influenza and chicken pox. In January 1878 two pupils were absent with 'hooping [*sic*] cough', and were unfit to return to school until four months later. And if all that wasn't bad enough, a logbook entry from November 1880 states that 'A few scholars have their shoes just now at the shoemaker's and cannot attend school till they return'. For all their sporadic attendance, Rowantree pupils performed fairly well in the annual government examinations. Inspectors during 1874 reported an average daily attendance of seven pupils, five of whom had been presented for the external tests. Four of these candidates had achieved a pass in Reading; three in Writing; and similarly three in Arithmetic. 'The school,' reads the inspector's report, 'appears to be taught with a fair measure of success, *the character of the attendance considered*'. In June 1876 the results were better still. 'I found the school in good order,' wrote the inspector, 'and scholars well prepared for the examination.' Sewing, he indicated, was not taught.

It took a considerable time for this deficiency to be remedied when, following a sixteen-year absence, John McSkimming returned to the Rowantree School in 1892, now as a fully-qualified teacher. His wife took up the task of teaching needlework and knitting to the girls. McSkimming comes across as a humane man who was genuinely committed to exposing his pupils to a wide and ambitious curriculum. Under his instruction, they became involved in map-making; studied history and poetry; performed calculations using weights and measures; and they participated in enjoyable diversions such as singing and 'drill'. Committed to engaging his pupils' interest, in September 1893 McSkimming put on record that he 'gave an object lesson on coal and peat'. Prizes were on offer 'as a stimulus to [pupils'] progress'. In spite of his enlightened approach, McSkimming had no compunction about the use of corporal punishment in those rare situations where he deemed it necessary. 'Inflicted corporal punishment on a boy today,' he wrote in March 1894, 'for throwing stones at the others during the dinner break.' The following year he 'punished two boys with a hazel rod on the palm of the hand for carelessness'. Firm but unmistakably dedicated, McSkimming's methods appear to have worked well since at the end of the 1894 school session he found himself in a position to record that 'attendance has been excellent during the year'.

It is unlikely that when John McSkimming's successor, James Campbell, arrived at the Rowantree School in October 1896 he would have been remotely unsettled by his new workplace's isolated location, being himself a native of the wilds of north Sutherland. If the observations of a member of the Barr School Board are to be believed, the new teacher soon settled in and became highly popular with his pupils. Visiting the school in June 1898, M. Kennedy commented warmly on the 'friendship [that existed] between teacher and scholars'. Campbell's wife, Flora, continued with the girls' sewing instruction and all of the couple's own five children were entered on the school roll during their time at the Rowantree.

Sadly the lives of James Campbell and his family were touched by tragedy a few months after he took up his post. On 16 April 1897 the schoolmaster's entry in the log shows that no classes had taken place that week following 'the sad and sudden death and burial of [his] youthful and beloved daughter, Lavinia'. On Saturday 10 August the child had fallen prey to an accident through which she had sustained serious burns - perhaps, we might surmise, her clothing had caught light from the fire. Despite her father's best efforts to save her, the little girl's injuries were so severe that she passed away two days later. We can scarcely imagine how sad Thursday 15 August, the date of Lavinia's funeral, must have been for her parents, siblings and for the wider Rowantree community. As a consequence of the tragic event, Campbell himself was obliged to seek medical attention, having injured his own hands while attempting to beat out the flames. Understandably his wife, Flora, was too distressed to resume her sewing instruction for some time afterwards.

It is likely that James Campbell experienced mixed emotions eight months later while distributing Hogmanay presents to his pupils with no Lavinia present to receive her small gift. The toys and sweets, he tells us, came courtesy of Mrs Emily Verdin, the wife of Conservative politician and High Sheriff of Cheshire, William Henry Verdin, who happened to be the shooting tenant on the nearby Glencaird estate. The Verdins remained part of the Rowantree scene for a number of years, providing 'entertainments and tea' for the pupils a year later on 30 December 1898. A 'sumptuous feast' was served in the schoolhouse, followed by two hours of singing and dancing - with which, Campbell wrote, the children were 'highly delighted'.

At the close of 1899 seasonal celebrations were postponed until the dawn of the new century, possibly the unavoidable consequence of three weeks of heavy snow during December. Once again the festivities were sponsored by the Verdins to whom the children accorded 'a hearty vote of thanks'. It appears that the Cheshire family must have moved on from the area before the following year's treat which was provided now by Robert Mein-Austin, the wealthy proprietor of the shooting-lodge at Black Clauchrie, recently constructed on a wild stretch of moorland south-west of the school. As part of the celebrations, every pupil on the roll was presented with the gift of a book. Eighteen months later, after five years' teaching at the Rowantree, James Campbell took the decision to retire. We might imagine that the tiny school felt fairly desolate for a while after the schoolmaster, his wife and four remaining children - Donald, James, Flora and Mary - departed to take up new lives in Edinburgh. As James Campbell

Black Clauchrie House

turned the key in the schoolhouse door for the very last time, his thoughts must surely have turned to little Lavinia whom he had no option but to leave behind.

Of course, life continued at the Rowantree School much as before. A change, however, occurred in August 1907 when the school's first lady teacher, Mary Brown, arrived and stayed for a year. In January 1909 a new pupil enrolled - John Templeton, whose father was employed as a shepherd at the lonely outpost of Tunskeen. Given the remoteness of John's home, the Barr School Board was obliged to arrange lodgings for him at Tarfessock farm, less than a mile from the school, and agreed to pay out two shillings and sixpence (just under 13p) per week as its contribution to the cost of his board. For all that, it is almost certain that John Templeton, a boy of primary school age, would have made the trek home to Tunskeen each weekend, crossing in all weathers the gruelling 2,000 foot hill-pass known as the Nick of Carclach in order to spend time with his family. Whether his father might have had sufficient free time to accompany him seems unlikely.

Almost certainly John would have assisted in a gardening project that was carried out at the school that year and the chances are that he was also one of those who took part in a mid-June treat when Rowantree pupils joined forces with their fellows at Barr and Clashgulloch Schools for a summer picnic. Bad weather, however, was never far away that year. When a footbridge over the Minnoch was damaged by floods, the Pringle children from Kirriemore had no option but to stay at home until it could be repaired. Finding an alternative crossing, it was noted, would have increased the children's customary seven-mile round trip to school to a total of more than ten. When George V came to the throne in 1911 the Rowantree School was not forgotten with each of its pupils receiving a coronation mug. Drawing lessons were provided around this time by a peripatetic art teacher, Thomas Bonar Lyon, whose landscape paintings command high prices today.

During the war years of 1914-18 the school logbook is curiously silent about the conflict raging on the far side of the English Channel. Its weekly entries continue in their usual bland style - 'Perfect attendance', 'Weather still rough' etc. - but if we are tempted to conclude that the war had left the Ayrshire and Galloway hill-country untouched, then the village war memorials at Barr and Bargrennan tell a different tale. In the post-war period, gaps open up in the logbook when the Rowantree School closed its doors, sometimes for several years at a stretch, before reopening sometime later - probably when the school's catchment area had accumulated sufficient scholars once again.

In response to a question posed at an Ayrshire Education Committee meeting in June 1920, the Director of Education, Dr John Third, confirmed that the Rowantree School had the lowest roll of any school in the whole of Scotland. A year later it was decided that the situation was no longer tenable and the decision was taken to close the school. The only child of appropriate age in the catchment area was a little girl living with her elderly grandfather who refused under any circumstances to allow the child to be boarded out in order to attend another school. He claimed to have hired a servant-girl, a recent school-leaver, with whose assistance he was convinced that his grand-daughter's education could be completed satisfactorily. The School Management Committee arranged for a qualified teacher to pay a weekly visit to the girl's home to provide her with individual tuition.

But that wasn't the end of the story for the Rowantree School. By November 1925 classes were up and running once again following the recent arrival in the district of new shepherds and their families. The roll

Rowantree School as it is today

stood at a healthy fifteen and the logbook at that time started to reflect modern developments. 'School dentists called today', the teacher, Mrs Lundie, wrote in June 1926, breezily adding that three of the children were sent home early after having teeth pulled. Pain-relief was not mentioned. Thankfully, there were plenty of happy days to compensate. When Mrs Lundie organised a Halloween party, she was surprised to find that her pupils were unfamiliar with what she called 'dipping for apples'. On the last day of the summer term in June 1927 she brought in her gramophone and instigated a communal sing-song with her pupils. In March of the following year the children were driven by motor-car to Barr where they were treated to tea and cakes, with an afternoon performance by a magician thrown in for good measure. A winter outing was organised, again by car, to allow the Rowantree pupils to view the Christmas tree at Barr, a tremendous novelty at the time.

In September 1929 Mrs Lundie's replacement, Mrs Stirling, recorded a red-letter day in the life of the school. The pupils, she wrote, had a 'delightful surprise' when the Lord Mayor of London, Sir Kynaston Studd, and his wife, the Lady Mayoress, plus two friends, paid an unannounced visit to the school. They had, it transpired, been touring the local area. The school's illustrious visitors donated a number of 'magazines and periodicals' - well-thumbed, no doubt - and the Lord Mayor was heard to make complimentary remarks about the purity of the local air and the children's healthy appearance. As far as the Rowantree pupils were concerned, we might imagine that their upper crust English visitors were as unfamiliar as beings from an alien planet.

When Mrs Stirling moved on to Clashgulloch, her replacement, Donald Campbell, arrived at the Rowantree in April 1931, having been transferred from the newly-closed school at Loch Doon. For Campbell it may have felt a bit like a homecoming since a quarter-century earlier both he and all his siblings had attended the Rowantree School as pupils. His father, James, it will be recalled, had been the schoolmaster at the time of his daughter, Lavinia's, fatal accident. A holder of the Military Medal, it seems certain that Donald Campbell had seen service in the trenches during the First World War and, that being so, it is easy to understand the attraction of a quiet, rural backwater where his principal enemies were no more sinister than the boisterous forces of nature. One winter Campbell reported being confronted with four feet of snow inside the school porch, a substantial quantity of which had made its way into the classroom where it showed no inclination to melt. There was no school that day, nor indeed for the rest of the week. At the other extreme, a drought once gripped the local area so tightly that the school water supply dried up. 'Drinking water,' Campbell reported, 'has to be carried a distance in a jug'.

Clearly it wasn't so bad or Donald Campbell would never have lasted at the Rowantree School all the years that he did. In August 1949, however, his health took a worrying dip. Pupils arriving back from their summer break found the school closed and were told that they would be notified when classes were due to resume. It was mid-November before Donald Campbell returned to work, recently discharged from hospital, and he noted his concern in the school logbook that his pupils had received no education since late June, a period of nearly twenty weeks. Given the timescale involved, it looks very much as though his health was in a precarious state. It wasn't the only cause for concern. In August 1950 the school roll sat at four; a year later it dropped to two where it remained at the start of the new session in 1952. On Christmas Eve that year Campbell reported in the logbook that he had closed the school for the seasonal holiday in line with normal procedure. After the final entry for 1952, there is nothing but a succession of blank, unmarked pages.

Barely a fortnight later, Donald Campbell died, aged 64, on 8 January 1953, having given more than twenty years of his life to the Rowantree School and its pupils. When a successor proved elusive, Ayr County Council availed itself of the opportunity to close the school for good. The parents of the two remaining pupils gave consent for their children to be driven daily to Bargrennan where they would complete their primary education. Campbell's death was the undeniable end of an era, though his family's connection with the Rowantree School was not yet severed entirely. Following his death, his brother, James, lived on in the schoolhouse along with his sister, Flora, earning a modest income from driving local children to and from their new school at Bargrennan. It is interesting to note that, such was the lure of the Rowantree School, that it had drawn three of the four Campbell siblings home to Ayrshire from Edinburgh. Their parents, James and Flora, were no different, ending their days by the shores of Loch Doon where they had settled in the home of their son.

When it was first established during the Victorian era, the Rowantree School lit a beacon of learning that shed its light over the remote south Ayrshire hills for the best part of a century. The school represented a new age, an age when lowly children in one of the quietest corners of the land were considered, perhaps for the first time, worthy of an education. With Donald Campbell's passing, that light went out.

8 Scotland's Wild West

When Buffalo Bill and his *Congress of Rough Riders* descended on Ayrshire in 1904, it wasn't the first experience that local people had had of American showmanship. Five years earlier, in October 1899, Barnum and Bailey's *Greatest Show on Earth* had set up shop at Struthers farm, Kilmarnock, as part of a five-week, twenty-town Scottish tour. Billed as 'The World's Largest, Grandest, Best Amusement Institution', the show was vaguely Western-themed in its conception but well watered down by such tasteless nineteenth-century add-ons as its *Stupendous Collection of New Prodigies and Human Curiosities* - put frankly, a 'freak show.'

As excitement mounted, schools in the local area closed for the day and many pits ceased production. However, despite Barnum and Bailey's much-vaunted 'Twelve New Waterproof Pavilions', the show fell foul nonetheless of the vagaries of the Scottish climate. In a day of relentless wind and rain, the opening procession had to be abandoned, the main marquee proved impossible to erect and both of the day's scheduled performances were ultimately called off. Happily, the self-styled 'Mighty Metropolis of Wonderland' fared rather better the following day at the Dam Park, Ayr, where it was noted that visitors from Kilmarnock formed a significant part of the audience.

Any lingering memories of soggy socks and collapsed umbrellas appeared to have faded by the time Buffalo Bill followed on in 1904. As a legendary figure of the Old West, William Frederick Cody's credentials were impeccable. Born on a farm near Le Claire, Iowa, on 26 February 1846, during his boyhood Cody's family were among the first wave of settlers to migrate west and occupy the newly opened-up Kansas Territory. At the tender age of fourteen Cody found employment as a rider with the Pony Express, the legendary mail-delivery company, and it was during this time that he was reputed to have completed the longest non-stop ride in the history of the organisation - something more than 300 miles from Red Buttes to Rocky Ridge, Wyoming, and back, an epic journey which kept him in the saddle for more than 21 hours and involved a similar number of horses.

The next phase of Cody's life was the one that gave rise to the nickname by which he quickly became immortalised. Employed in 1867 as a buffalo hunter, by his own account he slaughtered something in excess of 4,000 head of the beasts over an eighteen-month period, their meat destined for consumption by the gangs of railway labourers who were engaged in construction of the new Pacific Kansas line. During the late 1860s and early '70s, at the height of the wars with the plains Indians, Cody held the position of Chief of Scouts in the Fifth US Cavalry.

When he embarked on his Scottish tour of 1904, it wasn't by any means the first time that William Cody had taken his show on the road. His transition from outdoorsman to theatrical showman had begun decades earlier when newspaper reports of his exploits on the frontier prompted adventure writer, Ned Buntline, to place him centre-stage as the real-life hero of a serialised novel, *Buffalo Bill, the King of the Border Men*, whose first instalment appeared in December 1869 in the *New York Weekly*. The novelist would later claim that it was he who had devised the famous moniker by which Cody quickly became known.

The next step toward stardom was one that Cody took only reluctantly, if reports are to be believed. Whatever means of persuasion were applied, in December 1872 he headed east to Chicago where he embarked on a theatrical career, performing in Buntline's Wild West melodrama, *The Scouts of the Prairie*, in which he was cast - presumably rather oddly - as himself. The apparent ease with which Cody metamorphosed from rugged frontiersman into show business celebrity was not perhaps something that might have been expected.

As it turned out, his new incarnation proved a rousing success. Following his stage debut, the next few years of Cody's life must surely have been fairly schizophrenic, scouting throughout the summer months on the endless sweep of the plains before heading back east in autumn to tread the boards for spellbound theatre audiences. It is a measure of the success of Buntline's show that it continued touring successfully for a total of ten summer seasons, numbering among its Western stars the legendary gambler and gunfighter, Wild Bill Hickok. As the Indian conflict in the west gradually subsided, Cody placed a growing emphasis on his stage career which took a major leap forward in 1883 when the mammoth theatrical extravaganza of Buffalo Bill's Wild West show took to the road for the first time, incorporating among its performers a number of genuine native Americans. In a bizarre meeting of old enemies, Chief Sitting Bull - the architect of General George Custer's infamous defeat at the Little Bighorn - joined Cody's troupe for the 1885 season.

Following wide acclaim in the USA and Canada, in March 1887 the Wild West show shipped - lock, stock and barrel - across the Atlantic, making the journey to England aboard a specially-chartered vessel, the Clyde-built *SS Nebraska*, and staging performances in London, Birmingham, Hull and Manchester. Scotland had to wait until the autumn of 1891 when Buffalo Bill completed a two-month European tour before drifting north to perform in Glasgow throughout the winter months.

Glasgow audiences were presented with a series of dramatic tableaux depicting key scenes from the history of the Old West whose dubious accuracy probably did little to detract from the enjoyment of most spectators. Unsurprisingly, the highlight for many proved to be the involvement of native-American performers, decked out in feathers and finery, though even they were unable to put legendary female sharpshooter, Annie Oakley, entirely in the shade. At the close of a fourteen-week run in Glasgow, the Wild West show had proved a rip-roaring success but Buffalo Bill for one was reportedly less than heartbroken at the prospect of leaving, suffering, it was said, as a result of the city's dank winter climate.

In spite of the rapturous reception he had been accorded in 1891, Cody delayed his return visit to Scotland for another thirteen years until July 1904. Throughout the late summer and early autumn his *Congress of Rough Riders of the World* undertook what must surely have been a fairly gruelling seven-week, 29-venue, 28-performance tour that spanned the nation from Stranraer and Dumfries in the south-west to Inverness and Fraserburgh in the north-east. Supported by an estimated 800 crew as well as some 500 horses and ponies, the show rolled into Ayrshire in September 1904, its opening venue at Saltcoats.

In anticipation of the Wild West show's arrival, it would appear that north Ayrshire had no hesitation in entering wholeheartedly into the spirit of things. Local newspapers published the story of how a nine-year-old William Cody, armed with nothing more than a pistol, had single-handedly fought off a gang of bandits, shooting their leader dead in the process. It was an undeniably colourful addition to Buffalo Bill mythology but in all probability was entirely fictitious - a minor detail that did nothing to deter the local populace from flocking to Saltcoats Public Park on Friday 9 September, their numbers swelled by visitors from outlying areas as well as passengers arriving from Largs by special train service. The scope of the Wild West show had broadened considerably since its last visit to Scotland. With three entire trains required to transport its crew and equipment, the show's emphasis remained squarely on Cody's trademark 'cowboys and Indians' but a distinctly international flavour had crept in through the inclusion of equestrian acts from around the world - Russian Cossacks performed alongside Imperial Japanese Cavalrymen - ironically, their respective nations currently embroiled in hostilities in the Far East. Bedouin riders had been brought from the dunes of the Sahara, gauchos from the Argentinean pampas, while a quartet of American frontier girls on horseback added a touch of female glamour. In what was perhaps the most bizarre performance of all, 'Carter the Cowboy Cyclist' thrilled audiences as he hurtled at great speed down a ramp, from whose upward-curving tip he launched both himself and his bicycle some twenty-odd feet into the air, describing a giant parabola before descending once again to earth. Undoubtedly 'Looping Through Space' was an impressive and hazardous undertaking which consistently went down well with spectators, though what Carter's 'cowboy' credentials might have been was not made wholly clear. In addition to the main event, spectators were treated to a 'freak show' (shades of Barnum and Bailey) plus a variety of novelty acts, some featuring performing animals. Clearly the Wild West show had developed into something more akin to a circus but, despite the variety of acts on offer, the Saltcoats performance was not an unmitigated success. The show's advance-publicity materials had promised a performance 'rain or shine', but the audience's pleasure was reportedly marred by wind, rain, and muddy underfoot conditions.

The following day the show moved on to Kilmarnock where, in a well-practised operation, Cody's canvas city sprang up once again, this time on a field at Wardneuk farm, Beansburn. Not long after, conspicuously-dressed performers were to be seen, going about their business in the town in what was presumably a well-planned publicity stunt. Prior to the afternoon performance, what were said to have been the largest crowds ever seen in Kilmarnock converged on the showground, in spite of local competition in the form of music hall legend, Harry Lauder, who was billed to appear that same day at the town's Corn Exchange (now the Palace Theatre). Not everyone who attended the Rough Riders, however, came away impressed. A *Kilmarnock Standard* commentator reported grumpily that the American-Indian performers 'sang a war song, but it wasn't overpowering [and] danced a war dance, but it lacked originality.' Curiously churlish in his assessment, perhaps its author might have been happier with a ticket for Harry Lauder.

There is no suggestion, however, that the majority of spectators were anything less than satisfied, and it was noted that the show-crowds were tractable and well-behaved, ably shepherded, of course, by officers of the local constabulary. Inevitably, however, there were one or two exceptions whose cases were heard at the Burgh Police Court two days later on Monday 12 September. One related to the theft of an elderly gentleman, John Morgan's, wallet containing 30 shillings (£1.50), stolen shortly after the victim and his daughter had arrived at Kilmarnock railway station around 10 a.m. Later in the day, the culprit, Thomas Shaw of Sheffield, aroused the suspicions of two plain clothes police officers and, placed under arrest, was readily identified by the aggrieved John Morgan. The missing wallet and its contents were recovered from a railway carriage by a member of the public and handed over to police. Guilty as charged, Shaw found himself facing the prospect of 60 days in gaol.

A second case related to an attempted theft from a local minister - Rev. James Armstrong of St Marnock Street Church. Catching a well-dressed young man in the act of purloining his gold pocket-watch, the feisty clergyman forcibly detained the would-be pickpocket, ignoring his struggles to escape until police officers could be summoned to the scene. The thief identified himself as John Graham, a clerk residing in Greenock, though it turned out that he was unknown at the address he had provided. Sentenced to 60 days' imprisonment, the convicted man was said to have smiled at the presiding magistrate, Bailie Pearson, and uttered the words: 'Thank-you, sir. God bless you.' Whether his tone was one of sarcasm we can only guess.

While the two pickpockets cooled their heels in the cells at Kilmarnock, the Rough Riders' caravansary moved on once again during the early hours of Sunday morning, its arrival in Ayr a short time later coinciding with the annual fun-fair in Newton Public Park where the two entertainments found themselves setting up side by side. As if that wasn't enough, it happened in addition to be the week of Ayr's Western Race Meeting with horseracing scheduled for Wednesday, Thursday and Friday. Neither of these rival attractions, however, appeared to dent the Wild West show's appeal any more than Harry Lauder had managed to do in Kilmarnock and it was reported that on Monday 12 September huge audiences attended both afternoon and evening performances in spite - once again - of bad weather. Especially well received was Carter the Cowboy Cyclist, and Cody himself was accorded a rousing ovation. In the aftermath of the big event, however, opinion appeared to be divided as to the show's significance. One local newspaper correspondent gushed that 'Buffalo Bill's Wild West is a living, breathing definition of the words [...] Courage - Dash - Daring,' while a less enthusiastic fellow commentator observed dryly that 'Buffalo Bill was but an incident in a crowded week.' From Ayr the Wild West show travelled south to Stranraer, then on to Dumfries, its last Scottish venue, where Provost Joseph Glover presented William Cody with a gold medal, funded by subscription and inscribed with the words - 'From friends in Bonnie Scotland.' Leaving Dumfries, the Wild West show crossed the border and departed, never to return to Scotland.

A century or so on, what are we to make of Buffalo Bill and his Scottish sojourns? One thing, at least, seems clear. Of William Cody's drive and energy there can be no doubt, likewise his skill in enterprise and organisational ability. Yet, for all that, there are matters that we might choose to take issue with. For all its claim to 'Perfect Historical Accuracy', what the Wild West show actually presented was frequently anything but. In a curious reversal of the norm, the 'Truthful Reproduction of the Memorable Battle of the Little Bighorn' was history rewritten by the losers, investing General George Custer with a noble stature to which he was scarcely entitled and painting his native-American victims as the unambiguous villains of the piece. Scottish audiences could hardly have known that the desultory half-dozen bison that Cody chivvied around the show-ring for their entertainment were among the last of their kind, the once-vast herds now depleted and hunted to the verge of extinction by men like him. Nor were they in a position to recognise that the 'Indian War Dances', re-enacted for their amusement on stage, were in reality the death throes of an ancient culture that Buffalo Bill's generation of white Americans had been instrumental in obliterating. Commercial success notwithstanding, it is hard to avoid the conclusion that much of what the Wild West show did was to repackage the native-American people's tragedy as popular entertainment and to pave the way for the stereotyped heroes and villains who would populate Western movie sets throughout much of the twentieth century.

9 The Coming of the Tattie Howkers

It happened every July, regular as clockwork, when an old coal lorry from Girvan rumbled into the farmyard at Clachanton to disgorge its cargo of trunks and cases, pots and pans, baggage and bedding, plus a mixter-maxter assortment of some 30 'tattie howkers' to boot. Under the watchful eye of their patriarch, old John Gallagher of Sligo, the new arrivals would scramble down and organise themselves for their stay at Colmonell, stuffing their pillow-cases and mattresses with fresh straw from the hayshed and laying them out on bed-frames made from upturned wooden potato-boxes - the men in one byre, women in another. Meanwhile one or two of the more mature ladies would be busy in the cookhouse and soon the entire company would be seated at trestle-tables and tucking in to a feed of newly-boiled potatoes.

Such familiar scenes were played out every summer when bands of Irish migrant workers arrived on the Ayrshire coast to harvest the early potato crop. Situated a few miles inland, Clachanton grew 'second earlies' and the tattie howkers would turn up each year in mid-July, once the 'first earlies' along the shore had all been lifted. A fortnight or so later they would up sticks and move on once again, this time to the Kirkoswald district where the harvest followed on a little later. When they finally left Ayrshire, they continued to follow the harvest north and east until they found themselves in Perthshire, Fife and Angus during the late autumn when the maincrop in those areas was due for lifting. Many workers returned year after year to farms where they were known and during the 1950s and '60s John Gallagher and his crew were regulars at Clachanton.

Gallagher was one of a body of Irish 'gaffers' who were appointed by Scottish potato merchants to oversee the Irish end of their operations. As the harvest season approached, the gaffer's first task was to attend to the recruitment of workers, often by making his presence known at community events in Ireland, such as fairs and festivals, where he could be approached by those seeking employment. The gaffer might choose to spend time on the road, travelling around his local area in search of suitable candidates, or alternatively he might place an advertisement in the local press. In an effort to prevent local rivalries from surfacing, it was generally preferred to recruit from within a fairly restricted geographical area and a high percentage of the Irish workers who found employment on Ayrshire farms were residents of the north-western counties of Donegal and Mayo. The great majority were Roman Catholics and it wasn't unknown for some to be Gaelic speakers who stepped ashore in Scotland with barely a word of English.

The majority of the squads consisted of between 20 and 30 individuals, though on very large farms the total might well climb to well over 100. In general tattie howkers tended to be relatively young, often in their teens, and it was common for several family members to sign up together, the younger workers to be supervised throughout the season by an older relative. In the early years of the twentieth century it was not uncommon for children as young as eleven to be found working alongside their elders in the fields. Neighbours and friends too often banded together to companion one another in the potato squads, typically more than half of whose members would be female, for the most part unmarried women and girls.

Once a gaffer had assembled his team, his next job was to arrange their transport to Scotland. Normally members of the squad would meet up at an agreed time and place - possibly a railway station or a seaport - and travel on from there as a group. In the early days workers in remote areas had no option but to make their way to their meeting point on foot but by the 1930s travel by bus was usually feasible. Sometimes special trains were put on with 'fourth class' tickets for sale to migrant workers without much cash to spare. As an alternative to travel by rail, it was possible in later years for a gaffer to charter a bus specifically to transport his workers to the ferry terminal.

The majority of tattie howkers departed from ports in north-west Ireland, though a good number of sailings also left from Dublin. Almost invariably the crossing would be crowded and uncomfortable, sometimes with no division in the hold between human passengers and livestock. There are reports of disorderly behaviour as fights broke out between drunken men, and gaffers attempted to poach one another's employees. The first that most of the tattie howkers saw of Scotland was likely to have been either the docks of Greenock or Glasgow, though a more fortunate few sailed directly to Ayr or Stranraer in specially chartered vessels. For those arriving at ports on the River Clyde, special trains were laid on to convey

Colmonell (Dane Love Collection)

them to railway stations in Ayrshire where they were met by horse-drawn wagons which carried them to their ultimate destination on the farms. After the Second World War it became more normal for merchants to organise transport in open-topped lorries - less than ideal, you might imagine, in rainy conditions.

Not all of the work force, however, had travelled from across the water. A small number of potato diggers were enlisted from the population of Ayrshire's own towns and villages, a slightly larger percentage from bigger urban centres such as Glasgow and Paisley, but the bulk of the labour force consisted of those who had crossed the North Channel to spend their summer in Scotland. No strangers to agricultural work, the sons and daughter of small farmers in north-west Ireland were generally seen as the most efficient tattie howkers and they were regularly praised for their industrious habits and civilised behaviour. Only on rare, isolated occasions did any trouble occur.

During their stay in Scotland, the tattie howkers' gaffer accompanied his squad, supervised their moves from farm to farm, resolved any problems that might arise and distributed wages on behalf of the potato merchant who was their employer. It was quite common for the position of gaffer to pass from father to son, as it did at Clachanton when John Gallagher grew too old to continue. There was a similar tradition among the tattie howkers themselves and sometimes two or even three generations of a family would return to the same farm over a period of many years.

Before the spread of mechanised harvesting, lifting the potato crop involved a clear division of labour. One of the most demanding - and consequently prestigious - jobs was that of the digger who used a specialised three-pronged 'graip' to unearth potatoes from the drills where they had been grown. A job that demanded strength and stamina, it was normally (though not invariably) carried out by a man. Once the digger had brought the potatoes to the surface, it was up to the gatherer to collect them up, clear them of any adhering soil and place them in a 'spail' basket - one traditionally woven from thin wooden slats but which was supplanted in time by wire and plastic equivalents. If no worker was specifically tasked with 'riddling' the harvested potatoes, the gatherer might also be expected to grade them as she went along, separating 'ware' or sound tubers from those known as 'brock' which were damaged, diseased or undersized. It might not have required the muscle of the 'graip' man but the work of gathering - often carried out by females - was undeniably backbreaking. In wet weather the entire process proved heavy-going: digging became harder; the tattie-shaws (and, of course, the workers) became utterly drenched; and the task of ensuring that the potatoes were clean became even more burdensome than usual.

A particularly strenuous job was carried out by the 'tuimmer' who emptied - or 'tuimmed' - the contents of full potato baskets into hefty one and half hundredweight (50kg) barrels which then had to be hoisted on to the back of a cart. It was customary to place green tattie-shaws on top of barrels destined for the market as an indication of the freshness of the crop. In time barrels were superseded by one hundredweight hessian bags which were subsequently replaced in turn by paper sacks which were capable of holding a half hundredweight of potatoes. Traditionally it was the responsibility of the farmer to ensure that the harvested crop was delivered to the nearest railway station until the 1940s when road transport took over. Inevitably, as time went on, the spread of various types of mechanised digging equipment led to a loss of specialisation within the work squads with manual labour mostly required for gathering. The old ways, however, did not fade overnight. Hand tools remained part of the Ayrshire scene until well into the twentieth century and it is on record that the traditional three-pronged 'tattie graip' was still in use in the parish of West Kilbride as late as the 1950s.

By no stretch of the imagination could tattie howking be thought of as easy money. In the early part of the twentieth century the harvesters worked a ten-hour shift, six days a week, regularly starting at 4 a.m. or even earlier in order to ensure that potatoes were able to reach the market on time. Wages were customarily lower than in other forms of seasonal farm-work, principally because of the high percentage of women and teenagers in the potato fields. Accommodation didn't always come as standard and late nineteenth-century tattie howkers were expected to lodge in towns and villages as close as possible to their place of work and then find their way there each day on foot. Change came at the start of the new century when a major potato grower, John Hannah, made arrangements to provide on-the-spot accommodation at his farm of Girvan Mains and the practice gradually became widespread. There were, however, no enforceable standards and records suggest that many workers found themselves housed in sub-standard premises that had no sanitary facilities and even in extreme cases had to be shared with farm livestock. Pressure for regulation began to mount, spearheaded in large part by Ayrshire's Roman Catholic clergy, but not until after the First World War were statutory standards for migrant workers' accommodation on farms laid down by law. Where good accommodation existed, however, it was a boon to the work force: taken alongside the other perquisites of the job - bedding, fuel for heating and cooking and a supply of potatoes for eating - it meant that a sizeable proportion of a tattie howker's earnings could be remitted back to Ireland via the nearest post office.

Although much of the pressure for reform came from the Roman Catholic church both in Scotland and Ireland, that is not to say that the potato diggers made no efforts of their own to improve their lot. The only real weapon that they possessed was the ability to withdraw their labour and strikes were called on a number of years during the early twentieth century, focusing mainly on levels of pay as well as on living and working conditions. As the First World War drew to a close, an expansion in potato cultivation put the harvesters in a strong bargaining position and in June of 1918 many of them stayed at home until significant concessions had been wrung out of the potato merchants. Quite clearly the sight of 'horses […] standing idle in the stable for want of men' had served to focus minds. A few years later the Scottish Women Farm Servants' Union saw fit to establish a Potato Workers' Section but, all in all, the tattie howkers were never quite able to coordinate their actions so as to flex real muscle. Much of that failure may be down to their youth and inexperience, as well as the isolated nature of their upbringing in rural north-west Ireland.

That decent standards of accommodation were crucially important was amply illustrated in the early hours of Sunday 21 September 1924 when fire broke out at Kilnford farm, Dundonald. Eleven potato diggers, employees of the Scottish Co-operative Wholesale Society, were asleep at the time in three apartments located one storey up in the barn loft - two earmarked for men, the third for female workers. The first (outer) room was the only one with direct access to the outdoors via an external stone staircase and once the fire took hold the flames quickly spread, effectively trapping the occupants of the inner apartments, most of whom were too fearful to force their way through smoke-filled rooms to make their escape. One of the male workers, John Greenan - a 32 year-old ex-army man from Kilwinning - had been sleeping in the front room when he became aware that fire had broken out. Rather than saving his own life, he turned back into the blazing building where he was successful in rescuing one of the women, twenty year-old Susan Cree. Sadly, while attempting a second mercy mission, Greenan himself fell victim to the flames. Equally courageous, seventeen year-old John Ormsby perished while trying to assist his grandmother, Annie Dunsmuir, to safety. At age 70, Annie was the oldest worker to perish in the fire. By the time that the farmer, John Smith, scrambled up a ladder and burst open the rear door of the blazing loft, the fire had already completed its deadly work. Arriving too late to preserve human life, members of both Ayr and Kilmarnock fire brigades directed their efforts at saving the farmhouse and the remaining outbuildings. Eight Clydesdale horses were able to be led from their stable to safety - all of them, in the words of the farmer, John Smith, 'trembling like aspen leaves'.

A total of nine workers - five women and four men - lost their lives in the blaze at Kilnford farm, it was believed by suffocation. All of the dead were Scots, five from surrounding districts of Ayrshire. At a fatal accident inquiry, held three weeks later at Ayr Sheriff Court, a survivor of the tragedy,

James Murray, remembered his workmate, John Greenan, having placed a lighted candle on top of a potato box beside his bed. Without any alternative form of lighting in the barn loft, it would surely not have been the only one and it is easy to see how loose straw, spread across the floor as bedding, would have easily caught light. When it further emerged during the inquiry that no formal note had been kept of the tattie howkers' names and addresses, a representative of their employer, the Scottish Co-operative Society, ventured to suggest that 'to give an accurate record of this class of workers would be too heavy a burden'. Sheriff Broun, in charge, was not impressed. 'These people seem to be treated as if they were hens or cows,' he thundered. 'We might at least have their names.' When we think of John Greenan's desperate heroism; of the loyalty and affection shown by young John Ormsby for his elderly grandmother; and of the anguish of Susan Cree, the only female survivor, who attended the fatal accident inquiry dressed in mourning for the two sisters whom she had lost in the blaze, the words 'this class of workers' can only be viewed as stupefyingly insensitive. Among ordinary people, however, the incident elicited a wave of sympathy and in his poem, 'The Hero of Kilnford', it might be supposed that the Riccarton milkman and amateur versifier, John Hose, spoke for many when he railed at conditions under which human beings should have been 'herded in their hovels like a farmer's swine or kye'. As its title indicates, the poem is a tribute to the valiant efforts of John Greenan.

Unfortunately the Kilnford tragedy wasn't the last incident of its type. A similar catastrophe occurred thirteen years later at Kirkintilloch, Dunbartonshire, in which ten Irish tattie howkers - all male - lost their lives in a fire. The recommendations of a fatal accident inquiry at the time were confirmed in law the following year and made inspection of seasonal workers' accommodation mandatory for all of Scotland's local authorities. During the post-war decades progress was made with water closets and hot water for washing beginning to feature in the byres and bothies used by tattie howkers. What is likely to have been an unforeseen consequence of improving standards, however, was a steady reduction in the number of farms which provided accommodation for seasonal workers due to the increased cost involved. To some potato farmers, investing in new machinery which would reduce the need for a manual labour force was starting to look like the more attractive option.

Given the long hours and the arduous nature of their work in the fields, a certain proportion of what little leisure time the tattie howkers enjoyed was devoted to rest and recovery but certainly not all of it. Impromptu sing-songs would sometimes materialise in the evenings when one of the more musical members of the company took it upon himself to coax a tune out of an old fiddle or a battered accordion. Larger-scale dances took place, normally at weekends, when a number of squads within a local area would come together to exchange news and socialise and, with so many young unmarried people thrown together, it is hardly surprising that a good deal of courting took place at such events. The visiting workers might pay a weekend visit to their nearest town for shopping, entertainment or to send money home to their families in Ireland and it wasn't unknown on such outings for some of the men to treat themselves to a small refreshment in a convenient public house. On Saturday evenings and Sundays, the thoughts of many turned to more sacred matters and there was a notable occasion in July 1911 when upwards of 400 Irish tattie howkers were reported to have attended a mass in Girvan, conducted by Father Flanigan of Springburn. On a less elevated note, it has been observed that some of the potato workers made profitable use of their leisure hours by rat-catching on behalf of their host farmers, a 'ha'penny' bounty reportedly being paid in 1905 for each rat's tail produced as evidence.

There was a time when as many as 2,000 Irish men and women spent their summers harvesting Scottish potatoes but the aftermath of the Second World War saw their numbers wane and they dropped yet further, this time more dramatically, in the decades that followed. There were a number of reasons for the decline. Improved economic conditions boosted job prospects at home, and for the first time unemployment benefit provided Irish citizens with the security of a safety net. Meanwhile, at the Scottish end of the business, advances in farm machinery steadily eroded the need for an extensive labour force and so the tradition gradually dwindled and died. That the work of the tattie howkers was hard, dirty and gruelling is undeniable and we cannot begrudge the people of north-west Ireland their increased prosperity. But, for all that, it is hard not to feel that, when the tattie howkers' summer migrations came to an end, Scotland's farming calendar lost something of its seasonal colour.

TROUBLED TIMES

10 An Irvine Witch-Hunt

Modern-day Irvine bears little resemblance to the ancient burgh, steeped in continuity and tradition, where a young Robert Burns arrived in 1781 for his abortive attempt to learn the trade of flax-dressing. A bustling seaport since medieval times, the town had already amassed a considerable history by the time it was portrayed by Rev. Micah Balwhidder, the pawky narrator of John Galt's classic nineteenth-century novel, *Annals of the Parish*. One of the royal burgh's less illustrious chapters, however, took place sometime earlier when the Irvine authorities were notably zealous in persecuting hapless women who, on whatever slim pretext, came under suspicion of witchcraft.

One such case occurred in 1618 whose principal protagonist was a young woman by the name of Margaret Dean, *née* Barclay, whose husband, Archibald, was a burgess of the burgh. The problem began, it seems, when Margaret found herself facing an accusation of theft by her husband's sister-in-law, Janet Lyle. Outraged at what she insisted was a groundless allegation, she brought a charge of slander before the kirk session, a customary course of action at the time, which resulted - ostensibly at least - in a public reconciliation during which the two women agreed to set aside their differences. In Margaret's mind, however, the process had resolved nothing at all and, in agreeing to shake hands, she had been simply going through the motions. Her resentment against Janet Lyle and her husband, John Dean, continued to simmer.

As part-owner of an Irvine trading vessel, *The Gift of God*, John Dean must undoubtedly have been a prosperous citizen. Shortly after the apparent resolution of his wife's dispute, Dean set sail for France, accompanied on the voyage by various local merchants, among them Andrew Train, the provost of Irvine, who also, as it happened, owned a part-share in the vessel. As his ship slipped over the horizon, John Dean could hardly have guessed that he had provided Margaret Barclay with a perfect opportunity to vent her bile and, in so doing, unwittingly sow the seeds of her own destruction.

Around the time of the ship's departure, Margaret was heard to call down curses upon the entire venture, praying to God (perhaps surprisingly) 'that sea nor salt-water might never bear the ship, and that partans [crabs] might eat the crew at the bottom of the sea.' Possibly Margaret's poisonous remarks would initially have been put down to the meaningless ravings of a resentful woman but two significant events occurred a little later which cast her comments in a different light. The first involved a mysterious figure named John Stewart - a vagrant, it seems, who materialised on the doorstep of Andrew Train's residence, claiming knowledge that the provost had lost his life when *The Gift of God* had gone to the bed of the sea. As it turned out, the tramp's assertion was confirmed in due course when two members of the crew arrived back in Irvine, sole survivors, so they reported, of a shipwreck that had taken place on the southern English coast near Padstow. Naturally suspicion fell immediately upon John Stewart, whose premature knowledge of the ship's dismal fate was inexplicable by normal means, but also, of course, on Margaret Barclay, whose rancorous utterances had not been forgotten.

Arrested and questioned, John Stewart claimed that sometime previously he had been approached by Margaret who had sought from him instruction in the dark arts - 'in order that she might get gear, kye's milk [and] love of man.' Surely damning enough, but what followed was even worse. According to Stewart, Margaret had been anxious further to acquire the ability to impose 'her heart's desire on such persons as had done her wrong.' To a seventeenth-century listener, a connection with events in Cornwall would have been virtually automatic. At this point in his testimony, Stewart's story grew increasingly bizarre.

Shortly after the departure of *The Gift of God*, Stewart reported having arrived one night at Margaret Barclay's house - the reason for his visit never made clear - where he found a strange activity in progress. Two female companions were assisting Margaret in fashioning figures of clay, the women's skill sufficient, apparently, to endow one of the effigies with a clear resemblance to Provost Andrew Train. The human figures duly completed, a clay ship then followed. At some point the company was joined by the devil himself who had, for the occasion, taken the form of a black lap-dog which accompanied Margaret and her companions to an empty building close to the harbour. Moving on to the shore itself, the women proceeded to consign their clay figures to the waves which instantly began to surge and boil, according to Stewart, and to turn to a lurid shade of red.

Picked out by Stewart as one of Margaret Barclay's accomplices, a local woman, Isobel Insh, did her best to deny any involvement but it went badly for her when her own young daughter spoke out against her. Employed as a servant in Margaret Barclay's household, the eight-year-old was prevailed upon, by whatever means, to back up Stewart's outlandish claims and even went so far as to contribute additional details of her own devising. According to the child, on the night in question a black man had appeared alongside the supernatural dog which had, she insisted, illuminated proceedings by periodically emitting flashing lights from its mouth and nostrils. Her mistress, she revealed, had promised her a new pair of shoes as an inducement to keep silent about the events she had witnessed. She also took the opportunity to implicate a fourteen-year-old girl who lived nearby and for whom, we might conclude, she felt little affection.

The obvious discrepancies between her little daughter's version of events and that previously described by John Stewart did nothing to ease the pressure on Isobel Insh. Presumably in an attempt to save his own skin, Stewart was quickly persuaded to go along with this new account though he appears to have misjudged badly when he boasted of possessing magical powers of his own, acquired, he revealed, from his frequent companions, the fairy folk. What induced him to make his strange admission is not on record. The ministers and magistrates turned their attention next to Isobel Insh who eventually gave in to pressure and confessed to having been present when the clay models were cast into the sea. Such was the poor woman's desperation that she scored a spectacular own-goal when she indicated to Bailie Dunlop, also a seafaring man, that, if only he were willing to release her from custody, his business affairs would assuredly thrive thereafter. Wide open to misinterpretation, it was a remark that the authorities lost no time in leaping upon. Weary and drained, Isobel gave an undertaking that the following day she would be willing to make a clean breast of all she knew.

Whether she had any intention of keeping her word can never be known. Despite being weighted down with 'iron bolts, locks and fetters', Isobel succeeded that night in escaping via a window of the church belfry where she had been incarcerated and in scrambling up to the roof of the building, from where - accidentally or on purpose - she plunged headlong to the ground. In spite of severe bruising, she survived the fall and her interrogation resumed once again, ending five days later when she finally expired. By the time of her death, Isobel had reneged on her earlier statements exacted under duress and she is said to have protested her innocence to the end. Rumours circulated concerning the involvement of poison, though administered by whose hand is not recorded.

The death of Isobel Insh was only the first loss of life arising from the Irvine authorities' witch-hunt. Next to suffer was John Stewart who, for fear of possible suicide, had been confined in a 'safe lockfast booth' where he was kept under close watch and with his arms tied. The self-professed sorcerer was visited by two local ministers - Mr Dickson of Irvine and Mr Dunbar of Ayr - who raised the prospect of God's grace if he were prepared, even at this late hour, to renounce his former ways. Stewart, the clergymen reported, appeared receptive to prayers, offered up on his behalf. All the more surprising, then, when a short time later the prisoner was found hanging in his cell. Though signs of life were still evident, he proved impossible to resuscitate. The cord which he had used to hang himself was 'not above the length of two span long' and was believed to have been either his garter or alternatively a string with which he was in the habit of tying his bonnet.

With two of the principal witnesses - Isobel Insh and John Stewart - no longer in a position to testify, the decision was taken to subject Margaret Barclay to torture in the hope of securing a confession in advance of her trial. The chosen method involved securing her feet in stocks and then laying on her bare shins an increasing weight of heavy, iron bars - a 'most safe and gentle' torture in the considered view of Lord Eglinton whose credentials for making such an assessment we might feel entitled to question. For reasons that are not hard to fathom, Margaret saw things differently and pleaded for the weights to be removed, indicating that she was now prepared to tell the truth as they wished to hear it, but, as soon as her pain was relieved, she immediately recanted and proclaimed her innocence once again. When her ordeal recommenced, however, the situation quickly became intolerable and she is said to have cried out - 'Tak aff, tak aff, and befoir God I will show ye the whole form!' Clearly the torture had brought Margaret to breaking-point. In the presence of clergymen and local officials, she proceeded to make a full confession of how she had planned the wreck of *The Gift of God* and the deaths of her brother-in-law, John Dean, and Provost Andrew Train. That her statement, exacted under such trying circumstances, could ever have been judged reliable by educated men is almost beyond belief.

During the course of Margaret's forced confession, another unfortunate soul became implicated in the case (who may have been the third unnamed woman in the testimony of Isobel Insh's daughter). When confronted with an accusation of witchcraft, shock was possibly responsible for Isobel Crawford's immediate capitulation. Tortured nonetheless, she displayed great fortitude, suffering silently when a weight of more than thirty stones was laid on her shins. When the position of the iron bars was altered, however, the pain became too great and her resolve finally crumbled. Rather than endure further anguish, Isobel Crawford chose to confess to having consorted with the devil over a period of several years. Sentenced to death, however, she immediately recanted and at the time of her execution was said to have shown no sign of contrition, continually interrupting the prayers of the minister and refusing to pardon the executioner, as was customary in such cases. It should hardly have come as a surprise if the poor woman's wits had become totally disordered.

The fate that awaited Margaret Barclay was no more enviable. It went against her when she was found to be in the habit of carrying a piece of rowan-wood and a scrap of coloured thread as a means of inducing her cow to continue giving milk when the creature showed signs of going dry - evidence surely of nothing more sinister than a superstitious streak. Those sitting in judgment of Margaret chose to disregard the fact that such harmless items were routinely viewed, not as charms to facilitate the casting of spells, but rather to combat *against* the effects of witchcraft, a belief which gave rise to a traditional rhyme:

> Rowan tree and red thread
> Keep the devils frae their speed.

In her testimony, Margaret did her best to exculpate Isobel Crawford whom she had entangled in the affair - perhaps inadvertently - but to no avail, as we have seen. By the time that her husband, Archibald, put in an appearance in court with a lawyer in tow, she appeared listless, perhaps already defeated. 'Ye hae been owre lang in coming,' she is supposed to have said. With stupefying heartlessness, the jury rejected the notion that Margaret's confession had been made under duress, the iron weights having at that time been newly removed from her legs and still within easy reach. Following the inevitable guilty verdict, Margaret Barclay was executed by strangling and her body burned on a pyre. A young woman whose greatest crime was probably being foolish enough to utter ill-judged, spiteful words, she left behind a small child.

The Irvine authorities were by no means alone in pursuing their obsession with witchcraft. For well over a century women and, less commonly, men across the breadth of Scotland were harried, persecuted and put on trial, often based on nothing more than hearsay and the flimsiest of evidence. Witchcraft-hysteria reached its high-water mark during the middle years of the seventeenth century with some fifty cases brought before the Irvine authorities within a single three-month period, twelve of which resulted in executions. Things were no better in Ayr with a total of sixteen alleged witches put to death between March and May of 1650. It has been estimated that, during the years of persecution, something approaching two hundred unfortunate souls throughout Ayrshire faced the ordeal of being tried for witchcraft, the last to do so being Marion Brown of Kilmarnock in 1709, before the witch-hunt finally ended a quarter-century later when the laws relating to black magic were at long last repealed.

11 Guests from the North

When King Charles II reneged on his promise to the Scots, he set in motion a whole disastrous train of events. Having previously undertaken to establish a Presbyterian form of religion in Scotland whereby individual congregations were entitled to appoint their own ministers, in the event he balked at an arrangement which, in his view, smacked far too much of people-power and sought to impose in its place an Episcopal system whereby decisions were taken by bishops who were ultimately answerable to himself. Roughly one third of the Scottish clergy reacted by declining to swear an oath of loyalty to the king and were duly ejected from their churches. Many of these ousted ministers took to preaching at illegal, open-air services which often drew large crowds of their followers, known as Covenanters. Viewed by the authorities as highly seditious, these 'conventicles' were ruthlessly suppressed and many innocent lives were lost as a result.

The situation reached crisis-point in November 1666 when a Covenanting army, deriving in the main from the south-west of Scotland, marched on Edinburgh under the leadership of an experienced professional soldier, Colonel James Wallace of Auchans, near Dundonald. Ultimately, however, the protestors' mission proved abortive when they were defeated in the Pentland Hills by the numerically-superior forces of Tam Dalyell of the Binns whose ruthless cruelty in the aftermath of the battle earned him enduring ignominy. But, in spite of Bluidy Tam's victory, fears of future rebellion were not allayed and the problem rumbled for another decade or so until in the autumn of 1677 a move was made by the government to resolve matters once and for all. The decision was taken to quarter a large force of Highland clansmen in the trouble-spots of the south-west until such time as local landowners could be persuaded to sign a document - subsequently dubbed 'the Black Bond' - under whose terms they accepted responsibility for suppressing conventicles on their lands. For understandable reasons, many of the south-west's lairds displayed little enthusiasm for appending their signatures to a bond whose provisions they would be singularly incapable of enforcing. Therefore, in the new year of 1678, some 6,000 clansmen descended from the north, their numbers boosted by approximately 2,000 government militiamen. It was a force that came in time to be known as the 'Highland Host'.

A strange, old tale has survived - most likely in large part apocryphal - which gives a flavour of those unsettled times. It centres on a widow, Elspeth Wallace, who lived alone in an isolated cottage on the Cassillis estate, her only companions her pet cat and her milk cow, Doddy. Elspeth's days, we are told, were spent in tending her kailyard, the produce of which she used to feed her cow, and in cultivating a tiny plot of barley which she used to brew small quantities of a mild form of beer known as 'tippeny'.

Elspeth had been widowed, so the story goes, little more than a year after her wedding-day. Working in the gardens at Culzean, her husband had met with an unfortunate accident when he was struck by a falling tree-limb and died soon after. Born a short time later, Elspeth's child only ever knew one parent and naturally, as the child grew up, mother and daughter were very close. On reaching working-age, however, Jessie was obliged to leave her mother's home and to go into service on a neighbouring farm. For both mother and daughter, we might imagine, the wrench must have been considerable.

Only on Saturday nights did Jessie have sufficient free time to allow her to return home to spend a few hours in her mother's company. It was on one such occasion - a February evening of keen frost - when the two women had just finished supper and were settling down by the fireside to talk over a proposal of marriage which Jessie had recently received that the peace of the occasion was rudely shattered. With a loud bang, the door of the cottage burst open and in stepped two men in Highland plaids, one of whom laid hold of Jessie while his companion ensured that her mother was securely tied-up. In spite of Elspeth's loudly-voiced protestations, the Highlanders made off into the night, taking with them not only her daughter but also her milk cow, Doddy, whom they led away at the end of a rope.

This was the time when members of the occupying Highland army were billeted at nearby Blairquhan Castle. Jessie, it appears, had caught the eye of Lord Airlie, the local commander, and, hoping for a closer acquaintance, he had promptly dispatched two of his men on a kidnap mission, offering them as incentive the reward of her mother's cow. To the two brawny brothers, Donald and Archie Campbell, their assignment probably sounded like child's play but, as things turned out, it proved a good deal trickier than they might ever have imagined.

Returning through the darkness to Blairquhan, the two Highlanders found themselves struggling to master a spirited girl on the one hand and an obstinate beast on the other. Matters finally came to a head when, part-way to the castle, Doddy decided to dig her heels in and refused point blank to take a step farther - loyalty to her mistress probably less of an issue than the memory of a cosy byre. Jessie's outrage is easy to imagine when, before they turned their attention to the recalcitrant cow, Donald and Archie tied her ankles firmly together and planted her for safekeeping on top of a boulder in the middle of a nearby burn. Meanwhile Doddy continued with her policy of non-co-operation, forcing the two rapscallions to conclude that the best option open to them would be to slaughter the beast where she stood and carry off as much of her meat as they could manage. But how to carry out the deed? Probably well aware of the brothers' shady character, Lord Airlie had expressly instructed them to go on their mission unarmed

The present Blairquhan Castle

and they couldn't even produce a pocket knife between them. The solution that they finally came up with involved a joint effort whereby Donald agreed to hold Doddy firmly by the horns while his brother, Archie, prepared to brain the unfortunate creature with a rock retrieved from the burn.

Predictably the Highlanders' harebrained scheme didn't go to plan. As Doddy lunged and twisted in Donald's unfamiliar grip, Archie found himself unable to strike a clean blow and, growing increasingly frustrated, he finally plunged the rock downwards with all his might but, instead of making contact with the cow's broad forehead, it smashed instead his brother's skull. And so the old legend draws to a close, its moral obvious to all, as the villainous Archie weeps over the corpse of his dead brother. A short afterthought strikes a cheerier note when it informs us that both cow and girl were quick to flee the scene and that one of the two was happily married within the space of a month.

On the face of it, it would be hard to argue that Elspeth and Jessie's story makes for anything other than a highly improbable yarn, its superficiality quite apparent. But there may be a bit more to it than that. Behind the salutary tale of Donald and Archie Campbell lies the outline of another story, older perhaps and with a recognisable make-up: a solitary woman who lives alone in the woods, her only companions her pet animals; a beautiful and virtuous girl, threatened by villains who are narrowly thwarted; a happy conclusion with the prospect of a marriage to come. It is tempting to surmise that the story of Donald and Archie, blockheaded representatives of the reviled Highland Host, might well be a piece of crude seventeenth-century propaganda which has been superimposed on top of a traditional folk-tale.

And it is hardly surprising if the people of the south-west were disposed to demonise their unwanted guests, given the treatment they experienced at their hands. After mustering at Stirling, the Highland army had marched first to Glasgow and thence to Ayrshire where it set about the task of disarming local people and prosecuting any believed to have attended a conventicle, requisitioning all horses deemed to be above £50 in value and burning to the ground all unofficial places of worship. Individual Highlanders were quartered in the households of ordinary folk while larger groups were garrisoned at the mansion houses of those landowners who still held out against the Black Bond. By Privy Council dictat, the occupying forces had total immunity from prosecution for 'killing, wounding, apprehending, or imprisoning such as shall make opposition' - a conveniently vague catch-all, you might think, that could be made to mean virtually anything. According to the eighteenth-century historian, Rev. Robert Wodrow, the Highlanders arrived in the south-west equipped with 'good store of iron shackles, as if they were to bring back vast numbers of slaves; and thumb-locks, as they call them, to make their examinations and trials'. Small wonder, then, if the members of the Highland Host spread fear and revulsion wherever they went.

A remark attributed to the Duke of Lauderdale, the Secretary of State for Scotland at the time, is equally chilling: 'It were better that the west bore nothing but windlestraws [withered grass] and sandy-laverocks [sand-larks],' he is reported to have said, 'than it should bear rebels to the King.' Clearly Lauderdale viewed the Host as a good deal more than simply a peace-keeping force and, if his words are to be taken at face value, he was quite prepared for the visiting clansmen to make a desert of the south-west. Lauderdale had powerful backing. 'The King,' he was assured, 'does extreamly approve the course you have taken.' The Duke of Hamilton, on the other hand, was an unwilling recipient of Highland soldiers and wrote of his concern that they 'should not only have frie quarter bott liberty of plundering, and iff they pleased to settell themselves there as a new plantation and possess the countrey for a reward'. The nightmare scenario that he appears to envisage is tantamount to ethnic cleansing.

Even if the Duke of Hamilton's fears did not fully materialise, it would be hard to deny the welter of reports detailing the Highlandmens' cruelty and excesses. Countless properties were ransacked for provisions and valuables, highway robbery became rife and protection money - known as 'dry quarter' - was exacted as a matter of course. It escaped nobody's notice that the Highlanders evinced an apparent sixth sense in sniffing out hidden valuables to the extent that they were suspected by some of possessing the 'second sight'. The Earl of Cassillis - who at the end of the day was never prevailed upon to sign the Black Bond - complained that 'not onely free quarter, but dry quarter, plunder and other exactions, with many insolencies and cruelties, too tedious and lamentable to report were committed' by the 1,500 Highlandmen who were billeted in the Carrick district, many on his own lands. An estimated bill for the Earl's unwanted guests puts the amount at £32,000 Scots while the losses sustained for Ayrshire as a whole were reckoned to be closer to £200,000 Scots.

A serious hardship for the country people was the confiscation of their horses, the animals' loss felt all the more keenly at this vital season in the farmers' calendar when ploughing should have been underway. In a letter to the Marquess of Ormonde, Lord Granard wrote during the first week of March 1678 that 'multitudes of [local people] are so plundered by the highlanders that they have left their habitations and have not put plough in the ground this year'. Cattle, it was noted, were needlessly slaughtered, sometimes out of spite, and some of the inhabitants of the land had been harried to the extent that they chose to flee across the North Channel to Ireland.

People in the towns suffered too. On the Sunday prior to their leaving Kilmarnock, the resident Highlanders indulged in a plunderous spree which was only brought under control when their officers were paid by desperate townsmen to intercede. Particularly badly affected during the occupation was William Dickie, a Kilmarnock merchant, who had been obliged to accommodate nine clansmen for a total of six weeks. When his guests finally departed, he got his thanks when they carried off his household goods by the sackful as well as a considerable sum of his money in silver. Worse by far, however, was the fact that one of the Highlanders wounded his pregnant wife with a dirk, causing her to die from the injury soon after. Dickie himself suffered two broken ribs as a result of a beating. These weren't isolated incidents. While remonstrating with marauding Highlanders, Rev. Alexander Wedderburn of Kilmarnock received a blow to the chest from the butt of a musket which was widely believed to have led directly to his death. A few miles away, John Wallace of Crooks, Dundonald, lost a hand when it was severed by a Perthshire trooper.

Much has been made by writers and commentators of the vast gulf that divided the members of the Highland Host from the lowland population with whom they were billeted. 'The Highlanders were most feared [...] on account of their strange dress, their different tongue, their diverse manners and customs', wrote John R. Elder in his comprehensive account of the Highland Host, and Rev. Alexander Shields went further, stating that 'they brought down from the Wild Highlands a host of Savages, more terrible than Turks or Tartars'. A degree of caution, however, might be in order, bearing in mind that accounts of the period were penned largely from a committed lowland, Presbyterian standpoint. Routinely disregarded is the fact that the lonely corners of the Carrick hills still retained a form of Gaelic during the seventeenth century and it is not impossible that in some districts the oppressors shared a common language with those whom they oppressed. Ayrshire's last recorded native-speaker of Gaelic, Margaret McMurray of Cultezeoun, near Maybole, lived in advanced old age until 1760, more than 80 years after the departure of the Host. But, be that as it may, there is certainly no evidence that any linguistic affinity had the effect of softening relations between the people of south Ayrshire and their parasitic guests.

The sense of relief must have been palpable when the main body of the Highland Host was recalled in late February, the result, it has been suggested, of representations made to the king by prominent landowners such as the Duke of Hamilton and the Earl of Cassillis, or perhaps simply because the clansmen's absence from their ancestral lands had created an uneasy vacuum in the north. 'You would have thought by their baggage that they had been at the sack of a besieged city', wrote Rev. James Kirkton in his description of the Highlanders as they made their way home, laden with plundered clothing, shoes, bedclothes, pots and pans, items of furniture, bales of cloth and linen, and as many horses as it would take to carry them. At Glasgow they faced an unexpected setback when students held the bridge across the flooded Clyde against them, demanding that they hand over their booty and, surprisingly, it seems that many of them readily co-operated. Just north of the city trouble flared when the retreating clansmen were attacked by several hundred locals. A number of the Highlanders sustained injuries in the fracas that developed and one man, Alexander McGregor of Breadalbane, lost his life.

At the end of the day, Lauderdale's method of subduing the Covenanters of the south-west by his deployment of an occupying Highland army was one that proved singularly unsuccessful - indeed, spectacularly backfired. Far from crushing the spirit of protest, the Host's intimidatory tactics had rather the effect of hardening the rebels' resolve and galvanising a desire for revenge which found expression barely a year later in the Covenanting victory over government forces at Drumclog. Success for the protestors, however, proved short-lived and within a few short weeks they suffered a dramatic reversal of fortune at Bothwell Brig before hunkering down and weathering the long, hard years of oppression that would later become known as 'the Killing Time'. The persecution finally ceased at the time of the Glorious Revolution in 1688 when Charles II's successor - his brother, James VII and II - was driven into exile in France. With the accession to the throne of William and Mary, the Presbyterian case in Scotland was won.

12 The Murderous Mackillups

Motorists nearing the head of the Stinchar valley are faced with a choice. Go left at the South Balloch T-junction and you will soon head steeply uphill, looping and turning in the shadow of The Pilot and counting the milestones till Crosshill. If, on the other hand, you opt to turn right instead, things grow even more dramatic as, curling around the farmhouse at Pinvalley, the single-track road rises within a short distance to the Nick of the Balloch, a spectacular 1,300-foot pass among some of the grandest scenery in the entire south of Scotland.

The eighteenth-century map-maker, Andrew Armstrong, marked out the area for special comment. Alongside the Nick of Darley - another ancient hill-pass, now half-forgotten - he warns the unwary traveller that 'the Road leads on the Side of a very steep Hill, its [sic] not above two feet broad and if you stumble you must fall almost Perpendicular six or seven Hundred Feet.' The nearby hills he describes as 'exceeding barren & rocky', adding that 'on them are found the beautiful white Moor Fowl called the Termagant, and no where else South of Stirling.' Sadly, the bird in question has retreated from its former haunts but, even in the ptarmigan's absence, the landscape still inspires. This was the wild setting, so we are told, for a series of grisly events that took place sometime before Captain Armstrong arrived in the hills with his map-making equipment.

The most detailed version of events is perhaps that provided by Joseph Train, the eighteenth-century folklorist, whose account appears to be based largely on local knowledge. Train's story begins at the annual spring fair of Kirkdandie as a young pedlar, Charlie, sets out to return home to Minnigaff in Galloway. Having survived the boisterous shenanigans for which the fair was notorious, Charlie must surely have assumed that his two-day hike home would present few problems. His journey, however, did not go entirely to plan.

Life had not all been plain sailing for Charlie and his family. His father, whom Train identifies as 'Kie of Aldinny' (almost certainly the present-day farm of Aldinna), had been troubled for some time by unexplained losses from his flock and, suspicious of foul play, rose early one morning in hopes of catching the sheep-stealers red-handed. When he failed to return that night, exhaustive searches and inquiries were carried out but no clue ever emerged over the ensuing days and weeks to the missing man's fate. In time it became accepted that, whatever had happened, by now Charlie's father was likely to be dead and accordingly the lease of his farm was taken on by neighbouring farmers, the Mackillups of Craigenreoch. Obliged to flit, Kie's widow removed her family to Minnigaff where she subsisted on the charity of friends until, at the age of twelve, her eldest son, Charlie, could be put to work as a pedlar. Selling small items from his pack, the trip to Kirkdandie Fair was said to have been the boy's first away from home.

Whether trade was brisk we can only speculate but as the fair wound up for another season, it is easy to imagine Charlie's feeling of pride at the conclusion of his first independent venture. The first few miles of his homeward journey would have paralleled the Stinchar, passing through the village of Barr before, taking leave of the riverbank, Charlie would have climbed into hillier country to the south. To cross the Polmaddie range, he appears to have avoided Armstrong's vertiginous route, opting instead for the Nick of the Balloch whose gentler gradients possibly made up for its slightly higher altitude. Perhaps he took a breather at the pass, quenching his thirst at the Brandy Well before shouldering his pack once again and striding downhill with the infant Water of Minnoch trickling by his side and the high, rolling ridge of the Galloway hills filling the far horizon.

By the time he passed the lonely Rowantree Toll, daylight must already have been fading. A little further south, the farm of Craigenreoch (today more commonly spelt 'Craigenrae') may well have struck Charlie as his last opportunity to avoid spending the hours of darkness curled up in the lee of a heather-tussock. As he veered from the main Minnochside track and presented himself at the farmhouse door, the boy-pedlar could hardly have guessed that his story was about to step out of the commonplace and into the realm of the bizarre.

The tenants of Craigenrae were those same Mackillups, Nicol and Neil, who had stepped in at the time of Charlie's father's disappearance to take over the lease of Aldinna. 'A wild, savage race,' in the words of Joseph Train, their early ancestors were reputed to have arrived in far-off times from Ireland and it was widely rumoured in the locality that the two brothers continued in the same lawless tradition as their forebears, regularly boosting their income through the proceeds of crime. The men's father had drowned some time back while attempting to cross the swollen Minnoch - an event many attributed to black magic when he was unwise enough to fall from his wife, Madge's, favour. Notoriously unsociable, the Mackillups were willing nonetheless to accommodate any passing traveller who, unfamiliar with their reputation, was prepared to hand over a few coins in exchange for a dry corner of the steading where he might lay his head overnight.

A local boy himself, the chances are that Charlie understood the set-up at Craigenrae well enough as garrulous old Madge Mackillup fed him braxy ham and bannocks before showing him to a heather-bed in the 'spence' - a small room adjacent to the byre - where he would spend the night. With his modest pack and meagre takings, he probably believed himself beneath the Mackillups' notice. Madge's two sons, he noted, were absent from home - who knows where? - and had not yet made an appearance by the time that darkness descended and he bedded down for the night.

Sometime later Charlie awoke with a start. Subdued voices were coming from the room next door. Rising silently from his bed, he peered through a narrow gap in the flimsy partition to see by the light of a dim candle that the Mackillups had returned home, each brother manhandling a live goat which, from the ongoing conversation, he ascertained had been captured on the hills above Palgowan. For fear of interruption by late-going travellers, the brothers made it clear that they intended to waste no time in dispatching the stolen animals - puzzlingly, Joseph Train offers no explanation as to why two such seasoned villains would not have already slaughtered the beasts out on the open hill. Just as the brothers were about to do the deed, however, their old mother, Madge, intervened. It is likely that Charlie's blood ran cold when he heard her propose that her sons' first priority should be to silence their overnight guest, producing as she spoke a large knife which she had laid aside for the purpose.

How Charlie kept his nerve is impossible to say as the Mackillup brothers crept silently into the spence and Neil held a lighted candle within inches of the pedlar-boy's face. Though wide-awake, Charlie focused on remaining motionless, keeping his eyes tightly closed and maintaining the steady rhythm of his breathing. His ploy proved successful. Satisfied that their guest was sound asleep, the brothers retreated from the spence and resumed the task of slaughtering the goats - a mistake, they would soon realise. Meanwhile, cowering in his heather-bed, Charlie heard a pathetic bleat as the first animal's throat was cut, followed immediately by the sound of old Madge cackling as she reminded her sons of the death-cry of their late neighbour, Kie of Aldinna. With a jolt, Charlie realised that the mystery of his father's disappearance was solved at last. And if he was to avoid a similar gruesome fate, then he knew that decisive action was called for.

His heart pounding, Charlie got up from the heather-bed and, hoping that the Mackillups were still preoccupied with the second goat, slipped silently from the spence into the adjacent byre. Peering through the gloom, he reckoned that his only hope of escape lay via the space where the 'grip' exited the building (the channel used to drain away the cattle's dung and urine) and the present circumstances left no room for fastidiousness. As he squirmed through the grip-hole on his stomach, Charlie wouldn't have given the question of hygiene a second thought.

Nick of the Balloch

It didn't take the Mackillups long to discover that their bird had flown the coop, leaving behind only his outdoor clothing and a meagre bundle of possessions. Conscious possibly of having given the game away, old Madge, however, was not yet outmanoeuvred. There was at Craigenrae a 'sloth-hound' - a dog trained in the art of tracking - and, after allowing the animal to snuffle at Charlie's abandoned belongings, Madge released the dog which promptly vanished into the night. Probably close to exhaustion, when Charlie heard the bloodhound's baying drawing steadily closer, he must surely have feared that his number was up but, as it turned out, all was not yet lost and his life was saved in rather an unexpected way. In his hurry to escape, Charlie had left behind his shoes and, stumbling barefoot, he was probably unaware of having cut his foot, possibly on a sharp stone on the moor. When a few moments later the sloth-hound reached this spot, it stopped to lick up the blood and, believing its work complete, turned immediately for home. Back at Craigenrae, when the dog returned and Madge and her sons saw the beast's bloody jowls they drew the obvious conclusion that their fleeing guest had been silenced for good.

Instead, the young pedlar was retracing his steps up and over the Nick of the Balloch and down along the Stinchar to Barr where, cold and weary, he arrived at the village alehouse and recounted his shocking tale to its late-night drinkers. Clearly action was called for. Forming a posse, the men armed themselves and, apparently led by Charlie himself, they made their way to Craigenrae where the Mackillups were presumably surprised at the reappearance of a boy whom they had assumed to be dead. One of the brothers, Nicol or Neil, sprang at Charlie with a dagger but was restrained by the men of Barr before he was able to inflict any injury. The Mackillups, we are told, put up a determined struggle but eventually all three were secured and bound and conveyed over the hill-passes to Maybole where they were placed under lock and key, their fate now in the hands of the Earl of Cassillis.

Joseph Train specifies no timescale for the events of his story but readers are left with the distinct impression that its main proceedings - from Charlie's departure from Kirkdandie Fair up to the point where the Mackillups are taken into custody - all took place within the space of twenty-four hours. Given the considerable distances involved, the inhospitable terrain, not to mention the physical and emotional demands on poor Charlie, we might be inclined to take this timing with a fairly generous pinch of salt. That said, unquestionably Train's account has a more authentic feel than an anonymous predecessor, published some fifteen years earlier in *Blackwood's Edinburgh Magazine*. Appearing in 1829, this alternative account is notably shorter on local detail, yet a good deal more lurid in its content. The story's pedlar-boy, for example, remains unnamed, as do his predatory hosts and the location of their house of horror. Common to both stories, however, was the cut-throats' chilling method of disposing of their victims' bodies and - thanks largely to the efforts of a celebrated nineteenth-century novelist - it occupies to this day a unique place in the lore of south-west Scotland.

Whatever the pressure applied at Cassillis House, the Mackillups soon confessed to the murder of Charlie's father. Apparently the very 'jockteleg' (large clasped knife) which had ended the shepherd's life was produced as evidence and it was revealed that, after the murder, his body had been dumped in the 'murder-hole' - a natural chasm, filled to the brim with water, which was located in rough ground to the north-east of the steading at Craigenrae. The anonymous contributor to *Blackwood's Magazine* states that, in total, nearly fifty unfortunate souls had died - some by drowning - at the sinister pool, several of whose skeletons were later able to be recovered. Probably more reliable is the story that in 1818 a local man, Alexander Murray of the Rowantree, used a weighted line to plumb the depths of the murder-hole and was forced to spool out some eighty feet of twine before his dangling weight finally settled on the bottom.

What alerted the wider world to the phenomenon of the murder-hole was the publication in 1894 of S. R. Crockett's adventure novel, *The Raiders*, in which the author takes the liberty of moving the moorland tarn out of Ayrshire and into his native Galloway, repositioning it some seven miles away as the crow flies, at the western end of Loch Neldricken. The unfortunate soul who falls among thieves is not Charlie, the pedlar-boy, but rather the novel's youthful hero, Patrick Heron.

In some respects Patrick's story follows the tale in *Blackwood's Magazine* fairly closely. Abducted by a band of ne'er-dae-weels, his headstrong sweetheart, May Maxwell, has been smuggled into the remote heart of the Galloway Hills and, during his efforts to track her down, Patrick stumbles in darkness across an isolated hovel on the shores of Loch Enoch.

His arrival at the Shieling of Craignairny arouses a degree of suspicion among the house's surly inhabitants who are kept in order by an elderly, white-haired woman - a 'witch-wife', according to the novelist - who quizzes Patrick concerning his journey. Claiming to be a humble pedlar, lost and forwandered on his way to Dalmellington, Patrick retires for the night but is horrified to find bloodstains on his bed-sheets. His subsequent discovery of a fresh corpse, stashed in a large wooden chest, does nothing to steady his nerves.

Things, however, look up. A brief note, fluttering from a crack in the ceiling, alerts Patrick to the presence of his sweetheart, May Maxwell, held captive in a room above. By forcing a skylight window, he secures her release and the reunited couple then flee into the night, indignant cries and the baying of bloodhounds ringing in their ears. From a high vantage point, May directs Patrick's attention to a flat area to the west of Loch Neldricken, as level as a bowling-green, in which Patrick sees 'a black round eye of water, oily and murky, as though it were without a bottom.' 'That is their Murder Hole,' May informs him, 'but if we are to lie there we shall not lie without company.'

Thankfully, the young couple's future turns out rather more rosy, though the same cannot be said for the villainous inhabitants of the hovel by Loch Enoch shore. Some months after fleeing their evil clutches, Patrick Heron and an enigmatic companion, Silver Sand, are once again in the high hills, having rescued a kidnapped child, Marion Tamson, from the same band of scoundrels. Before they are able to return the child to her parents, however, the men are forced to sit out an epic snowstorm - the infamous 'Sixteen Drifty Days' - in a secret howff where an isolated spearhead of Ayrshire plunges south into Galloway. 'The best hiding-place in all broad Scotland,' boasts Silver Sand, adding that the cosy refuge has seldom seen a visitor since the days of the Covenant when it provided sanctuary for many a persecuted wanderer. Even now, in the twenty-first century, the rocky peak of Mullwharchar is still remote, a good five-mile tramp from the nearest tarmacadamed road.

During the time that Patrick and Silver Sand are snowbound, their peace is shattered one day by a gargantuan rumble as though Mullwharchar itself were coming down upon their heads - 'a most michty hurl of stanes,' concludes Silver Sand. When the roar dies down and is not repeated, they put the matter from their minds until the morning of the seventeenth day when the storm has finally blown itself out. When the men emerge from their snowy prison, what they see amazes them. The only splash of colour in an otherwise white world is a savage red and grey scar on the brae-face opposite, marking the place where a massive rock-fall has broken away from the flank of the Dungeon Hill and plummeted down the hillside, obliterating in its progress the Shieling of Craignairny and burying its unfortunate inhabitants under countless tons of rock and snow. Patrick and Silver Sand gaze in wonder, knowing full well that anyone caught in the path of that mighty juggernaut is by now beyond all mortal assistance.

Such, then, was the exit that the novelist, S.R. Crockett, devised for his fictitious villains - dramatic and well-deserved, no doubt, but different entirely from the cut-throats' fate in other versions of the tale. According to *Blackwood's Magazine*, as soon as their confessions were extracted the old woman and her two sons were hanged without delay on gibbets erected on the moor. Joseph Train, on the other hand, has the three murderous Mackillups hanged on the infamous 'dule-tree' at Cassillis House - the last executions to be carried out, he observes, by order of an Earl of Cassillis. The manner of the criminals' demise wasn't the various storytellers' only point of divergence. Crockett places the action during the eighteenth-century glory days of the Solway smugglers; Train in the early part of the same century. *Blackwood's*, however, takes a different view, locating the events of the story as far back as the turn of the sixteenth century.

The plain truth is that no-one can say for sure and nothing in the story of the murder-hole is capable of being verified. It has even been suggested that the basis for the whole lurid tale was nothing more than an opportunistic murder committed by two tramps who robbed their unwitting victim at some unknown time in the past, then discarded his body on the moor, but were caught and hanged for their pains. Just such a brutal crime would surely have been meat and drink to local storytellers, thus putting the oral tradition into overdrive. Even the name 'murder-hole' may not be all that it seems. The last of the old Gaelic language slipped from local people's lips during the eighteenth century and the term 'murder-hole' may simply be a fanciful echo of a similar-sounding Gaelic name but with a different meaning entirely.

Whatever the reality, the location of the Craigenrae murder-hole is now largely forgotten, lost within an extensive stand of Sitka spruce. But even before the Forestry Commission's post-war transformation of the countryside, the demise of the murder-hole had already been reported, filled in - for all its reputed depth - by a local shepherd who had grown weary of fishing out drowned sheep. So the murder-hole's final victim was not, it appears, some solitary traveller, waylaid on a lonely by-way, but rather an unfortunate sheep, grazing unwarily on the Minnochside moors.

13 Troubles on Lady Isle

Strangely, one of the least-visited spots in Ayrshire is located within clear sight of several major towns, few if any of whose inhabitants will ever set foot on its meagre, windswept turf. A mere three or so miles south-west of Troon harbour, Lady Isle is roughly circular in shape, a mile and a half in circumference and measures little more than 600 yards across. At no point does the islet's low-lying terrain rise higher than twenty feet or so above the level of the surrounding sea. Diminutive though it may be, Lady Isle possesses nonetheless a group of still smaller satellites - Half-Tide Rock, Scart Rock (*scart* being Scots for cormorant) and Seal Rock - the names an indication of some of the wild creatures to be found along its rocky shorelines. But although Lady Isle sustains healthy wildlife populations, all under the protection of Scottish Natural Heritage, of human habitants there are none.

That isn't to say, however, that the island has been entirely disregarded over the years. Sadly, no trace remains of a pre-Reformation chapel, dedicated to the Virgin Mary and with links, it has been suggested, to the ecclesiastical establishment at Ladykirk, near Prestwick. This, some would have it, was what gave rise to the island's name, though an alternative theory proposes that it derives rather from the Gaelic *laidh*, denoting a ship's course across the waves. Perhaps the chapel's ancient masonry was removed during the 1770s, recycled for use in erecting twin-beacons which, once lined up, signalled a safe anchorage for shipping on the east side of the island. Some suggest that the magistrates of Glasgow were responsible, weary perhaps of losses for which Lady Isle's rocky reefs were deemed responsible, while others take the differing view that it was the island's proprietor, the Laird of Fullarton, who was the man behind the pillars' construction. It is possible, I suppose, that both parties had a hand in what might have been a joint-venture.

Whoever was responsible, their efforts did not prove wholly successful. During a storm in December 1811 a vessel was spotted, stranded on rocks alongside the island, and, by peering through a spy-glass, a number of survivors could be made out on the island itself. The Revenue Cutter, *Prince of Wales*, set out in an attempt to effect a rescue but, thwarted by high winds and heavy seas, the skipper, Captain Wallace, had no option but to turn back to Troon where he reported that a dozen or so of the stranded vessel's crew had succeeded in lighting a fire on the island and that they had erected for themselves a makeshift canvas shelter. From the numerous bags of cotton and large wooden casks which he had observed, floating on the waves, Wallace surmised that the beleaguered vessel had been on a return journey from the West Indies when she came to grief.

The following day the wind dropped sufficiently to allow *The Prince of Wales* to make a second attempt with the result that all fourteen marooned sailors were successfully rescued from Lady Isle. In confirmation of Captain Wallace's theory, it emerged that the *Ellen* had been returning home from the West Indies to Port Glasgow with a cargo of sugar, coffee, rum and cotton aboard when, during the hours of darkness, she had struck a rock amid the pounding surf of Lady Isle. In order to prevent the wind from catching in the rigging and making a total capsize more likely, the crew had used axes to chop down the masts and, by sheer good fortune, the main mast had fallen in just such a way as to form a bridge between the wreck and Lady Isle, enabling all members of the crew to scramble across and reach dry land. The *Ellen* herself, however, was not so fortunate. The bulk of her cargo proved irrecoverable and on 7 January 1812, three weeks after the night of the great storm, the ship's effects were disposed of by public roup, including - as reported in the local press - 'Masts, Spars, Sails, Standing and Running Rigging, Anchors, Cables, Guns, Copper-Sheathing etc. Also a Parcel of Pig-Iron and Shot, all as they lie at present on the Lady Isle.'

By the opening years of the nineteenth century, the Lady Isle's proprietor, Colonel William Fullarton, had fallen on hard times - the result in part of his ill-advised bankrolling of three entire army regiments - to the extent that in July 1804 he was forced to put his Ayrshire estates up for sale. A year later the Marquis of Titchfield (later Duke of Portland) parted with £79,500 to acquire the Fullarton lands, at which point the impoverished colonel departed for London where, still in his early 50s, he passed away less than three years later - the last member of a family whose association with Lady Isle went back the best part of five centuries.

Lady Isle from above Troon

On the face of it, the maritime part of the Duke of Portland's new acquisition might have seemed fairly isolated, but it soon became clear that that wasn't sufficient to keep intruders at bay. In 1811 the Duke's tenant, William Allasson, bemoaned the mistreatment of the flock of sheep which he grazed on the island, as well as the fact that trespassers had been poaching its wild rabbits, in demand at the time not only for meat but also for their pelts which were used in the manufacture of fashionable top-hats. Further problems a decade later prompted the Duke to put up a reward of five guineas, a considerable sum in June 1821, for information leading to the conviction of 'evil-disposed persons [who] have lately set fire to the surface of the Lady Isle near Troon.' According to a notice published on the Duke's behalf, fire had 'consumed the greater part of the [island's] Turf and Pasture.'

When Provost William Fullarton of Ayr - a relative of Lady Isle's former owner - took over the tenancy of the island in June 1829 he requested in the local press that 'no person landing [on Lady Isle] shall take any dogs ashore, as all the Rabbits have been destroyed.' The notice further intimated that the provost had introduced 'a few more pairs and hopes that neither these shall be destroyed, nor the little vegetation that there is.' The island's enthusiastic new tenant soon embarked upon an ambitious programme of improvements. In the half-century or so since they had been erected, the island's twin pillars had been become weathered and indistinct, so Fullarton arranged for them to be restored and freshly whitewashed. He ferried boatloads of earth and dung out from Ayr - an expensive enterprise surely - in an effort to restore the island's ravaged vegetation and before long sheep were once again grazing on the island pastures.

A simple wooden hut, erected to provide shelter for the provost's workmen, may well have been the first new building that the island had witnessed since the construction of St Mary's Chapel untold centuries before. A more solid structure of stone and lime followed a little later, attached to the taller of the two beacons in the centre of the island, which served as accommodation during visits by Fullarton and his guests but - initially at least - was said to have been left unlocked as a useful refuge for anyone in need. His establishment of a landing-place enabled easier access for small boats, something perhaps that Provost Fullarton would later come to regret.

Almost inevitably, there were those who had no scruples about taking advantage of the provost's magnanimity, and it soon became necessary for the lodge to be secured during its owner's absence. In April 1831 Fullarton offered a reward of two guineas for information relating to an incident in which 'the House situated on the Lady Isle was feloniously Broken Open.' Sadly, it was no isolated occurrence and over a two-year period the property was said to have been burgled on no fewer than four occasions, the locks on the lodge burst open, goods stolen or destroyed, and sheep and the island's rabbits slaughtered. In January 1832, Provost Fullarton was once again driven to offer a similar reward following yet another break-in.

Whether the money was ever claimed is not on record but what is certain is that four local men were soon apprehended and charged in connection with the break-in. John Gray, senior, and John Gray, junior - presumably father and son - appeared in due course in the dock at Ayr Sheriff Court alongside two more Grays - James and William - all members of the same family of Troon fishermen. As it happened, it was by no means the first time that the Grays had become embroiled in a dispute concerning Lady Isle.

Trouble had flared five years previously in 1827, when the island's owner, William Cavendish-Scott-Bentinck, 4th Duke of Portland, petitioned Archibald Bell, Sheriff of Ayrshire, with a view to disputing the right of John Gray, senior, John Gray, junior, and James Gray - as well as other 'sea fishermen residing at Troon' - to fish for lobsters in the waters adjacent to his lands, claiming such exclusive rights for himself. For their part, the Grays asserted that they had operated in these waters 'uninterrupted' for more than 40 years - and that, furthermore, the Duke had frequently observed them at work and had even, on occasion, bought from them their catch. Once it came to court, the case dragged on over a period of several years as arguments for the 'pursuer' - the Duke of Portland - and the 'defenders' - the Grays - were bandied back and forth. In the end the outcome of the case hinged - a little bizarrely - on the question of whether lobsters might reasonably be classed as 'semi-domesticated animals' - comparable, say, to 'pigeons in a pigeon-house [or] bees in a hive'. If so adjudged, the Lady Isle lobsters would automatically be considered the Duke of Portland's property. Unresolved at Ayr, the case was referred to the Court of Session in Edinburgh which finally concluded in May 1832 that, based on a lobster's 'power of locomotion' - no less! - the creature might reasonably be deemed a wild animal and, therefore, 'not the subject of property till caught.' As a result of the learned lawlords' ruling, the court found in favour of the Troon fishermen who were not, it was further noted, to be held liable for expenses.

It was a landmark judgment, a striking victory for the Grays though, as may be remembered, it was only one of two court-battles that they had on their hands during the spring of 1832. Things had gone rather less favourably when they appeared before Ayr Sheriff Court on 18 April to answer a charge of burglary on Lady Isle. It was alleged that, on New Year's Day of that year, John Gray, senior, John Gray, junior, James Gray and William Gray had forced the locks on Provost Fullarton's lodge where, on entering, they had proceeded to carry out various acts of vandalism including the destruction of certain articles of furniture. While the accused men were prepared to admit to having entered the property and - as it emerged - tucked into a meal of potatoes there, they flatly denied responsibility for any damage. In spite of the testimony of two prosecution witnesses, ultimately it proved impossible to make the charge in its entirety stick as the possibility could not be discounted that the damage to the lodge might have been perpetrated by an earlier intruder prior to the fishermen's arrival. Whether the Grays had indeed broken up an old chair or two, perhaps to feed a fire, is now impossible to know but, on the basis of what some might see as a technicality, all four men were issued with a fairly modest fine - five shillings each - before being returned to Ayr jail pending payment. Following their rap on the knuckles, the Grays continued for many years afterwards to set their lobster-creels in the waters around Lady Isle - as had been demonstrated beyond question they were perfectly entitled to do.

Hazards on Lady Isle could materialise in guises other than those of wind and wave as a curious case in September 1857 demonstrated all too clearly. Two Newton-upon-Ayr fishermen - John McPherson, and his nephew, William Taylor - had landed a party of visitors from Edinburgh on the island when a mid-afternoon downpour, accompanied by flashes of lightning, forced the group to take shelter in the lee of one of the old beacons. Because the tide was receding, however, William Taylor took responsibility for moving the party's boat out to deeper water and, in an effort to stay dry, it appears that he then wrapped himself in a length of sail-cloth and lay down on the floor of the boat in order to allow the squall time to pass. When the rain finally eased and Taylor's companions emerged from where they had been sheltering, they were puzzled when he did not likewise reappear on deck and their concern mounted yet higher when he failed to respond to their repeated cries. When a member of a second party from Troon, also visiting the island that day, was enlisted to investigate, the sad truth emerged. On drawing near, the Troon man discovered that the mast of Taylor's boat had been shattered by a bolt of lightning and, tragically, a hole burnt through the sail in which the fisherman had wrapped himself. Sadly, the dead man left behind a widow and three children.

As the nineteenth century wore on, the need for modern lighting on Lady Isle became increasingly pressing. On 3 February 1854 a coal-laden schooner, *Dispatch*, was wrecked on rocks at the north end of the island while *en route* from Ayr to Belfast. No loss of life occurred, the entire crew being rescued by a tug-boat from Troon, but the vessel herself was thought to be irrecoverable. A quarter-century on, the brig, *Caros*, of Whitehaven ran aground in November 1880, though once again the crew survived. It was another twenty years before work got underway to erect a stone tower in the centre of the island on the site of one of the eighteenth-century beacons, the new structure to be 63 feet in height and with a conspicuous light placed on top. When the work of construction was complete, Messrs. McDonald and Muirhead of the Northern Lighthouse Commissioners' staff duly arrived on the island on the morning of Tuesday 27 January 1903 where they removed the screens that had partially obscured the light during testing. It was hoped that the blinking white light, visible an estimated fifteen miles away, would prove of great benefit to passing ships.

There was, however, no instant panacea. A mere eighteen months after the new tower beamed its first light across the waves, a steam yacht, *Donna Henrietta* - the property of Mr Welsh, a brass-polisher in Ayr - came to grief after striking a submerged rock while on a cruise around Lady Isle in broad daylight. The yacht's hull was badly holed but, by using her own small dinghy, all of *Donna Henrietta's* dozen or so passengers and crew succeeded in reaching the island in safety. When distress signals were spotted from the mainland, William McNeill set sail from South Beach on his steam launch and brought the shipwrecked party back to Troon. The following morning McNeill and Welsh returned to inspect the site of the wreck and, though able to salvage certain of its fittings, they held out little hope for *Donna Henrietta* herself, lying as she was in a particularly exposed position.

Twenty years later, a 1,200 ton steamer, *Marjorie Seed*, set sail from Rothesay Dock, Clydebank, shortly before midday on Christmas Eve 1924 in what was considered favourable weather and calm sea conditions, carrying a cargo of coal bound for Huelva in southern Spain. Why, some six hours later, the vessel should have run aground on the Scart Rock was never satisfactorily explained. But strike the rock she did, incurring damage to the extent that she filled rapidly with water. An SOS was sent out by wireless and the bulk of the crew - twenty men in all - were soon picked up by the Troon tug and lifeboat, including the ship's master, Captain Smith, who became unwell shortly after the collision and had to be taken by ambulance to Ayr County Hospital - the product, we might speculate, of stress. Four crewmen remained aboard to make an assessment of the damage done but they too were taken off around 10 p.m., bearing with them the depressing news that seawater had penetrated the engine room to a depth of four feet.

Any notion of re-floating the beleaguered vessel in the days that followed was put paid to by a succession of violent gales that swept in from the south-west. Gradually the ship's funnel was swallowed up by the waves and within a week or two all that remained visible from the Troon shore was the topmost portion of her masts. An underwater investigation, carried out in early February 1925, confirmed that, such was the damage that the vessel had sustained, she was now quite beyond recovery. The consensus appeared to be that the *Marjorie Seed* had come a cropper as a result of a fundamental navigational error.

During the 1930s steps were taken by Ayr County Council to protect Lady Isle's seabird population through granting the island bird sanctuary status. The Council's measures were, however, limited in their effectiveness but were further strengthened in February 1951 when an Order under the Wild Birds Protection Act was endorsed by the Secretary of State for Scotland, Hector McNeil, under whose provisions the island became one of the few places in Scotland at the time which afforded total protection to wild birds and their eggs. Lady Isle remained during this time the property of the current - 7th - Duke of Portland but which he leased each year to the Royal Society for the Protection of Wild Birds in return for a nominal rent, an open-handed arrangement that his parsimonious nineteenth-century predecessor, the 4th Duke, would surely have viewed with a degree of disapproval.

14 The Battle of Bridge Mill

The two opposing armies met face to face near the old corn mill that operated on the Water of Girvan. Those several hundred marchers who had arrived from the north, brandishing banners, swords and staves, were fronted by a handful of men bearing firearms. Directly ahead, their opposite numbers made up for their lack of fire-power by a hail of rocks which they rained down upon the visitors' heads while the two groups' leaders engaged in negotiations. Struck on the face by a flying stone, one of the northern gunmen finally snapped and, raising his weapon to his shoulder, took careful aim before firing. In the pitched mêlée that followed a goodly number of combatants on both sides were to suffer grievous injuries and not everyone would emerge from the fracas with his life intact. So - a scene dating from late medieval times, perhaps, as competing clans fought out a turf-war in a bid to establish local precedence? Not so. For the Bridge Mill confrontation took place less than two centuries ago, a few short years before a youthful Queen Victoria acceded to the British throne.

The lead-up to the disturbance at Bridge Mill was a time of great unrest. Parliamentary reform was in the wind and up and down the land its supporters were engaged in conducting meetings and congregating in marches and processions. With the permission of the authorities, pro-reformers in Girvan picked out a local holiday, Monday 25 April 1831, to march through the town, holding aloft the radical political symbol of a tricolour on which the words 'Reform' and 'Loyalty' were emblazoned. Not everyone, however, was in agreement with the marchers' aims. At that time the population of Girvan totalled some five thousand, an estimated two thirds of whom were believed to be Irish in origin. For some of the Protestant Irish the passage through parliament two years earlier of the Roman Catholic Relief Act - under whose terms Catholics were entitled for the first time to hold many public offices, including that of Member of Parliament - had already been a step too far, and they viewed with displeasure the prospect of further parliamentary concessions, the principal beneficiaries of which, they believed, would once again be Catholics.

For these reasons Girvan's community of Orangemen resolved to take action. During the course of the April demonstration, they intercepted the pro-reform marchers at the street known as the Sandy Raw (now Duncan Street), tore down their tricolour and carried out a number of violent assaults. In a show of defiance the pro-reformers regrouped the following day and once again hoisted the tricolour with a view to resuming their march but they found their way barred a second time by Orangemen wielding sticks, pokers and hammers. At this point the local authority stepped in, calling a meeting on Wednesday 27 April during which all future processions were banned in an effort to stem further disorder. The injustice of the decision outraged many local people and, following a fairly widespread indignant reaction, the ban was quickly revoked with the result that on Thursday 28 April a large pro-reform procession, with a body of magistrates at its head, marched through the streets to a mass rally at Girvan Green. Flags were displayed - tricolours among them - as well as banners proclaiming pro-reform slogans. Speeches were made and three cheers raised for eminent local reformers, such as Thomas Francis Kennedy of Dalquharran and Dunure, the popular MP for Ayr Burghs, and Richard Oswald of Auchincruive, a future Whig member for Ayrshire. The event passed off without incident and, when proceedings were complete, the crowds dispersed in an orderly fashion. This time the local Orangemen kept their distance, the occasion perhaps a little too grand for their brand of bully-boy tactics.

Trouble wasn't inevitable. Around the same time as Girvan's problematic march, Kilmarnock staged a similar event on what can only have been a highly impressive scale. A mile-long procession of several thousand marchers, attended by 100 men on horseback, made its way through the town streets with representatives of Kilmarnock's principal trades to the fore, each displaying its own distinctive flag and emblem. Numbers were swelled by pro-reform delegations from much of the surrounding area - from Ayr, Cumnock, Fenwick, Galston, Irvine, Kilmaurs, Newmilns, Stewarton and Tarbolton - and the vast throng that assembled on the site of the present-day Howard Park was estimated at considerably more than 10,000. The crowd was addressed by various pro-reform speakers, and rousing musical entertainment was provided by local bands.

Arguably the day's most poignant moment came about immediately after the voice of the final speaker fell silent. In a dramatic and moving gesture, a vast array of 130 pro-reform banners were simultaneously unfurled and held aloft while the sonorous sound of a drum-beat rolled out across the park. A sense of fate seemed to hang in the air - of change for the better within reach - and, when the rally dispersed, it was noted that there were no instances of drunkenness or disorder and that the pro-reformers returned to their homes in a sombre and law-abiding fashion.

What happened at Kilmarnock was by no means unique. At the northern end of the county, the town of Largs hosted a pro-reform rally during which some 500 marchers and sixty mounted men expressed their political opinions in an unfailingly orderly manner, while 1,100 turned up at a similar event in Beith. At Cumnock more than 1,000 people, many of them elderly and at least one man walking assisted by crutches, took to the streets in order to demonstrate their hunger for change. In an echo of an earlier display of people-power, some of the pro-reformers carried swords and banners that dated back a century and a half to the days of the Covenanters, and one of the flags in use was said to have been flown at the Battle of Drumclog in 1679. Another flag, borne aloft by the people of Ochiltree, was reputed to have been carried by Richard Cameron, immediately prior to his martyrdom at Airds Moss in 1680. Meanwhile the townspeople of Stewarton expressed their gratitude to Colonel Charles McAlester for having cast his vote in the recent general election for a pro-reform candidate by unyoking his carriage and drawing it manually through the town streets. As they hauled him all the way from Stewarton to his home at Kennox House, a distance of more than three miles, a piper accompanied the procession and struck up the cheerful tune of 'Charlie Is My Darling'.

But at the southern end of the county resentment continued to smoulder. Still smarting from the Orangemen's spoiling tactics in April, Girvan's pro-reformers drew up plans to thwart traditional Orange celebrations on 12 July to commemorate King William III's victory in 1690 over his Catholic rival, James VII and II. Learning of their intentions, the Orangemen, for their part, made contact with sister-lodges at Maybole, Crosshill and Dailly, inviting their members to show solidarity by swelling the Girvan Orangemen's ranks. When councillors were presented with representations from concerned members of the public, they immediately issued a statement prohibiting the march but, apparently fearful that their ban would be disregarded, they also sent word to the Sheriff Substitute for Ayrshire, William Eaton, alerting him to the potential for conflict.

Responding to their nervy communication, Eaton arrived for an overnight visit to Girvan on Monday 11 July, a mere 24 hours before the scheduled time of the march. He spent time in discussions with local magistrates before meeting leading figures in the Orange community whom he cautioned, both face to face and in writing, about the risk of serious disorder if the procession were to go ahead as planned. A deal was struck when the Girvan Orangemen agreed to call off their march. As it was too late now to cancel arrangements already made with the Maybole and district lodges, they undertook to intercept the visiting Orangemen at Bridge Mill and convey them to the Doune Park by a route through the town which avoided the principal thoroughfares. After refreshments, the Maybole Orangemen would follow the same route out of Girvan. The chances are that the Sheriff Substitute breathed a mighty sigh of relief when his eleventh-hour efforts appeared to bear fruit. The truth was that he had no other card up his sleeve, having been advised by the Solicitor General in Edinburgh that he had no legal means at his disposal to ban the procession outright. In addition, the council's request that a military force be dispatched to Girvan in order to keep the peace had been declined, for all that the two opposing parties were known to be making preparations for armed conflict.

In the absence of military assistance, responsibility for maintaining order fell entirely to the town's special constables and, following negotiations with William Eaton, an additional 100 Girvan residents were co-opted specifically for duty on 12 July. Accompanied by one of the town bailies, James Henderson (a local slater and plasterer), and equipped with staves and batons - but without firearms or swords - these were the men who were posted to await the Maybole Orangemen's arrival at Bridge Mill. Behind them trailed a small army of townsfolk, consisting, it was said, mostly of women and children.

When the Maybole Orangemen first appeared they were seen to be marching in orderly fashion, four or five abreast, bearing colours and accompanied by fifes and drums. Despite the presence of a heavily-loaded cart, dispensing generous shots of whisky, the mood was hardly festive: of an estimated 200 or 300 marching men, roughly half were described as being armed with weapons that ranged from swords and bayonets to pikes and guns. When the marchers reached Bridge Mill they stopped 100 yards short of the waiting constables, two of whose number stepped forward to inform the Orangemen's leader of the change of plan as agreed by the Girvan lodges. It looked as though there might be a peaceful outcome when the chief Orangeman agreed to the constables' demands and made to redirect his men accordingly. But things started to crumble when it became obvious that not all of the men under his command were willing to cooperate.

During the wrangling that ensued, a number of stones were lobbed from behind a hedge towards the stalled procession. Predictably the Orangemen responded in kind with the result that, despite the special constables' best efforts, a barrage of missiles was soon raining down on both sides. The stone which struck one of the Orangemen and possibly broke his jaw was the one fated to ignite the touch-paper. Witnesses recounted how a lean man, no longer young, stepped out from the fifth or sixth file of Orange marchers, raised his rifle in a methodical manner and took careful aim before firing. At this stage in proceedings the Girvan constables were a mere ten or fifteen yards away and the unfortunate soul on the receiving end of the Orangeman's bullet was Alexander Ross, a fisherman to trade, who was heard to utter the words 'Oh! I've been shot' before crumpling to the ground with his hands pressed to his stomach. Ross died within minutes with a bullet lodged in his spine.

As several more shots rang out, panic seized the crowd whose members scattered and fled, some into the fields, others back towards the town, while a smaller number made good their escape by swimming the River Girvan. One of those who did so, a blood-spattered constable, was stoned by the Orangemen as he struggled across, fortunate possibly to reach the far bank without drowning. It was only a single instance of what quickly developed into an inexplicable wave of brutality. Finding the remaining constables powerless to halt their advance, the Orangemen surged into Girvan, rampaging through the streets and wreaking havoc wherever they went, egged on, it was later alleged, by Irish Protestants living locally. Anyone unfortunate enough to come within reach - whether man, woman or child - was viciously attacked. While attempting to disarm Alexander Ross's killer,

Alexander Ross's Memorial, Girvan

Alexander Stevens was struck on the head from behind and knocked unconscious. An elderly man, Gilbert Davidson, was accosted as he attempted to make his way out of the town in order to work in the fields. Assaulted and left for dead, remarkably the old man survived. A weaver, David McQueen, lost the sight of one eye as a result of a stab-wound but perhaps the most shocking case of all related to a constable by the name of Orr who was assaulted close to the council buildings. Knocked to the ground by his attacker, he was battered and slashed before a second assailant entered the fray and set about unleashing repeated kicks to his body. Orr's worst moment, however, was yet to come when a third attacker discharged a pistol in his face but by sheer good fortune the bullet merely grazed the side of his head, thus enabling the beleaguered constable to survive by the skin of his teeth.

When the marauding Orangemen arrived at their destination at the Doune Park they were received as guests by representatives of Girvan's Orange lodges. Meanwhile the rest of the town's inhabitants set about arming themselves as best they could in anticipation of the mob's return. To this end a four-pounder cannon was hauled from Bailie Anderson's garden, loaded chock-full of grapeshot and set up in a prominent position overlooking the municipal buildings. But the townsfolk's anxieties, as it turned out, proved unfounded. Whether word had reached the Orangemen concerning Bailie Anderson's formidable ordnance or rather they were already sated with gratuitous violence, in the event they elected to leave Girvan via the back door, ironically by following the route that had been allocated for their arrival.

As the dust gradually settled, feelings throughout the town continued to run high. Throughout the entire episode, the Sheriff Substitute had been persona non grata for his perceived inaction. Handfuls of gravel had been thrown at the window of his accommodation in the King's Arms Inn and he had been harangued in the streets to the extent that he was forced to retreat to his lodgings. Leaving Girvan in the aftermath of the riot, his carriage was pelted with stones and his coachman mistreated by the angry townspeople. As darkness fell, armed citizens patrolled the town's bullet-scarred streets but peace had once again been restored and no further trouble was encountered. Of Girvan's resident Orangemen there was nary a trace. Fearful of recriminations, it was believed that they had abandoned their homes and fled to the country.

It would be entirely understandable if the Sheriff Substitute was a little put out by the rough handling he had been subjected to at Girvan but, whether or not, he still had a job to do and a killer remained at large. Eaton's first stop was at Maybole where he orchestrated the arrests of ten men who were suspected of involvement in the recent atrocity. The following day 21 men, some displaying obvious injuries, were transported by cart from Maybole to Ayr where they were secured under lock and key. A suspect had emerged for the shooting of Alexander Ross and the Sheriff Substitute dispatched a party of men in his pursuit. It appeared that Samuel Waugh, an Irishman living in Maybole and a former soldier with the Downshire Militia, had taken to the wild hills beyond Barr, making for Newton Stewart, possibly in the hope of ultimately finding a passage across the Irish Sea. Some accounts suggest that Waugh's pursuers caught up with him at the Suie, an isolated shepherd's house on the very fringes of Ayrshire. Arrested and escorted back to Ayr, it was noted that his jaw had been broken in two places - whether from his involvement in the riot or the result of his resisting arrest is impossible to know. Following investigations by Sheriff Archibald Bell (who had by now travelled to Ayrshire from his base in Edinburgh), Sheriff Substitute William Eaton, and the local Procurator Fiscal, Samuel Waugh was charged with the murder of special constable Alexander Ross. The acknowledged leader of the Orange procession, John Ramsay, faced an identical charge, while a number of other men from the Maybole district were charged with offences relating to mobbing, rioting and assault.

It was three or so months before Waugh and Ramsay appeared before the Court of Justiciary at Ayr in late September. Proceedings soon ground to a halt, however, when counsel for the accused made representations on his clients' behalf, requesting that their trial be removed out of Ayrshire to a neutral venue where opinions were liable to be a little less entrenched. It transpired that the presiding judge, Lord Gillies, was willing to assent - probably aware that sectarian tension in Ayrshire showed no signs of easing. A number of Girvan Orangemen and their families had been obliged to seek refuge in Maybole, having allegedly been forced from their homes. There were those, however, who characterised events rather differently, suggesting rather that the Orangemen had left Girvan by choice and had decided to instigate a little trouble prior to departing.

Around the same time, Alexander Goldie, an Orangeman facing charges in relation to the riot who was currently released on bail, and his wife, Margaret Davidson, fell victim to what appeared to be a savage tit-for-tat attack on a country road near Girvan Mains, as did another Irishman, William Young, who was assaulted at the place known as 'Blue Sky', near Houdston Farm. So severe were Goldie's injuries, it was said, that he had to be transported to Ayr by cart. Two weavers, Alexander McBroom and Andrew McGarva, were subsequently convicted of the assaults and each was sentenced to a nine-month jail term. Robert Sloan, a juvenile who had also been party to the crimes, received a lesser sentence of three months' imprisonment. All three were bound to keep the peace for a further five years.

A relatively new phenomenon to Scotland, Orange sectarianism was regarded sufficiently seriously as to merit parliamentary attention at Westminster. A House of Commons select committee report into Orange institutions expressly refers to events at Girvan - Alexander Ross is named specifically - as well as noting the curious detail that, unlike other Scottish counties, a significant proportion of lodge members in Ayrshire were not Irishmen by birth but native Scots. No reason for this is suggested. The report's authors were clear in their observation that for the most part Orange lodges were concentrated in the west of Scotland and this circumstance is likely to have influenced the decision to relocate Samuel Waugh and John Ramsay's trial to Edinburgh.

Their case came to court during the dark days at the tail-end of the year. As well as mobbing, rioting and assault, both men were charged with having been responsible for Alexander Ross's murder, Waugh with having pulled the trigger and Ramsay having given him the order to do so. Both pled not guilty. Given the chaotic conditions at Bridge Mill on 12 July and the entrenched positions of most of those present, sifting fact from fancy was never likely to be easy and much of the evidence provided by witnesses proved conflicting. During his testimony, special constable James McClure stated his firm belief that none of the townsfolk had been armed with a gun but a witness from the Orange party was equally adamant that the first shot had come from the Girvan side. Asked to substantiate his opinion, he insisted in all seriousness that he had seen with his own eyes a puff of smoke produced by the gunshot. A number of eyewitnesses denied categorically that John Ramsay had ever issued any order to shoot, one man going so far as to recount how he had seen the Orange leader step in to obstruct an Orangeman who was in the act of firing. Constable McClure, on the other hand, confidently asserted that Ramsay had given the command to fire. A further bone of contention cropped up over the question of whether Samuel Waugh had been struck by a stone before or after Ross's death - or indeed whether he had been struck at all. Whatever the truth of the matter, Gilbert Gray of Fauldribban, near Girvan, had no hesitation in confirming Waugh as the man who had fired the fatal shot. From the Orange side, James Farrell described how he had watched Waugh load his weapon carefully prior to the shooting but the Crosshill weaver stopped short of confirming that Waugh's bullet had been the one responsible for ending Ross's life.

For all the confusion, there was enough sound evidence to convince the jury. By a majority verdict, Samuel Waugh was found guilty of murder and sentenced to be executed at Ayr on 19 January 1832, his body to be subsequently given over for medical dissection. On learning his unhappy fate, the prisoner reportedly remained impassive. His co-accused, John Ramsay, fared a good deal better when the charge of murder against him was unanimously found 'not proven' - perhaps more a reflection of the conflicting evidence than of the jury's faith in his innocence. In relation to the lesser charges that he faced, the court accepted the Orange leader's plea of not guilty to the charge of assault and sentenced him to nine months' imprisonment for his part in the mobbing and rioting at Girvan. Four weavers similarly accused were given jail terms that varied between nine and twelve months.

For Samuel Waugh it looked as though the game was well and truly up but one final straw remained to be clutched at. In a last-ditch bid for clemency, an account of the circumstances relating to his case was commissioned by the Lord Justice Clerk and sent for consideration by government officials in London. The fact that as many as six out of the fifteen Edinburgh jurors had judged the accused man guilty of no more than culpable homicide had provided his supporters with a glimmer of hope but it was quickly dashed when word came back from the south that there was to be no reprieve. Although he was said to have received the news with stoicism, it seems that Samuel Waugh was never able to reconcile himself to his own culpability and insisted to the very last that 'his own blood and the blood of Alexander Ross lay upon the people of Girvan'. Not everyone, of course, would agree that the pitching of stones merited gunfire in response.

Alexander Ross's grieving friends and family were not the only ones whose lives were damaged by Waugh's crime and the convicted murderer's own nearest and dearest also suffered collateral damage. While awaiting execution, the Orangeman received a final visit from his distraught wife, her distress compounded, it was reported, by the recent loss of her only child. Waugh's sisters also travelled to the prison to say their last farewells. Attended by various clergymen, the prisoner freely admitted to having fired the shot that struck down Alexander Ross but persisted in his claim that his intention had never been to kill either him or anyone else. During his time in jail, Waugh was described as remaining remarkably calm, declaring himself ready to meet his maker and confident of a fair hearing in the world to come.

The prisoner's last earthly journey took place on Tuesday 10 January, just over a week before the date assigned for his execution, when he travelled from Edinburgh back to Ayrshire. He was met at the county boundary by a company of the Ayrshire Yeomanry plus a deputation of local officials including the Chief Constable of the county and the Sheriff Substitute, William Eaton, into whose custody he now passed. Given the publicity surrounding Waugh's case, it is hardly surprising that his execution generated a good deal of interest in the local area. In line with standard practice, the scaffold was erected outside Ayr prison the night beforehand and from first light onwards on the day of the hanging itself the first members of the public started to congregate. Given the current sectarian tensions, a heavy security presence had been put in place in the form of a squad of armed constables, some specially sworn in for the occasion, plus a detachment of soldiers on horseback. During the day local officials, including the Sheriff and Provost, took their places among the spectators whose estimated number had risen to more than 5,000. It was early afternoon before the condemned man finally appeared and, as he was seen ascending the scaffold's fateful steps, a hush descended on the crowd. For a man whose previous actions might indicate an uncertain temper, it was reported that Waugh proceeded to his death coolly and with no theatricals. He was granted a few quiet minutes to prepare himself for what was to come before the hangman, John Murdoch of Glasgow, drew back the bolt and, as he plunged from the scaffold, Samuel Waugh paid for his inexplicable moment of rashness with his life.

15 A Poor Man's Disease

On Monday 20 February 1832 a married couple were walking from Glasgow to Kilwinning in search of employment when suddenly the woman was taken ill. Unable to go further, they were forced to stop off at Doura, a small coal-mining settlement to the east of Kilwinning, where by sheer good fortune they had an acquaintance who was willing to take them in. Sadly, however, the pregnant 25 year-old woman's condition deteriorated to the point where it became clear that her life was beyond saving and, when she finally passed away late the following evening, poor Flora Johnston earned for herself the unenviable distinction of becoming Ayrshire's first recorded fatality during the cholera epidemic of 1832.

It had been clear for some time that trouble was brewing beyond the horizon. Towards the end of the previous year there had been disturbing reports of a cholera outbreak in the English town of Sunderland, prompting preparations for the possible spread of the disease into Scotland. Town and village health boards were formed with a view to improving standards of local sanitation and putting procedures in place for the relief of vulnerable groups, such as the poor, the elderly and the infirm. Handbills were distributed, promoting personal and domestic hygiene, and a number of the poorest citizens were issued with articles of warm clothing and blankets. Soup-kitchens opened their doors and in some cases hand-outs of coal were provided for those in greatest need. Watchmen were charged with specific responsibility for keeping tramps and beggars at bay, all such travelling people being viewed as potential carriers.

Before the year was out cholera had travelled to other areas of northeast England, including the city of Newcastle, and by January 1832 it had crossed the border for the first time. The earliest Scottish fatalities were recorded in east coast towns such as Haddington and Tranent, and not long after the disease made its way into Edinburgh itself. It took a little longer for cholera to move west, its first unfortunate victim a ten year-old boy, Neil McMillan, from Kirkintilloch. Further fatalities in the locality followed, principally among the elderly and the very young, and it did not escape notice that Kirkintilloch was located on the banks of the Forth and Clyde

Canal where barge-loads of goods routinely arrived for unloading from the north-east of England.

At the first sign of worrying symptoms - vomiting, diarrhoea, bodily spasms - sufferers were advised as a matter of urgency to take an emetic consisting of ingredients such as mustard and salt in equal measures, both to be dissolved in hot water. Sympathy, it has to be said, was neither instant nor universal and it took time for the prejudice to fade that cholera victims were in some way responsible for their own sad plight, as though poverty and squalid living conditions were simply a matter of choice. A significant proportion of fatalities, it was noted, related to the indigent residents of municipal workhouses and, in more affluent circles, it was convenient to pigeonhole cholera as a poor man's disease.

Paradoxically, there were those for whom the disease, and the panic it engendered, represented nothing short of an opportunity to be grasped and exploited. A curious case occurred at South Walton Farm, just south of Glasgow, in the moorland parish of Mearns. When without warning the farmer and his wife became violently ill, understandably they suspected the worst. But, as the severity of their symptoms gradually eased and their initial fears lessened accordingly, the possibility dawned on John and Margaret Gilmour that their bout of illness might rather have been related to the potato soup which they had consumed earlier in the day. What happened next defies belief.

As a means of putting their food-poisoning theory to the test, the Gilmours served up platefuls of the same potato soup to three of their employees, two of whom instantly became unwell while the third, who was observed to have eaten sparingly, remained largely unaffected. What was left of the soup was then fed to two pigs, one of which expired on the spot while its more fortunate companion vomited up its recent meal and survived. The contents of the dead pig's stomach were analysed by a local doctor and, based on the outcome of his investigation, the farm was subsequently visited by Sheriff Campbell, the Paisley procurator fiscal, at which point the farm-worker who had escaped illness was found - strangely enough - to have absconded without trace. What the entire episode tells us about relationships at South Walton where servants made attempts on the lives of their employers, and those employers in turn tested tainted food on humans before livestock, is possibly a moot point.

A few miles further south, it had become clear that Flora Johnston's death would not be the end of the matter at Doura. Several local people, most of whom Flora had been in contact with, developed cholera symptoms, including Dr Anderson, the physician who had attended during her last, sad hours. Anderson's replacement was Dr Ramsay of Kilwinning who took the radical step of taking up temporary residence at Doura in an effort to prevent the spread of the disease. He was joined there by a Mr Buller, a noted expert in the treatment of cholera based on experience gained in England and Poland, as well as elsewhere in Scotland. A soup-kitchen was set up, clean bed-clothes issued and medicines distributed to those in greatest need.

Fortunately the measures bore fruit, and within the space of a few weeks the outbreak appeared to have been stemmed. The knotty question of interment, however, remained. Among the townspeople of Kilwinning there was reluctance to grant access to the local churchyard, while back at Doura there was an equal and understandable conviction that the deceased were entitled a dignified and respectful burial. Eventually the stalemate was broken through the intervention of the local landowner, Lord Eglinton, who offered to make available a plot of land on his estates. Thus, in the corner of a muddy field on one of His Lordship's farms, the dead of Doura found their final resting-place. Out of an estimated total population of 170, some 30 or so residents had fallen ill and, for six of them, their symptoms had proved fatal.

But if fears gradually subsided at Doura, news arriving from further afield offered few grounds for optimism. The disquieting story broke in late June of a cholera outbreak which was most notable for its tragic and unusual location. On Friday 18 May the emigrant ship, Brutus, had set sail from Liverpool bound for Quebec, its 330 passengers intent on building new lives in Canada. A week into the voyage, however, illness broke out among the passengers which the ship's doctor quickly identified as cholera and, despite his best efforts, the disease rapidly spread. When a number of crew members succumbed, Captain Neilson took the decision to turn around and, by the time Brutus docked once again at Liverpool on Thursday 14 June, more than one third of those aboard were suffering from cholera symptoms, of whom 81 ultimately perished, their dying agonies reportedly compounded by heavy seas. At least one of those who lost her life was a

Scot - Mary Henderson of Glasgow - and four members of a single family, the Greens of Oxfordshire, breathed their last aboard ship. Even for those passengers fit to step ashore on the quay at Liverpool, the weeks they had spent at sea must surely have seemed a living hell.

With events at Doura fresh in people's minds, small wonder then that Ayrshire found itself caught in an uneasy limbo. The nearest confirmed cholera cases - at Glasgow, Paisley and Greenock - were a good deal too close for comfort and from time to time the fears of the population bubbled to the surface. A story circulated of how the skipper of an Irvine brig, the *Harmony*, had succumbed to the disease, and a little later, in mid-May, rumours of a fresh outbreak at Maybole were played down by the medical authorities. Through the long days of May and June and on into the early part of July, Ayrshire held its breath, fearful, you might imagine, of a storm about to break.

In Ayr, it started fitfully. By 12 July cholera had reached Kilmarnock, twelve miles away, but for the time being the county town remained unaffected. Things changed, however, on 18 July when a 70 year-old woman, variously named as Steven or Gibson, turned ill in her lodgings close to the town centre. Like Flora Johnston before her, the woman had

The Cholera Memorial, Howard Park, Kilmarnock

some days earlier arrived from Glasgow where, by her own admission, she had assisted in preparing the bodies of cholera victims for burial. Her condition deteriorated with shocking rapidity and within 24 hours of her tucking into a hearty repast (herrings and new potatoes, it was reported, washed down with beer and buttermilk) all signs of life had departed. Living in fairly crowded conditions, her neighbours were removed to a 'house of seclusion' on the South Quay at Ayr harbour where they were placed under conditions of quarantine. The empty houses they had left behind were then fumigated and limewashed, and it was observed with some satisfaction that no associate of the dead woman subsequently fell prey to the disease.

It was, however, a little too early for complacency. Within a matter of days a second, unrelated case cropped up, the threat on this occasion arriving by sea. It emerged that a sick seaman, the master of a trading vessel, had been slipped ashore at the mouth of the River Ayr and secretly conveyed to his home at Newton Green. Medical assistance, it appears, was summoned too late to affect the outcome. When the circumstances gradually became known, it transpired that the dead man had recently visited Greenock where he had spent time nursing a friend who was terminally ill with cholera. Moves were made to prosecute the harbour pilot who had carried the invalid ashore - allegedly inebriated at the time - but, as it turned out, the man himself fell ill and died of cholera a day later. As in previous cases, the pilot's home was sanitised and his grieving relatives placed in quarantine.

Ayr's fourth victim was also found to have a Greenock connection, having returned from that town during the first week in August, two days before her death. A 34 year-old weaver was next to succumb, resident in a different area of the town and believed to have had no contact with any of the previous fatalities. The day prior to his falling ill, however, it was noted that the weaver had received a letter from Glasgow, informing him of the cholera-related death there of a number of his relations. Of Ayr's first five cholera victims, four were judged to be unconnected and on Thursday 26 August the local Board of Health issued a categorical assurance that there was no evidence of epidemic cholera in Ayr. Its timing could hardly have been worse.

Even before the Board's notice appeared in print, the disease had broken out at various locations throughout the town, striking down its victims apparently at random but laying a particularly heavy hand on the young and elderly. Many townspeople fled to the sanctuary of the countryside, businesses closed their doors and proceedings in the law courts ground to a halt while local churches offered up a plethora of desperate prayers for the town's deliverance. In a cruel irony, the spread of infection was believed to have been exacerbated by the street festivities which had marked the passing in parliament of the Scottish Reform Act, a significant and highly popular step towards universal suffrage. In the days and weeks that followed, the number of fatalities escalated alarmingly, reaching a highpoint when a total of 67 Ayr residents succumbed to cholera within the space of a single week.

At the height of the epidemic, scenes played out on the streets of Ayr which were more reminiscent of a medieval time of plague. Those unfortunates who developed symptoms were bundled from their homes and rudely stretchered to Wallacetown where an improvised hospital had been set up, and their clothing and personal effects were unceremoniously burned. For fear of contaminated air, burning tar-barrels were placed at intervals throughout the streets and the dead-cart was regularly to be seen, making its rounds by night and day to uplift the latest crop of corpses for mass burial. In order to prevent contamination, guards were posted outside infected properties but when cases became too numerous, the word *Sick*, chalked on the invalid's door, was made to suffice, to be replaced with *Caution* in the event of a death.

As cholera tightened its grip, suspicion and fear became its constant companions. Perhaps surprisingly, doctors fighting the epidemic were often viewed with mistrust, the belief being widespread that the bodies of the dead were at risk of being misappropriated for use in medical research. It wasn't the only off-beat notion to surface at the time. 'It is a singular fact,' proclaimed the *Liverpool Journal*, 'that wherever cholera prevails, the flies die. Never before were there so few flies in Liverpool.' It was a questionable news priority, you might think, at a time of such intense human suffering. Back in Ayr, however, the situation eventually started to ease as casualties slowly tailed off but it was the best part of three gruelling months before the epidemic finally burned itself out.

It was probably of little comfort to the people of Ayr that they had not been alone in their agonies. The cholera epidemic of 1832 exacted a grave toll on many Scottish communities, just as it did throughout much of the rest of the inhabited world. Just over 200 Ayr residents were reckoned to have perished between July and October, while losses in Kilmarnock came closer to 250 and smaller towns such as Beith and Dalry similarly experienced fatalities. Irvine got off relatively lightly with only 21 recorded deaths. By the beginning of 1834, however, the threat of mass cholera was deemed to have receded sufficiently to allow Ayr's Board of Health to be safely disbanded and, following a concluding meeting on 30 January, its goods and equipment were disposed of by public auction. In a poignant final gesture, the Board's four remaining coffins were donated for use by occupants of the local poorhouse at the time of their demise. Sadly, the pain and grief of 1832 were not to be the last occasion when the scourge of cholera was visited upon the people and communities of Ayrshire.

16 Politics and Poaching

In popular mythology the poacher is frequently represented as a solitary character of independent mind who strikes a blow on behalf of the common man with every hare or salmon lifted by moonlight. Rather than inviting censure, his iron nerve in flouting an unjust law is viewed instead as verging on heroic. And, whilst in times past there was probably no shortage of individuals whose activities conformed fairly closely to the stereotype, it certainly wasn't the poacher's only method of working. In the early part of the nineteenth century it was by no means uncommon for poaching to be a highly-organised activity, carried out on something approaching an industrial scale. Just such an instance occurred in the Cumnock district in 1833 which, as it developed, saw criminality and politics overlapping to the extent that soon they became hard to distinguish.

Towards the close of the previous year a band of poachers, believed to have amounted to as many as twenty-five individuals, had been known to be active on the estates of Auchinleck, Ballochmyle and Dumfries House. Thought to originate in Glasgow or Lanarkshire, the gang's *modus operandi* was to divide into smaller groups of between two and five men who then set about methodically clearing the countryside of game. Brazen and ruthless, the presence of gamekeepers deterred them not in the least as they carried out their operations with little attempt at concealment and in blatant defiance of the law. At least one case was reported where they went so far as to humiliate one of the estate gamekeepers, obliging him under threat to carry a bulging game-bag on their behalf.

In spite of the illegality of their operations, the gang found no apparent difficulty in disposing of game, making use of what looked like well-established supply chains to send the greater part of their spoils to be sold in Glasgow. An additional ready market was at hand locally, however, in the form of two public houses, in Auchinleck and Cumnock, within whose walls as many as twenty hares, plus countless partridges and pheasants, were reputed to have changed hands on occasion in the space of a single night. Their day's work duly completed, the poachers were in the habit of settling down most evenings for a spell of jovial carousal in one or other of the two hostelries.

The gang's illicit activities continued uninterrupted until early in the New Year of 1833 when the Marquess of Bute's gamekeepers at Dumfries House received a tip-off that the estate was due to be targeted on Thursday, 10 January. A systematic search was carried out on the day which revealed a solitary poacher at Roseburn who, despite his best efforts to escape, was finally apprehended a good mile away on the farm of Garlaff. Escorted to Cumnock, for reasons that seem inexplicable today the arrested man was granted a say in where he might be secured and he plumped in the event for the residence of a local grocer and publican, Hugh Campbell - a circumstance which apparently caused his host no small degree of embarrassment. It has been suggested that the poacher's choice might well have been based on the fact that Campbell's establishment was one of his associates' regular haunts and certainly when his three accomplices returned to Cumnock later that day they had no problem tracking him down here. It appears, in fact, that it was in Campbell's house that the three men were arrested themselves.

The poacher seized at Garlaff was removed in due course to the Dumfries Arms Inn whose accommodation doubled as a makeshift courthouse. During the official proceedings he refused point-blank to cooperate, declining to give his name (he was later identified as one John Mitchel [sic]) - or to pay the fine imposed following a guilty verdict. Pending the arrival of a cart to transport him to jail in Ayr, the convicted man attempted to escape with the result that he had to be tied up using ropes. By now news of the arrests had spread throughout Cumnock and, as a crowd of townsfolk had congregated whose sympathies were not hard to discern, the decision was taken to postpone the trial of the three remaining poachers. In an effort to maintain order, a number of special constables were posted at Hugh Campbell's house.

As it transpired, trouble broke out initially not at Campbell's establishment but rather outside the Dumfries Arms where between two and three hundred local people had gathered. By the time that a local carter, David Smith, arrived at around 6 p.m. to convey the prisoner to Ayr, feelings were running high. Resentment over the laws relating to poaching had bubbled over into an expression of wider political dissatisfaction, and

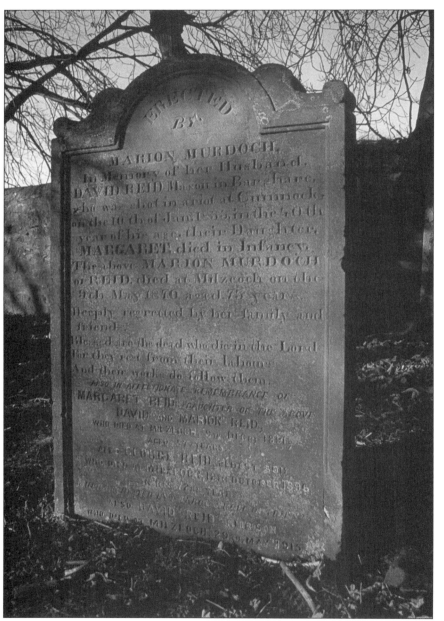

David Reid's headstone, Cumnock old cemetery

it was later reported that radical slogans and cries of 'Liberty!' were to be heard, emanating from the crowd. With the convicted man aboard, Smith's vehicle had not travelled far from the Dumfries Arms before its accompanying constables were attacked by the mob who successfully overpowered them and proceeded to liberate their prisoner. After being sported in triumph through the streets, the newly-sprung poacher promptly displayed a clean pair of heels as he wasted no time in fleeing the scene. He was last seen hotfooting it up a close beside the United Associate Church and scrambling over the top of a wall.

Flushed with its first taste of success, the mob now redirected its attention towards Hugh Campbell's premises where, in the absence of any lockfast public building, the remaining poachers remained under armed guard. Constables, supported by local gamekeepers, had been charged with responsibility for keeping order and preventing escapes - their job allegedly rendered more difficult by alcohol, supplied to the crowd from Campbell's hostelry (though this was something which the landlord would later vehemently deny, claiming rather that the spirits had been stolen from his establishment). Further inflamed, it was said, by the political utterances of mob orators who chose to portray the prisoners as blameless victims of an unjust law favouring the rich, the crowd grew increasingly restive until finally, despite the best efforts of the men on guard-duty, events spiralled out of control.

One of the special constables that evening, James Baird, recounted later how shouts from outside the building had left no room for doubt about the crowd's intention to liberate the men in custody. When an attempt was made to force open a back window, one of Baird's colleagues took up position with his back pressed firmly against the shutter but was unable to hold out when a second powerful onslaught propelled him across the room. Another of the constables, Peter Bannatine, did his best to keep the crowd at bay by firing a warning shot through the window over their heads but to no avail. Undeterred, the protestors burst open the door and muscled their way into Campbell's premises. The scene that followed rapidly degenerated into chaos.

And turmoil turned quickly to tragedy. During the course of the mêlée, Robert Collins, a gamekeeper at Ballochmyle, called out to the crowd, giving them due warning that his gun was loaded and cocked, but his words apparently fell on deaf ears. Another of the gamekeepers, George Patrick, later recalled that one of the poachers (whom he named as Lindsay) had made a grab for Collins's gun and, for whatever reason, the gun had then gone off with forty-year-old David Reid, a master-mason living at Barshare and one of the special constables on duty, squarely in the firing-line. It didn't take long for the head-wound that Reid sustained to prove fatal. Taking advantage of the resulting commotion, all three poachers made good their escape.

The dead man left behind a widow and five children, the tiniest of whom, Margaret, was less than a week old at the time when her father's life was abruptly curtailed. Official consequences, of course, were quick to follow. In the aftermath of the rioting the Sheriff Substitute and Procurator Fiscal visited Cumnock to conduct investigations which, once completed, resulted in a number of local people being charged with offences that ranged from deforcement (obstructing officers of the law in the course of their duties) to assault, mobbing and rioting. Those charged were engaged in a variety of trades and included a labourer, a nailer, two carters, a shoemaker, a plasterer, a sawyer, a weaver, and - perhaps a little surprisingly - a man employed as a sheriff officer. Facing the more serious charge of culpable homicide was Robert Collins, the Ballochmyle gamekeeper, whose gun had been responsible for the death of David Reid. By contrast, the lives of the poachers appeared entirely unaffected as they carried on with their activities as usual. On the very day when they had been due to stand trial at the Dumfries Arms these same men were busy poaching on Auchinleck estate, a couple of miles away, and during the weeks that followed they were seen to be active in the adjoining parishes of Sorn and Muirkirk.

Cases arising from the rioting in Cumnock were heard just over three months later, on 22 April, at the first available sitting of the Circuit Court of Justiciary at Ayr. The outcome was not perhaps quite what the prosecuting authorities might have hoped for. For a start, not all of the charges could be made to stick: John White, a carter, wriggled out on a technicality when his home at Stepends was found to be located, not in Old Cumnock parish as recorded in the court documentation, but in the neighbouring parish of Auchinleck. Hugh Murdoch, a sheriff officer, declined to put in an appearance and was promptly outlawed by the court. The cases against John Miller, weaver, and John Hunter (alias Hunter

Downie), labourer, were delegated to be heard by Ayr Sheriff Court at a later date. And if that wasn't enough, the defence contended that the original arrest warrant, signed by Justice of the Peace, Alexander Allason of Glaisnock, was without legitimacy on the grounds that nowhere in its terms were those individuals named who were to be detained. If the four poachers had not been legally held, the defence argument went, then the act of liberating them could hardly have been illegal. Members of the jury, it appears, were convinced. Following their deliberations, the case against the majority of the accused was found not proven and ultimately only a single conviction resulted from the charges relating to riotous behaviour. David Reid, a plasterer, was found guilty of having assaulted a constable, William Drennan, who had been in charge of the convicted poacher who was being transported from the Dumfries Arms in David Smith's cart. Reid received a nine-month prison sentence.

There remained, of course, a highly poignant case which had still to be heard. Deemed responsible for the death of a colleague - albeit indirectly - what Robert Collins's feelings might have been during the three months that he spent awaiting his appearance in court is something we can only guess at. On the day of the trial, however, it soon became apparent that his case was one that elicited a considerable degree of sympathy from all quarters. The Advocate-Depute made it clear that the 'distressing case' had been brought before the court merely in order to allow investigation of the circumstances that had led up to David Reid's death which, when the evidence was heard, appeared to have been 'purely accidental'. Lord Gillies, presiding, stated unequivocally that he believed the accused to be 'perfectly innocent' and, following deliberations, the members of the jury were happy to concur. Robert Collins walked out of court a free man, his ordeal to all intents and purposes at an end. Or so it might have seemed.

After briefly absconding, the two men still to be tried, John Miller and John Hunter (alias Hunter Downie) finally made an appearance at Ayr Sheriff Court two months later when the former was acquitted of all charges and the latter sentenced to two months' detention in solitary confinement. And, with that, the legal formalities arising from Cumnock's riot of January 1833 were finally concluded. Ironically, of course, all four poachers at the centre of the storm had got off scot-free, and for the two men convicted of riotous behaviour - Reid and Hunter - it was presumably only a matter of sitting out their sentences until they were released from custody and able to resume their old lives. But on Margaret Reid, née Murdoch, left without a husband, the day's events had imposed a life sentence as she watched her children grow up without their father.

It may also be the case that the day of disorder claimed a further unforeseen victim, a man whose painful recollections refused to fade. For, on 10 September 1833, precisely nine months after the events in question, it was reported that the Ballochmyle gamekeeper, Robert Collins, had lost his life when a double-barrelled shotgun which he was cleaning went off unexpectedly, injuring him so severely in the process that he died within half an hour. Apparently unbeknown to him, one of the gun's barrels had been loaded. When news of the tragedy broke, no doubt there was talk. As an experienced gamekeeper, Collins must surely have been a man well accustomed to handling firearms, raising the suspicion perhaps that his death was not quite the unfortunate accident that it first appeared. In spite of his earlier acquittal in court, could it be that his part in the death of a colleague - possibly a friend - had placed a weight on Collins's conscience that was simply too great for him to bear? It is impossible to say. For nearly two centuries now the truth has lain buried in the kirkyard at Catrine alongside Robert Collins's last earthly remains.

17 The Fortunes of Felix

From his surname we might reasonably deduce that, at some point in the past, Felix McCarron's forebears made the decision to strike out from their homeland for a new life in Scotland. In their native Ireland the name has a distinguished pedigree, dating back to the eleventh century when one Teag MacCarroon [sic] surfaces in the *Annals of the Four Masters*, a weighty compilation of medieval Irish chronicles, and by the sixteenth century Hobbert McCarron of Killenefaghna was recorded as being in possession of the family's ancestral lands on the east bank of the River Shannon. By the time that Felix's branch of the McCarrons washed up in Ayrshire, however, we may assume that the glory days had faded and that the family fortunes had taken a bit of a dip.

Born in Kilmarnock in 1812, during Felix's lifetime he was destined to travel a good deal farther than his Irish ancestors ever had. Little is known of his early years but by the time that he had reached working age it is on record that he was earning his living as the 'driver of an ass and cart'. Things appear to have gone awry during his late teens when he started to fall foul of the law. In November 1831 he appeared before Ayr Sheriff Court, charged with being responsible for a savage attack on a man and two women in Widow Dunn's public house in Strand Street, Kilmarnock. His male victim, James Dunn, had been assaulted with a poker while Janet Dunn and Janet Donaldson both sustained knife-wounds to the head and face. Pleading guilty, Felix received a sentence of four months' imprisonment, having already served two while awaiting trial. Almost certainly drink played a part in what happened but it is clear nonetheless that Felix McCarron was a violent and dangerous man.

The crunch came five years later in September 1836 when, along with a local weaver, John Gray, Felix faced a charge of having picked the pocket of Daniel Harvey, a hawker living in Fore Street, Kilmarnock, thus securing for himself the dubious prize of two pairs of braces. He had in addition redeemed various items of clothing pawned by his victim sometime earlier, presumably having acquired the pawnbroker's receipt from Harvey by similar sleight of hand. His co-accused, Gray, failed to turn up in court and was outlawed for his pains but Felix owned up to his crimes and pled guilty. Being by 'habit and repute a thief', the law came down heavily upon him. Sentencing him to seven years' transportation with penal servitude, the judge, Lord Moncrieff, lectured Felix on the importance of mending his ways and made a point of mentioning the good education which it seems he had received. Hoping for a change of heart, Felix's father, Patrick, petitioned the court, appealing for clemency on the grounds that his son had been lured from the straight and narrow through the influence of bad company. Referring to his own lameness, Patrick McCarron pointed out that he himself had no other option now than to support his son's two young children which would add considerably to the burden of his family responsibilities. (For whatever reason, no mention was made of the children's mother, presumably Felix's wife. It is, of course, possible that she was dead.) In spite of Patrick's best efforts, the court upheld its original decision and Felix's departure from Scotland was thus assured.

Felix McCarron was only one of a vast multitude of British and Irish people who were consigned during the eighteenth and nineteenth centuries to a life down under. In 1783 Britain's defeat in the American War of Independence had closed off North America as a convenient receptacle for the nation's criminal underclass and, following a search of the globe for suitable alternatives, the steamy jungles of West Africa were rejected in favour of a more distant southern land, only recently described by the explorer, Captain James Cook. Following this decision, over an eighty-year period hundreds of ships transported in excess of 160,000 convicts to Australia, an estimated 26,000 of whom were women and some 15-20,000 children under the age of sixteen. Viewed as a means of deterring crime - the difficulties of ever returning home were well known - the policy also supplied a convenient labour force for the new Australian colonies.

But even before a transported criminal was permitted to depart the British Isles there were considerable hardships to be faced. Prior to setting sail, convicts were housed, often for months if not years, on various unseaworthy vessels which had been taken into service as makeshift floating prisons. Described as 'hell on water', conditions on board these 'hulks' were invariably filthy, overcrowded and hazardous to health. In Felix McCarron's case, a total of nine months elapsed between his conviction at Ayr and subsequent embarkation for Australia, some part of which was spent aboard HMS Fortitude, a prison-ship which was moored on the River Medway in Kent.

Felix's wait ended in late May 1837 when he was among the passengers who set sail from County Down, Ireland, aboard the convict ship, *Elphinstone*, bound for what was then known as Van Diemen's Land - the island of Tasmania, some 150 miles to the south of mainland Australia. Of the 240 men to be transported on the *Elphinstone*, 44 had been given life sentences and 28 men - just over ten per cent of the total - had been convicted in Scottish courts, ranging from Ayr in the south to Inverness and Aberdeen in the north. In addition to Felix, the fate of another two transportees aboard the *Elphinstone* had been settled at Ayr. Hugh McClelland, a 'gentleman's servant and stone cutter', had been charged with breaking into the harness room at Craigie House and stealing £7 in cash, as well as a number of articles of clothing. McClelland admitted his guilt but added rather ruefully that his ill-gotten gains had amounted to rather less than £7 - more like a paltry £3. His protest, however, fell on deaf ears when Lord Moncrieff sentenced him to seven years' transportation. Also aboard the *Elphinstone* was a third man whose trial had taken place at Ayr. John Ross, a labourer originally from East Lothian, also received a seven-year sentence when he was found guilty of theft. But in one respect at least Felix stood alone. Among an abundance of Johns, Thomases and Williams on board the *Elphinstone*, the passenger manifest reveals one single solitary Felix.

The *Elphinstone* wasn't the first vessel to transport passengers convicted at Ayr - and she certainly wouldn't be the last. Found guilty of passing two forged Royal Bank of Scotland notes, David Earl of Patna sailed to Van Diemen's Land aboard the *Phoenix* in 1824. The peak years for transportation, however, came a little later, during the 1830s. In October 1837 Andrew Galloway of Ayr, an inveterate sheep-stealer, set sail for Van Diemen's Land aboard the *Neptune*. Based on his good behaviour, Galloway received his 'ticket-of-leave' in February 1842 which granted him additional freedoms but there is no suggestion that he ever set eyes on his wife, Elizabeth, or his two young children again. Convicted of stealing jewellery and a sum of money from a public house, William Stewart never made it to Van Diemen's Land, having died at sea aboard the *Sarah* in March 1837.

His accomplice, John McGregor, was more fortunate and survived the voyage.

Male convicts from Ayrshire were not the only ones to face banishment overseas. During a single session of the Court of Justiciary at Ayr in April 1845 no fewer than five convicted women received sentences of transportation. Forty year-old Mary Hamilton was a widow who earned her living by carrying out domestic jobs and needlework. Suspected of stealing hens from her neighbours, she was rumbled when the creatures made themselves heard, cackling beneath her bed. Mary Hamilton was sentenced to seven years' transportation. Thirty year-old Mary Baxter stole seven shillings and threepence plus a quarter-pound of tea from a certain James Richmond in Ayr. This, coupled with her previous convictions, resulted in transportation. A third woman, Mary Craig, had befriended Hugh McQueen, a Kilmarnock plasterer who had become a little worse for wear while on business in Ayr. The two retreated to a house in Isle Lane where they retired to a private apartment but sometime later, once McQueen was sufficiently sober, he discovered his wallet had vanished along with its entire contents of £12 in notes and change. When police officers were summoned, they quickly located Mary Craig, hiding quietly in a closet. Hearing her sentence of seven years' transportation, she was said to have lambasted the judge, Lord Wood, in spectacular fashion.

Twenty year-old Elizabeth Howard had been part of a group which preyed on Andrew Milligan, skipper of the *Peggy*, currently visiting Ayr from Carrickfergus in Ireland. She and two friends - Sarah Smith and Janet McCall - had inveigled the seaman into buying them drinks before, assisted by Elizabeth's boyfriend, they rounded on him in Fort Street and made off with his money. By the standards of the time, Janet, a first offender, got off relatively lightly when she was ordered to be confined in Perth Penitentiary for twelve months. Her three associates, however, all had previous convictions and were sentenced to seven years' transportation. With heavy sarcasm, Elizabeth Howard is said to have thanked his lordship profusely, informing him that she had expected a sentence that was twice as long.

Very likely Elizabeth knew what a taxing time she had ahead of her. In spite of medical advances, diseases such as scurvy, dysentery and typhoid presented a perennial problem to transportees who were fed a meagre diet and were obliged to endure long spells of inactivity in cramped and airless conditions. Ill-health, however, wasn't the only hazard to be faced during transportation, as had been demonstrated all too clearly in January 1835. The *Neva* had set sail from Cork in south-western Ireland, carrying 150 female prisoners, 33 child convicts plus various free passengers, all bound for Sydney, Australia. Four months later, tragically close to her destination, disaster struck. In the early morning of Wednesday 13 May the *Neva* collided with a reef in the vicinity of King Island, immediately north-west of the main island of Tasmania, and began rapidly to break up. Twenty-two shipwrecked passengers succeeded in reaching dry land by clinging to fragments of the vessel's shattered timbers, though seven of them died soon after from the effects of exposure. Those fifteen who survived - including the ship's captain and chief officer - were taken care of by a local seal hunter, John Scott, and his Aboriginal wife and children until they were picked up a fortnight later by the crew of the schooner, *Sarah Ann*. Of the *Neva's* 239 passengers, no fewer than 224 lost their lives during the disaster. It did not go unnoticed that the *Neva* was the third convict ship to be wrecked within the space of two years and it was observed at the time that, in the interests of economy, vessels of inferior size and quality had been brought into service for the transportation of convicts.

Fortunately for Felix McCarron and his fellow-passengers, the *Elphinstone's* voyage went rather more smoothly. Bearing in mind the costs involved in transporting convicts, it was normal for the authorities to go to considerable lengths to ensure their safe arrival in Australia. After 1815 all transport ships were expected to have a naval surgeon aboard whose responsibility it was to monitor the health of both convicts and crew. The *Elphinstone's* medical man, Campbell France, appears to have done an effective job as, when the ship completed her four-month voyage and reached Hobart in early October, out of the 240 convicts who had originally sailed from County Down a total of 239 stepped ashore in Van Diemen's Land. Contrary to what might be expected, the survival rate among transported convicts was rather higher than that relating to those law-abiding emigrants who had freely chosen to leave their native land to establish new lives in the antipodes.

Felix McCarron was one of those who made it. Information recorded on his arrival in Tasmania paints a picture of a man who was relatively short in stature - a few inches over five feet in height - with a dark complexion and similarly dark hair and beard. His eyes are hazel in colour with a scar below his right eye acting perhaps as a reminder that convict stereotypes are not totally fictitious. Felix's occupation is listed as 'carter' - possibly a designation that he chose for himself in the hope of securing an easier life than that of a common labouring man. If it was a ruse, then perhaps it worked since on arrival Felix was not placed in a work gang but assigned instead as servant to Thomas Bransgrove, an English butcher operating in the town of Launceston.

Bransgrove had arrived in Tasmania some twenty years earlier in similar circumstances to Felix. Convicted of cattle-theft, he had initially faced the death penalty before his sentence was commuted to transportation overseas. Like Felix, he had arrived in Van Diemen's Land aged 24, and since then things appeared to have gone his way. By the time that he had completed his designated seven years' penal servitude Thomas was held in sufficiently high esteem to be appointed overseer of William Lawrence's Formosa ranch in the Lake River region of Tasmania and, such was the trust that his employer placed in him, that when a violent assault and robbery were carried out on two local shepherds, Thomas was one of those tasked with identifying the masked men responsible. In a classic case of poacher-turned-gamekeeper, one of Thomas's duties at Formosa was to impound any stray livestock he encountered before attempting to reunite it with its owner. So impressed was he by the possibilities offered by life down under that he successfully persuaded his brother, William, to emigrate from England and in 1831 the two men set themselves up as partners in a butchery business in Launceston. Clearly a man of some ability, Thomas enhanced his respectability still further the following year when he settled down to marriage with a local widow, Elizabeth Hinckman.

Under Bransgrove's positive influence, it must be conceded that Felix McCarron did not completely turn over a new leaf. His record during this time is a little patchy though his brushes with authority appear to have been relatively minor and were thus lightly punished. In April 1838 he was admonished by the local police magistrate, Matthew Curling Friend, for being absent without leave. Two years later - in February 1840 - a complaint was made by a man named Lawton that Felix had been out after hours but the charge was dismissed for lack of evidence. Ten months later this same Lawton reported Felix for drinking, resulting this time in his receiving a severe reprimand. In June 1842 he was admonished once again for being out after hours.

In spite of the restrictions imposed on him, life had not by any means stood still for Felix. In July 1840 he had obtained the necessary permission to marry Catherine Edwards, a local woman in her late twenties, and the couple were blessed in due course with the birth of a son, Felix, born in 1842, followed four years later by a daughter, Catherine. None of the minor infractions that he had been guilty of had prevented Felix from securing his pardon in February 1843, several months before the end of his seven-year term, and he was now free to set himself up as a farmer at Musk Vale, east of George Town. In spite of his lately-found respectability, however, Felix was not an entirely reformed character and from time to time his old self resurfaced. Charged with threatening and intimidating a certain Patrick Brady in the street, he was cited to appear in August 1849 before a Justice of the Peace - the same Matthew Friend, as it happened, who had admonished him eleven years earlier. The reason for the alleged confrontation is now forgotten as is the outcome of the case. A bantam cock of a man, Felix's feisty temperament was always something that could be relied upon.

And almost certainly it was backbone and strength of character that enabled Felix to surmount the obstacles that life had placed in his path. Convicted in a system that was designed to protect the interests of the rich and privileged, he was forced to leave behind all that was precious - two small children in the care of a grandfather whose health appeared to be failing, and the painful memory perhaps of a recently-departed wife - and to endure a four-month voyage to a strange land with the prospect of seven years' hard labour at its end. For all that, Felix succeeded in creating a life for himself at the far end of the world and in building a family around him. When he died - too young - in 1859 that knowledge must surely have provided those close to him with at least some degree of comfort.

18 Encounters with Cats

Back in the 1930s, a gamekeeper employed by the Marquis of Ailsa made a remarkable find, deep in the woods of Culzean estate. Caught in one of a series of traps was what appeared to be a Scottish Wildcat which, laid out, measured a total of 38 inches from nose to tail, a very respectable size for an adult male. Long believed to have vanished from the Ayrshire countryside, it was an ignominious end for the county's last verifiable wildcat.

But nearly half a century on, during the 1970s, rumours of predatory cats, roaming the Ayrshire countryside, began to resurface. Encouraged by a series of big cat sightings in other areas of Scotland, Anne Lockhart of Crofthead farm, Kilmaurs, came forward with the story of how she had watched from an upstairs window while a large golden-coloured animal, roughly twice the size of a Labrador dog, bounded through her snow-covered garden before clearing the perimeter fence and vanishing into the fields beyond. The creature, she noted, had a conspicuously long tail that put her in mind of 'a young lioness', and she went on to claim that the paw-prints that it left in the snow showed clearly-defined claw-marks - a little unexpected, perhaps, since most felines are capable of retracting their claws while on the move. Regrettably, no other sightings were reported of the Kilmaurs lioness.

Some observers took the view that big cats, living wild in Scotland, represented a relict population that dated back as far as the last ice age. A more popular theory, however, held that the upsurge in sightings was a consequence of the Dangerous Animals Act which had been passed by Parliament in 1976 to address a growing trend among the rich and famous to keep exotic animals as pets. In the early- and mid-1970s big cats were viewed as a powerful status symbol in the world of high fashion, and the sight of a languid model leading a puma on a leash became a virtual cliché of the time. Openly sold in top-end London stores, cuddly puma kittens didn't stay that way for ever and, as their appetites expanded and their playfulness developed a bit more of an edge, what had seemed at first a chic and biddable pet could turn surprisingly quickly into a major headache for its owner. The last straw came for many when the 1976 Act introduced mandatory (and costly) licensing and insurance, as well as imposing heavy restrictions on conditions under which big cats were to be kept. Many cubs and half-grown animals were destroyed as a result but there were others which simply vanished off the radar - released, it was suggested, into any convenient patch of open countryside. In Ayrshire there were reported sightings of both black and tawny-coloured cats, ranging across the county from Fenwick Moor in the north to the Carrick Forest area, south of Straiton.

Perhaps it was one of these creatures that materialised near Pinmore Viaduct, not far from the junction of the Stinchar and Assel waters. Informed of a number of sightings of a large, black cat, local police took the matter seriously enough to turn up on the doorstep at Laggansarroch, a short distance down the valley, where the farmer, Dougie Wyllie, conducted an officer on a Land Rover tour of the surrounding hills. He took along a rifle - just in case - but in the event the two men drew a total blank, the big cat, if ever there was one, having apparently gone to ground.

Big cats in the wild were one thing, but even those kept in captivity created their own share of difficulties over the years. Back in the 1890s, there was no shortage of witnesses at Kilmarnock's annual 'Grozet Fair' when an allegedly 'untameable' lion decided to make a break for it. For the duration of the holiday period, a funfair had been operating within the precincts of the town's cattle market where, among the merry-go-rounds, shooting ranges and Aunt Sally-type stalls, one of the main attractions was a marquee housing 'Buff Bill's Menagerie' - a blatant attempt by Peebles-born showman, William Kayes, to cash in on the Wild West cult, typified by the genuine Buffalo Bill, that was sweeping the land. Among a panoply of creatures on display, the show's star turn was a burly male lion which was alleged to have 'demolished' its previous keeper the year before and was thus restrained behind a double set of bars. Unfortunately, however, while making his exit at the close of one of his evening performances, the current lion-tamer slipped up when he failed to secure the door of the inner cage properly, thus allowing the beast to thrust its head and shoulders into the narrow gap between the two doors alongside him. As members of the audience looked on in horror, the combined weight of the two eventually caused the outer cage-door to give way with the result that both man and snarling beast tumbled into the auditorium amid a confusion of flailing limbs. As men, women and children stampeded towards the exit, a number were knocked over, some sustaining minor injuries. The lion, meantime, wasted no time in identifying the entrance to the marquee as a possible escape-route and, following the fleeing crowd, he stepped out into the market in a bold bid for freedom.

His taste of liberty was all too brief. Faced with the noise and chaos of an unfamiliar world, the poor creature rapidly realised that he had bitten off more than he could chew and he promptly retreated beneath a caravan from where he refused to budge, growling menacingly at anyone who dared to approach. Harassed by the cracking of pistol-shots, however, he was finally forced into the open and herded back into the marquee where, their confidence restored, a crowd of onlookers assembled to enjoy the spectacle as local police officers assisted Buff Bill's men in their attempts to coax the disgruntled cat back into his cage.

Ignoring a succession of wisecracks from the crowd, the showmen stuck to the task in hand but were ultimately forced to resort to brute strength. Having succeeded in lassoing the wayward king of the jungle, they looped the other end of the rope through a skylight in the roof of his cage and, by this undignified means, the escapee was finally hauled along a gangway and through the open door of his cage. As the door clanged shut behind him, a series of hearty cheers arose from the crowd. Happily the situation had been brought under control with no serious injuries, though police later reported an assortment of hats, caps, gloves, umbrellas, scarves and shawls which had been abandoned during the scramble from the tent and were now waiting to be reunited with their owners.

An equally disturbing situation cropped up nearly twenty years later in Newton Public Park, Ayr, when a lion billed 'The Untameable Brutus' lived up to his ferocious reputation. Part of Albert Manders' Menagerie, the beast was claimed to be 'African forest-bred' - a fairly obvious fiction - but there was little doubt about his cantankerous nature. During the course of an evening performance, Brutus's keeper - a powerfully-built black man named Bert Maccomo - stepped into his cage, armed with no more than his usual stick and wooden chair. It soon became clear, however, that on this occasion his co-star was in no mood to cooperate, menacing Maccomo several times before launching a full-scale attack during which the keeper was severely mauled. In an attempt to fend the lion off, Maccomo retaliated with his stick but, completely undeterred, the creature seized hold of his right hand, virtually severing his index finger. As shocked members of the audience surged towards the exits, circus officials rushed into the cage bearing hot irons which they used to force the big cat back, enabling his injured keeper to make an escape. Thankfully Maccomo's injuries could have been a good deal worse and, following treatment by a local doctor, he was allowed home later that same night. It was subsequently reported that the 25 year-old keeper had only worked with the Menagerie for a matter of weeks and that, prior to his arrival, Manders himself had dealt with Brutus and had suffered several similar attacks.

It should probably be no surprise that a creature bred for the open savannah would react badly to a life of captivity, especially if its situation were compounded by mistreatment. Two years after the incident at Ayr, Manders and Maccomo faced a charge of animal cruelty when it was alleged that the keeper had deliberately terrified a lioness during the course of a run of performances at York's Martinmas Fair and that his employer had been complicit in his actions. As part of his act, Maccomo would offer to

Laggansarrroch Farm

'endanger his life' by stepping for a few moments into the cage of a lioness that was claimed already to have killed one lion-tamer and seriously injured two others. Prior to entering the cage, Maccomo was accused of frightening the creature into submission by making a series of deafening bangs and by thrusting red-hot iron bars into her cage. Once inside, he had continued the onslaught by repeatedly firing off blank cartridges. So disgusted was a member of the audience that she walked out of the show and immediately reported the matter to police. When the case came to court in June 1913, the judge at York agreed that the law had been broken and Maccomo was fined ten shillings (50p) plus costs and his employer, Albert Manders, twenty shillings (£1) plus costs. When we consider the treatment that the poor lioness had received, it is little wonder that she had come to see human beings as the enemy.

Mercifully, attitudes have moved on, with circuses following suit, and performing animals are now virtually a thing of the past. What has remained constant, however, is the periodically-recurring rumour of big cats living wild in the Ayrshire countryside. In summer 2009 the story broke of a horse which had been found injured in a field near Coylton whose wounds, according to veterinary experts, looked very much as though they had been inflicted by a predatory cat. It emerged that there had been a possible sighting of a big cat two months earlier in the grounds of nearby Sundrum Castle, and in early autumn a large black cat was reported to have been spotted at Sorn, ten miles or so to the east. What remains puzzling, however, is why any predator would have chosen to take on prey the size of a horse at a time when the surrounding fields were brimming with new-season lamb, surely a softer target by far.

There are other difficulties too. In spite of sightings across Scotland spanning several decades, to date there has been a dearth of compelling evidence (carcasses of prey species, for example, or images captured on film) and many reports have consisted of little more than a quick glimpse among undergrowth or a momentary flash across the headlights. When it comes to the possibility of big cats living wild in Ayrshire, it is hard to avoid the conclusion that the jury is still very definitely out.

19 The Freeze of 'Forty-Seven

Seldom has the truth of the old adage - 'as the day lengthens, the cold strengthens' - been quite so vividly demonstrated as it was in the late winter of 1947. During the early part of the year high pressure dominated, leading to untypically dry conditions in Scotland which were accompanied by very low temperatures. Though spared for a while the blizzards that had ravaged other areas of the country, Ayrshire did not escape the bite of winter entirely. On one day in early February the dubious honour of having the lowest temperature of any location in the British Isles was accorded to the (normally) balmy resort of Prestwick. By the middle of the month ice had been seen to form in Girvan harbour while, twenty miles inland, Loch Doon froze over completely. Change came in the last week of February when the dry spell finally gave way to the snowstorms that had already been affecting other parts of Britain.

At the top end of the county, the Largs district was particularly badly hit with both road and rail links to the town severely disrupted. When a service bus heading for Kilbirnie became snowbound, its driver, conductor and entire complement of five passengers left the sanctuary of their vehicle to battle their way back to Largs through drifts that were said in places to be chest-high. It was nearly midnight by the time that they arrived at their destination. Numerous private cars had to be similarly abandoned though the driver of Galbraith's grocery van opted to remain with his vehicle overnight, presumably to ensure the safety of his stock.

There was worse to follow. A fortnight later a second snowstorm whistled in, even more severe than the first, this time trapping an entire bus-load of 25 passengers on an exposed section of the same road. As temperatures dropped, the inmates' spirits were reportedly buoyed up by a chirpy former Wren (member of the Women's Royal Naval Service) by the name of Jessie Macpherson who took it upon herself to orchestrate sing-songs through the hours of darkness. (Her efforts were apparently well received. What with the cold and discomfort, there probably wasn't much sleep to be had anyway.) After struggling through wreaths of snow that topped the roadside hedges, a rescue party succeeded in reaching the bus the following morning, much to the relief of its beleaguered occupants. And if it looked as though bus travel offered poor prospects, the railways were no better. A train bound from Largs for Ardeer was stranded for several days in a cutting two miles south of Fairlie, its disgruntled passengers forced to disembark and trudge back to the village on foot.

It wasn't only transport that was adversely affected by the freezing conditions. The people of Largs were advised as an urgent priority to conserve water when levels in local reservoirs became worryingly low, the result, it was said, of their feeder burns in the hills being frozen solid for a protracted period. Towards the middle of the month the need for economy was highlighted yet further when it was reported that the Outerwards Reservoir, a few miles outside the town, was encased in a sheet of ice more than a foot thick and that an estimated ten days' supply of water was all that remained. It appeared that the wintry conditions spared no-one, not even the dead. Funerals in Largs had to be postponed after wind-blown snow filled up the open graves and, in any case, no cortege could have made it beyond the cemetery gates which were completely blocked by eight-foot drifts.

Even low-lying Kilmarnock had its transport links disrupted by the snow and in early March it was noted that the nearby New Farm Loch had been frozen solid for the last six weeks though few of the locals had turned out, as in former times, for curling or skating, prompting veterans of the sport to dismiss the current generation as mere 'feather-bed curlers'. The ready availability of indoor rinks was cited as a possible explanation. Farther away from any such modern facilities, the villagers of Ochiltree demonstrated a stronger attachment to old traditions and enthusiastic groups of skaters were regularly to be seen, gliding along a mile-long stretch of the frozen Lugar Water in a scene reminiscent of a Christmas card. As the mercury in the village plummeted close to -20°C, local curlers joined the skaters on the ice and took advantage of ideal conditions to compete for a variety of trophies.

But for others the consequences of the cold spell were a good deal more serious. Some distance east of Ochiltree, a fourteen year-old Hurlford boy got himself into difficulties during a visit to the home of his sister and brother-in-law at Cronberry. On Wednesday 19 March Peter McDonald (whose leg, it transpires, was still in a cast following a recent fracture) accompanied his sister's husband from Cronberry to Muirkirk but, when a snowstorm blew in, the older man left to return home on foot, leaving Peter in the care of friends. When the boy went out later that day, it was supposed that he had gone to the cinema but when he failed to return by 11 p.m. inquiries revealed that - in spite of his plaster cast - he had left Muirkirk with the intention of walking back to his sister's home, a journey over the snow-covered moors of just over seven miles.

When news of the missing boy reached Cronberry, the local schoolmaster, Alexander Sloan, set about organising a party of volunteers to scour the surrounding snow-covered countryside while Peter's brother-in-law and a friend left to conduct their own search. Meanwhile at the Muirkirk end, two local policemen, Sergeant Norman McLeod and Constable Charles Waugh, set out from the police station there and started to walk west but, with the road scarcely distinguishable from the surrounding snowy landscape, the task that faced them was akin to searching for the proverbial needle in a haystack. Both groups of searchers encountered atrocious conditions as they fought their way through enormous drifts, ten to fifteen feet deep in places, in an unremitting blizzard of sleet and snow. Given the circumstances, it was no small achievement that the two parties made contact at Wellwood, almost exactly mid-way between the two villages, but neither one was able to report any sign of the lost boy. Accompanied by the two Muirkirk policemen, the Cronberry search party turned around and made its way back to the village.

But it wasn't as though the Muirkirk men had any thought of giving up. Following a mere half-hour's rest, Sergeant McLeod and Constable Waugh left Cronberry in pitch darkness to resume their search. Four weary hours later the two officers were on the point of calling it a day when their efforts finally bore fruit. Investigating an isolated hut on the site of an opencast mine - as a last resort, it was said - they found huddled inside a man employed by the mine as a watchman and, with him, the lost boy, Peter McDonald. Understandably both of the hut's occupants were hungry and chilled to the bone, though it transpired that the kindly watchman had foregone his 'piece' for the benefit of his unexpected guest. Their job nearly done, the policemen completed the last weary miles to Muirkirk where they telephoned back to Cronberry with the good news. Food and warm clothing were speedily sent out to the isolated hut where Peter McDonald was judged none the worse for his misadventure. Once his family's relief subsided, however, it seems likely that the errant teenager would have found himself with some explaining to do. It wouldn't have taken much for his wintry escapade to have ended a good deal less cheerfully.

A few miles farther south, in a remote corner of Dumfries House estate, a shepherd by the name of John Waugh witnessed a disaster in the making which he was powerless to prevent. On the lonely farm of Glenmuirshaw 1,000 Blackface sheep faced the prospect of starvation when they were unable to break through the frozen carpet of snow to reach their grazing beneath. Prospects for the animals' survival looked grim - with the roads in their current snowbound state there was no possibility of hauling emergency feed up the winding, four-mile cart-track that provided Glenmuirshaw with its sole vehicular access. To all intents and purposes, the problem seemed intractable but the farm's tenant, Jacob Murray, came up with a thoroughly modern solution. Chartering a small six-seater aircraft, he loaded it up at Prestwick Airport with half a ton of animal feed and

Glenmuirshaw

directed the pilot towards Glenmuirshaw. Making his way up the narrow Glenmuir valley, Pilot C.N.S. McDermott held his machine steady, making the drop at the critical moment before revving hard in order to gain sufficient height to clear the hill ahead. It was a dicey manoeuvre and one which had to be repeated a total of nine times before the aeroplane's entire cargo of hay-bales and cattle-cake had been jettisoned and McDermott was free to return to base, his mercy mission completed in just 40 minutes. Back in the hills, there seems little doubt that John Waugh - a man whose occupation was as old as time itself - would have had ample reason to extol the virtues of modern technology. It was reckoned to be the first time in Scotland that an airlift had been used for such a venture and the entire operation cost Jacob Murray the princely sum of £21 and ten shillings (£21.50). When his tup lambs achieved top prices at Lanark Market six months later, it was shown to be money well spent.

In the hilly country of south Ayrshire what was perhaps a less predictable consequence of the cold, dry February was an outbreak of moorland fires. Three thousand acres were reported as having gone up in smoke to the south of Kirkoswald, with the shepherd's house at the Craigens only just saved from the flames in the nick of time. The lowe given off by the fire was reportedly visible from the tower at Kilmarnock Fire Station, some 25 miles distant. Farther south, near Barrhill, a mighty blaze destroyed an even greater expanse of moorland - in this case, a reported 10,000 acres. (It seems more than likely that the culprit was a stray spark from a steam locomotive, labouring up the line towards Chirmorie summit with the fireman laying on coal by the shovelful.) As in other parts of the county, things changed when the snowstorms blew in. As the roads became impassable, sea travel came into its own as foodstuffs, newspapers, mailbags and passengers were ferried by boat from Girvan to Ballantrae and then on to Stranraer. The residents of villages inland, however, found themselves entirely cut off and two Pinmore men were reported to have made a difficult journey to Girvan for provisions, hauling a sledge on a round trip of more than ten miles through hilly country. Wading through deep snow, their outward journey lasted two and a half hours but no record survives of how long they took to make the return trip, presumably dragging behind them a laden sledge. In an effort to start clearing the roads, teams of the unemployed and prisoners-of-war from Doonfoot Camp joined forces with local authority workers. It was said that, before getting down to business, a standard joke for members of the squads was to hang their coats up on a convenient telegraph line.

James McKean, a 71 year-old commercial traveller from Ayr, and a younger companion, John Milliken of the Black Bull Hotel, Tarbolton, had been motoring home from Galloway in the evening of Wednesday 12 March when the blizzard blew in. Battling through driving snow, eventually the two men came face to face with a particularly intractable snowdrift and their journey by car came to an end, five miles south of Dalmellington. The men now faced a quandary: whether to stay in the shelter of their vehicle, but with neither food nor heating; or alternatively to attempt to press on on foot. In the event, they opted for the latter but, given the weather and underfoot conditions, the older man in particular found the going heavy. He was nearing the point of exhaustion when, by sheer good fortune, they stumbled across an abandoned bus, so the decision was taken for him to take shelter there while John Milliken continued alone with the intention of summoning assistance. It is hard to imagine that James McKean got much rest, waiting in darkness inside what amounted to an unheated metal box.

When Milliken reached Mossdale farm, a mile short of Dalmellington, he made a telephone call to the local police station in which he explained the circumstances surrounding his friend's plight. With no time wasted, a small rescue party was assembled at Dalmellington who met Milliken at Mossdale and followed him back to where McKean had been left in the stranded bus. Any relief that John Milliken may have felt, however, must surely have flooded away when it became clear that, chilled and exhausted, hid elderly friend was too weak to move. The members of the rescue party made McKean as comfortable as they could and, thanks to the efforts of a local shepherd, James McNee of Glenmuck, who carried a small stove to the bus from his home, the patient was afforded at least a little warmth.

When daylight broke a second, larger party set out from Dalmellington, bringing with them a sledge, a stretcher and various flasks of hot tea. Their journey started by lorry but, with the blizzard still raging, the rescuers found their way barred by a colossal snowdrift, less than a mile south of the town. Forced to continue on foot, they trekked down the long trench of Glen Muck, skirting snow wreaths where possible and scrambling over others where they had no other option. On reaching the abandoned bus, their first priority was to attend to James McKean, wrapping him in blankets and securing him carefully on the stretcher. The return journey cannot have been an easy one as the men took turns at stretchering the elderly patient, with those not required at any given time making a point of huddling close by to provide what shelter they could.

Part-way to Dalmellington the rescue party encountered a local doctor who had set out on foot to reach the stranded bus and, following his advice, McKean was taken to the nearest dwelling - Mossdale farm - where slowly he began to revive in the warmth of the kitchen. A little later the doctor declared him fit to be carried to the waiting lorry and, arriving soon after at Dalmellington, he was put to bed in the Loch Doon Hotel, surrounded by hot water bottles. His recovery was fairly rapid. After a two-night stay in the hotel, McKean was fit to walk unaided to the railway station on the Saturday morning. By then he was able to joke about his ordeal, though it was clear that his gratitude to his rescuers was wholeheartedly sincere.

Perhaps the most dramatic incident arising from the bad weather occurred when the Glasgow-Stranraer train became marooned on high moors to the south of Barrhill. It wasn't the first event of its kind. Trains had previously come unstuck on the self-same stretch of track during the harsh winter weather of 1895 and then again in 1908. When the 5.10 p.m. service left Girvan on Wednesday 12 March 1947 all went well until the train was brought up short near Glenwhilly when it ploughed into a mammoth, 30-foot snowdrift and was quickly engulfed. The first night wasn't so bad as the train's heating and lighting continued to operate but when that came to an end the following day, the 57 passengers' ordeal began in earnest. Conditions were already less than comfortable when, to make matters worse, pressure of snow burst in a number of the carriage windows, adding to the travellers' woes and injuring two unfortunate souls who were cut by shards of broken glass. Thankfully, at least no-one needed to go hungry when food being transported on behalf of the Navy, Army and Air Force Institutes ('NAAFI') was allowed to be distributed to the passengers, supplemented by hot tea provided by railway staff at Glenwhilly. On Friday the stranded passengers managed to move into the station building which had the not inconsiderable virtue of being heated, though food was in short supply.

Relief squads bound for Glenwhilly were dispatched as a matter of urgency from both Ayr and Stranraer but before they could meet their objective 32 of the more determined passengers took matters into their own hands, marching away from the scene of their confinement and down the snowy track to New Luce. For those left aboard, the relief must surely have been intense when, on Saturday 15 March, railway workers from Stranraer finally made it through the drifts to within walking distance of Glenwhilly. There would have been few regrets as they gathered up their belongings and prepared to depart, their three nights of captivity now firmly behind them. Those passengers who were elderly or infirm were stretchered over the snow by German POWs. It took until Thursday 20 March before the train itself was dug out and enabled to complete its journey, finally pulling into Stranraer no fewer than eight days behind schedule.

When the three-month freeze finally eased and a thaw set in at the tail-end of March, understandably most of Scotland heaved a massive sigh of relief. During its arctic interlude, everyday life had become problematical, frequently impossible, and now at last it looked as though things might get back to normal. However, it wasn't quite that simple for everyone, and for a few individuals the relaxation of winter's grip simply led to a new set of problems. When the ice started to break up on the Water of Deugh, south-east of Dalmellington, a jam built up a short distance downstream, just over the Kirkcudbrightshire boundary. Forced to divert from its usual channel, the Deugh burst its banks, smashing down drystane dykes and flooding the steading at Waterhead farm to a depth of three feet where the resident Murdoch family were obliged to seek refuge in the upper storey of their home - in the company, so it was said, of a newly-born calf which they tethered to a bedpost. Mercifully the only casualties caused by the deluge were a number of unfortunate fowls which died by drowning. Situated on a slight rise, Darnshaw fared rather better though the farm buildings quickly became totally marooned on an island in a newly-formed loch. In an effort to restore order, an attempt was made to dynamite the ice-barrier upstream but, when this proved unsuccessful and it became clear that normal service at Waterhead and Darnshaw was still some way off, local shepherds rallied to assist in evacuating the two farms. The families affected were provided with temporary accommodation with their neighbours.

And undoubtedly this was the most heartening outcome of Scotland's wintry ordeal as a spirit of cooperation surfaced in communities up and down the land. To maintain deliveries, postmen willingly took to the fields in order to avoid deep drifts that impeded progress on many of the roads. With visibility down to virtually zero, a bus to New Cumnock was only able to complete its journey by crawling along behind a plucky individual on foot who guided the vehicle through a blizzard. When the branch line linking the Barony Pit with the main Glasgow & South-Western Railway became blocked, 100 miners volunteered their services to clear the line of snow, ensuring an uninterrupted supply of coal. A lady doctor travelled to Dunure by fishing boat to treat an elderly patient who had suffered three broken ribs in a fall. All in all, it seems that the trials of March 1947 brought to the fore some of our best human attributes. Today, in an era of supposed global warming, there are those who might suggest that these are qualities which are unlikely to be called upon in future years - but who can say for sure? The harsh winter conditions of 2010/11 stand as a sharp reminder that our Scottish climate may yet be capable of pulling a few unexpected tricks from up its sleeve.

HEROES AND VILLAINS

20 The King of the Randies

The story of Billy Marshall spills frequently into Ayrshire - or out of it, depending on which version you choose to accept. His obituary in the *Scots Magazine* of November 1792 describes the fabled gypsy king as a 'native of Kirkmichael, Ayrshire', though it must be allowed that counterclaims have been asserted equally by parishes in both Dumfriesshire and Kirkcudbrightshire. Less contentious is the location of Billy's final resting-place in the churchyard of St Cuthbert's, Kirkcudbright, where his headstone records rather impressively that 'William Marshall, Tinker, […] died 28th November 1792, at the advanced age of 120 Years.'

No doubt Billy's great age might be liable to raise an eyebrow or two but, when it comes to establishing hard facts, it doesn't help that no contemporary account of his life was ever written. On the contrary, a scattering of fragmentary references in books plus various anecdotes, passed down by word of mouth, are virtually all we have to go on. Born around 1670, of Billy's parentage nothing is known but like many another during the Covenanting era he may well have been baptised by an outlawed minister at a field conventicle. By his own account, during his late teens he travelled to Ireland where he soldiered under King William of Orange at the Siege of Derry in 1689 and the following year at the Battle of the Boyne. In the years that followed, he saw further spells of active service on the continent under the Duke of Marlborough but he was apparently in the habit of routinely deserting every summer in order to be home in time for the Kelton Hill Fair, near Castle Douglas, an annual spree that he is said never to have missed in more than a century.

The chances are that Billy's years of military hardening would have qualified him admirably for the path that lay ahead. For, army days behind him, he rose at home to become chief of the gypsies of Carrick and Galloway, a position that he is believed to have retained for upwards of 80 years. Claims have been made regarding Billy's 'royal' bloodline - as a descendant, some have suggested, of the ancient Pictish kings of Galloway - but, be that as it may, his rise to greatness was viewed in certain quarters with a degree of suspicion, and there were those who held that it took something more than mere chance to crown him. James Allan - the celebrated Northumbrian piper who happened to be Billy's son-in-law - left an account of a grisly occurrence which he claimed to have witnessed in the town of Maybole. First thing one morning, he tells us, he came across the butchered corpse of Billy's predecessor, Isaac Miller, with a bloodied dagger lying alongside him in his bed, the knife in question one which Allan had himself acquired at Ayr a year previously but which he had sold to Billy the very day before. According to Allan, Billy saw to it that the story was put out that the old chief had died as a result of suicide but was quick to ensure that the body was laid to rest in a sequestered spot among the Galloway hills without allowing time for further investigation. Allan's story is, of course, unsubstantiated.

However Billy's 'coronation' came about, his fame - or notoriety - spread widely in the years that followed. 'King of the Galloway Gypsies', 'the Caird [tinker] of Barullion' and 'King of the Randies' (men who followed their own instincts and appetites and despised the rule of law) are a selection of the sobriquets that he amassed in a dominion extending 'frae the Brig-en' o' Dumfries to the braes o' Glenapp' and out across the sea to the counties of Derry and Down which he and his band visited periodically. In prefatory remarks to his 1815 novel, *Guy Mannering*, Sir Walter Scott dubbed Billy 'King of the Gypsies of the Western Lowlands', a misnomer if ever there was one since the majority of the Marshalls' haunts and hideouts were located in some of the highest hill-country that southern Scotland had to offer.

Never one for half measures, Billy was recorded as having tied the marital knot no fewer than seventeen times during the course of his extended lifetime. He fathered innumerable offspring, including, it is reputed, four illegitimate children after he had passed his 100th birthday. Ever zealous of maintaining a respectable facade, he plied his trade as a skilled craftsman, an incorporated member of the Guild of Hammermen, who engaged in the repair of kettles, pots and pans and the manufacture of household items such as spoons, flat-irons for pressing clothes, brass and silver brooches and a variety of other articles from bee-skeps to bagpipes.

An accomplished carver well into his old age, it is on record that in 1788 Billy presented Dunbar Douglas, 4th Earl of Selkirk, with a finely-crafted horn mug and spoon, inscribed with their maker's initials and his age at the time of manufacture: 115. Quite irreplaceable, these objects have since found their way out of the hands of the Selkirk family and into a glass display-case in Kirkcudbright's Stewartry Museum.

Of course, fine craftsmanship is likely to have been a source of pride (why else would Billy have bestowed such a gift on the Earl of Selkirk?) but it is likely to have served a second, more devious, purpose. The chances are that roaming the countryside with horn spoons and innocuous metalwork would have provided Billy and his followers with the cover they needed for other more underhand pursuits such as forging counterfeit coins - an ideal occupation, you might imagine, for expert metal-workers. Meanwhile troupes of light-fingered Marshall women were in the habit of working town and village streets and marketplaces, drawn to wherever people congregated, while their menfolk secreted themselves by lonely roadsides with a view to intercepting late-going wayfarers and relieving them of the contents of their wallets.

Most conveniently for Billy, the smuggling trade in south-west Scotland was in its heyday during the eighteenth century and he was quick to exploit its possibilities, his men frequently operating as forwarders of contraband goods - principally tea, tobacco and brandy - which reached the Galloway coast usually via the Isle of Man. Despite his own enthusiastic involvement in the trade, it was wryly noted that Billy was not above blackmailing others similarly engaged. Near his base at Bargaly Glen he operated a series of illicit whisky-stills, tucked away among the lonely hills where highly-trained dogs would alert their master - without so much as a sound - to the presence of unwanted intruders. Such was Billy's authority that, as his followers combed the backwoods and byways of Carrick and Galloway, they were said to have felt at liberty to exact tribute wheresoever they wished, routinely in the form of fodder for their horses and provisions for themselves and their families. Few, it is suggested, dared refuse.

Yet, for all his unassailable strength in his heartland, a case is on record - dating, apparently, to 1712 - which found Billy guilty of allowing ambition to lead him into error. Seeking to expand his zone of influence, he led a band of his followers north, out of Carrick and into Kyle, until the men found their passage blocked at Newton-on-Ayr by a gang of rival gypsies, aided by a tough alliance of Irish seafarers and local miners. A violent fracas ensued which quickly became a rout, forcing those Marshalls still standing to pull back to the town of Maybole where, fortunately for them, the arrival on the scene of Irish reinforcements enabled them to fight a rearguard action and exit the situation without complete loss of face. A turf war too far, the lesson of Newton-on-Ayr was not lost on Billy and it was a strategic error that he was never to repeat.

Strangely, for all his apparent ruthlessness, Billy was regarded throughout the countryside with considerable affection, possibly because he was never one to overlook a favour nor did he make it his practice to prey upon the poor. In a letter to *Blackwood's Magazine* in Edinburgh in August 1817, James McCulloch of Ardwall, Gatehouse-of-Fleet, reported that Billy had been closely acquainted with three generations of his family, calling at Ardwall twice a year where he had been in the habit of proffering a gift of horn spoons before applying himself to the task of mending any household pots and pans that needed repair. McCulloch added that Billy would 'never

Horn mug and spoon made by Billy Marshall

tak' a farthin' o' the laird's siller' and when the gypsies were camped at Ardwall it was regarded as perfectly safe for washing to be left overnight on the line. Not a single missing hen or duck, he stated, could have been laid at Billy's door.

A second instance of Billy's capacity for neighbourliness was demonstrated when he and some 30 of his followers descended one day on a Galloway farm where they were known. Finding the harvest being brought in late, the gypsies pitched in and helped, asking no more as the price of their labours than a full stomach. Later, when enquiries were made as to whether the Marshalls had ever stolen from the farm, the reply was categorical: 'Not they; they were like the craws - they aye gaed awa' frae their nests to steal.' Perhaps surprisingly, Billy's connections were not confined to his own or to any particular social class. For whatever reason, an unexplained association with the Selkirk family resulted in his being granted a pension which helped sustain him through his extended old age.

Possibly it was enigmatic connections such as this that shielded Billy during his lifetime from the full weight of the law. In the spring of 1723 he combined forces with 'the Levellers', a band of desperate men and women who had been dismissed from their jobs and evicted from their rented homes as the Galloway lairds set about enclosing their lands with a view to pasturing livestock and - naturally - maximising their income. With the tacit support of certain local ministers, the only form of protest open to these voiceless individuals, many of whose families faced utter destitution, was direct action in destroying - or 'levelling' - the new dykes that had so disrupted the pattern of their lives. Initially under cover of darkness, and later as they grew bolder in the full glare of daylight, gangs of Levellers would space themselves at intervals alongside an offending dyke and, at a given signal ('Ower wi' it, boys!'), each would apply a strong wooden rod and push with all his might. Every time a dyke tumbled, the Levellers were said to have raised an almighty cry that carried far and wide across the countryside and must surely have brought a shudder to many a laird in his bed.

As a known leader of the rebels, Billy acquired a further title to add to those he already possessed. But why, we might ask, did the 'King of the Levellers' choose to ally his forces with the cottars and shepherds who had fallen victim to the greed of their landlords? Supposedly a descendant of the ancient Picts (Billy's men would still on occasion paint their faces) his demolition of the new dykes has been viewed by some as an atavistic blow, struck on behalf of his dispossessed forebears, the aboriginal inhabitants of the land. But, as so often in relation to events in Billy's life, it is a tricky business to sift out the reality and his motives may well have been rather more complex. As a supplier of illicit whisky to the dyke-builders, it would clearly have been in his interests to keep the gangs in the locality for as long as possible, engaged in repairing as well as in constructing dykes, and it is not impossible that, in toppling their handiwork, the wily Billy was running with the hare while hunting simultaneously with the hounds. Partial to a dram himself, when during his old age it was put to him that whisky acted like a 'slow poison' his response was fairly robust. 'It maun be damned slow,' he is said to have retorted, 'for I hae drunk it for a hunner years, an' I'm leevin' yet.'

Ultimately the Levellers' uprising proved unsuccessful and in October 1724 a small, ragged army of rebels made their last, futile stand on the banks of the Black Water of Dee where they faced a company of professional dragoons. Many of the Levellers were armed with little more cudgels, hayforks and swords dating back to the days of the Covenant and, in the brief conflict that developed, 200 of their number were taken captive and marched off to be gaoled at Kirkcudbright. At the end of the day, a mere twenty prisoners reached their destination, the others having melted into the surrounding countryside while their captors pointedly looked the other way. Billy was one of those who showed a clean pair of heels, apparently aided in his getaway by a sympathetic soldier of the regiment of Black Horse whose vagabondish tendencies were similar to Billy's own. It is believed that this Andrew Gemmell, a native of Cumnock, was the inspiration for Scott's character, Edie Ochiltree, in his 1816 novel, *The Antiquary*. Those Levellers who did reach the gaol at Kirkcudbright were put on trial and punished under the law, either through fining, imprisonment or even transportation overseas. If the last of these had been Billy's fate, his personal history - and a substantial portion of the folklore of south-west Scotland - would certainly have turned out quite differently.

An undeniably colourful character, Billy's actions and activities during his long and eventful lifetime made a major contribution to the history and mythology of Ayrshire and Galloway. But what are we in the 21st century to make of this King of the Randies and the contradictory depictions of his character that oral history has passed down to us? A principled protector of the poor, perhaps, who rose up at the forefront of the Levellers to challenge the greed and callousness of the lairds? Or alternatively a ruthless grasper whose vaulting ambition and consequent bloodletting propelled him to the top of the gypsy hierarchy? The truth, we might suspect, lies somewhere in between. The chances are that the real Billy Marshall was neither villain nor hero.

Billy lived through times when travelling people in Scotland routinely found themselves on the receiving end of prejudice and discrimination, and coping with the rigours of the road demanded both assertiveness and ingenuity, qualities which Billy possessed in abundance. When viewed against the backcloth of his people's daily hardships, the myriad small dishonesties that he stands accused of are inclined to pale a little perhaps and even his acts of violence can be placed in some sort of historical perspective. A sinner among sinners, Billy inspired genuine fondness but if we are tempted to view him as a Robin Hood-type figure, then we must do so in the knowledge that he was at best a flawed one.

21 A Case of Poisoning

Throughout the afternoon of Wednesday 15 March 1780, Lizzie Wilson worked at preparing her family's evening meal, stirring from time to time a large pot of 'sowans' - a porridge-like staple based on fermented oat husks - that was bubbling away on the kitchen fire. Her elderly mother, Elizabeth, sat close by, quietly intent on carding wool and spinning. When Lizzie considered that the sowans were ready, she removed the pot from the fire and proceeded to pour half of its contents into a wooden bowl, adding a little milk as she did so. What was left she set aside for her father, William, when he returned home from his hard day's work following behind the plough.

The farmhouse at Ploughland, Dundonald, accommodated two distinct households, the first consisting of William Wilson, his wife Elizabeth, and their two unmarried daughters, Lizzie, age 29, and 20-year-old Margaret, the four family-members sharing a living-room and adjacent kitchen, with both apartments also doubling up as bedrooms. Beyond a narrow passageway, a further single room was occupied by Wilson's son by a previous marriage, John, and his wife, Margaret Sinclair. It has been suggested that relations between the two households were not always entirely harmonious, with a degree of mistrust existing between John Wilson and his step-mother on the opposite side of the dividing wall.

After removing the sowans from the fire, Lizzie proceeded to tuck in heartily but her younger sister, Margaret, took relatively little by comparison - no more than a couple of spoonfuls - having eaten fairly recently beforehand. Though she would later claim that she had been aware of a peculiar taste, at the time Margaret said nothing. When the girls' father arrived home from the fields a little later, he was warned by his wife that there was 'something not canny' about the taste of the sowans but, despite appearing to laugh off her anxieties, he opted nonetheless to forego a second helping.

It didn't take long for the women's fears to be realised. Soon after their meal, Margaret and her mother began to feel unwell. Visiting from next door, Margaret Sinclair had also eaten a small portion of sowans and she too quickly became ill, as did her pet cat to which she had fed a few titbits from the table. The effect on Lizzie, however, was a good deal more dramatic. Becoming violently ill, she vomited twice in rapid succession and lost thereby the entire contents of her stomach - her earlier hunger, perhaps, what would ultimately prove her salvation. Meanwhile Lizzie's sister, Margaret, lit a pipe of tobacco in an effort to relieve her symptoms which prompted her to vomit and possibly saved her life by so doing. Sick himself by this stage, William Wilson set out for Dundonald on an errand to obtain sugar for the women's tea, a beverage widely regarded at the time as medicinal. His journey to and from the village was interrupted by periodic bouts of vomiting and by the time that he struggled back to Ploughland he was forced to take to his bed. Overnight matters grew graver still. First to expire was Wilson's wife, Elizabeth, whose life slipped away at around 10 o'clock the following morning. William himself lingered on for a few days more but ultimately he too lost his battle for survival when he passed away early on the Sunday morning.

Before leaping to over-dramatic conclusions, various fairly prosaic possibilities required to be ruled out. Summoned to Ploughland around midnight on 15 March, an Irvine physician, James Alexander, suspected initially that the Wilsons' meal had been contaminated with darnel - a poisonous weed, commonly found among cultivated oats - but he was assured by William Wilson's employer, Matthew Hay, that such a plant was unknown in the locality. Seeking an alternative explanation, the doctor went on to identify as a possible source of infection a grimy copper kettle in which milk was carried to Ploughland each day from the neighbouring farm of Girtrig. But when a second Irvine physician, Dr James Oliphant, examined the Wilsons' cooking-pot the following day, he detected traces of a white-coloured, gritty substance which he suspected at the time of being either sublimate mercury or possibly arsenic. Keen for a second opinion, Oliphant was joined a little later by James Alexander (who had by chance been treating Lady Eglinton at nearby Auchans House) and the two men carried out a series of tests which led them to conclude that the tiny white grains that remained in the pot were most likely to be particles of arsenic. Advised that no such poison was stored on the farm, the doctors were able thus to rule out accidental contamination and were left with no other option than to face up to the possibility that what they had on their hands was a case of wilful poisoning.

With foul play now a distinct possibility, the two doctors felt it necessary to inform a Justice of the Peace and, with no writing materials to hand, Matthew Hay's servant-girl, Betty Fulton, was dispatched to convey a message by word of mouth to Alexander Fairlie of Fairlie, the nearest such official. Overhearing matters from her sick-bed, Lizzie Wilson cried out at this time that 'it would be as good for you to send for no Fairlies', a puzzling interjection that was never subsequently explained. In any event, Betty Fulton arrived at Fairlie House a short time later only to be informed that Alexander Fairlie was absent from home. The next closest Justice of the Peace, Campbell of Newfield, happened to be unwell and unable to attend, so the decision was taken to send for Dr MacKerrell of Hillhouse.

Speculation now turned to the identity of who might be responsible. It was perhaps inevitable that the person who visited the farm most frequently and who had free access to the house on the day in question would find himself in the spotlight. Thirty-nine year-old Matthew Hay lived at the Holms, a 200-acre farm rented from Lord Eglinton, along with his wife, Ann, and the couple's four children. An efficient and prosperous tenant farmer, Hay's bountiful grain-crops were widely respected, harvested from fertile 'holms' that lay alongside the River Irvine and from which in times past the farm had presumably derived its name. A man with clear ambition, Hay leased a further 170 acres at the farm of Ploughland, a mile or so south of the Holms, which was managed on his behalf by his 'grieve', William Wilson.

Matthew Hay, however, was not quite the upright citizen that he might have appeared at first glance. Something of a dark horse, his farming income was known to be supplemented by the fruits of irregular activities with a band of local smugglers, of whom he was apparently a leading light. On top of that, he was believed to have dabbled in counterfeit currency. Some years earlier, in 1767, he had stood trial for plotting the murder of Alexander Gordon, a customs officer at Ayr, but, despite the testimony of several witnesses, a conviction proved impossible and ultimately he was acquitted. The farmer of the Holms was, then, a man with a chequered past but what was still unknown at the time of the poisoning was that the elder of Wilson's two daughters, 29-year-old Lizzie, was carrying Matthew Hay's child.

Early the previous month - February 1780 - Lizzie Wilson had broken news of her condition to Hay and the two had agreed to keep the matter under wraps until, closer to the time of her confinement, Lizzie would be removed to Edinburgh, her costs to be covered by the child's father. No further discussion of the matter took place until the forenoon of 15 March when Hay turned up at Ploughland to supervise the ongoing work of ploughing. He found Lizzie in the kitchen in the company of her mother but, in spite of the older woman's deafness, he avoided broaching the subject of Lizzie's pregnancy until her mother had left the room. When he inquired after her health, Lizzie replied with the disturbing news that, although only 'a quarter gone', she was already 'growing big'. Hay suggested that they discuss the matter further in two days' time but Lizzie replied that her sister, Margaret, would be leaving shortly for Corraith, thus providing them with an opportunity to talk in private. Hay agreed to this and departed for the fields where he remained with his men until around 1 p.m. when they unyoked the plough-horses and repaired to John Wilson's house for a midday break.

Hay had suspected for some time that his workers were inclined to prolong their lunch-breaks when unsupervised, therefore he waited while the men rested and tucked into their broth. When they finished eating and

Holms farm, Drybridge, today

left to return to the fields, he chose not to accompany them, remaining instead at Ploughland where, to quench his thirst, he dipped a jug into a container of water which was standing beside John Wilson's door. Noticing that the liquid appeared cloudy, he crossed the passageway to ask for clean water next door, an apparently innocuous action that would later raise a few eyebrows. Margaret Sinclair, for example, would claim that Hay had ignored her offer of clean water and it would also be suggested that he knew perfectly well from previous experience that the water in William Wilson's house was rarely fit to drink.

On entering the Wilsons' kitchen, Hay found Lizzie by the fireside, attending to the cooking-pot, with her mother spinning alongside. Invited by Lizzie to sit, he indicated that he preferred to remain standing and went on to ask for a drink of water. Lizzie replied that since the container had been standing a while its contents would be 'ill-tasted' and that she would have to fetch fresh water from next door. It would later be suggested that Hay's request for a drink was simply a ruse to ensure that Lizzie left the room.

Questioned afterwards, Lizzie's elderly mother recollected that, once her daughter stepped outside, Matthew Hay had taken a glance into the cooking-pot and given the contents a bit of a stir. For his part, Hay would recall that the old woman had called out at that time - presumably to her daughter - 'Lass, the sowans are too thick, you have been too long of eiking [adding water to] them.' To his knowledge, however, no water, or for that matter any other substance, had been added to the pot as a result. When Lizzie returned to the kitchen, carrying a container of water and milk, he took a drink, then immediately departed.

He didn't leave Ploughland straight away. A short time later Hay returned to the farmhouse - his third visit that day - this time to ask Lizzie to pass on his instruction that the 'close' (farmyard) must be cleaned up as a matter of urgency, adding that he would send a cart the following day to uplift the resulting muck. After he left the house, to Lizzie and Margaret's surprise, Hay paused in his tracks and stared back through the window - something both sisters in retrospect found a little disconcerting, as though he might have been conscious that this could be the last time he would see them alive. When Hay returned to Ploughland some hours later, his fourth (and final) visit of the day was ostensibly for the purpose of checking up on whether his instructions had been followed. By then, of course, illness had broken out and the house was in uproar. Amid the panic and confusion, Lizzie Wilson accused Hay of having slipped a pinch of snuff into the cooking-pot, maybe something worse. When the doctor arrived a little later from Irvine, it was an allegation that she would repeat in his presence. Matthew Hay, of course, flatly denied any wrongdoing.

As a married man with a young family, naturally there were certain matters which Hay might have preferred hushed up. Acquiring poison presented him with no difficulty. Perennially troubled by rats, he was in the habit of obtaining arsenic from a Kilmarnock apothecary, Thomas Corsan, whose premises he had visited only a fortnight or so before. The rat population in the Holms granaries had soared to something approaching plague proportions and, despite the best efforts of a local rat-catcher, the creatures' numbers had continued to rise. Hay's first priority at Corsan's shop was to settle his outstanding account but before leaving he went on to buy sixpence-worth (about 2p) of arsenic. The payment was made in cash and the quantity of poison so small that no written record of the transaction required to be kept.

Back at the Holms, Hay combined the arsenic with a quantity of crumbs swept up by a kitchen-servant, Mary Thomson, after baking, and proceeded to lay the lethal concoction out on wooden planks in the stable loft. The strategy appears to have been successful as, according to one of his herdsmen, Hugh Brown, 'a good many rats' were destroyed as a result. When exactly these events took place is a little tricky to pin down: the farm-servants recalled that Hay's persecution of the rat population coincided with the start of spring ploughing, a little later than normal that year because of a keen frost. The chances are that the rat-poison was laid out at the Holms a week or so prior to the Ploughland calamity.

On the face of it, Hay came across as genuinely concerned for the fate of his suffering tenants. To provide relief, he offered without hesitation to send wine and brandy and, following Elizabeth's death, he very reasonably suggested delaying the burial to permit a post-mortem examination to be carried out. Yet for all his show of concern, it couldn't be ignored that Hay had a powerful motive for wanting Lizzie Wilson and her swelling form effaced from the local scene and, based on the information provided by Thomas Corsan, the Kilmarnock apothecary, there is no doubt that he had at his disposal the means to remove her. With evidence piling up against him, Hay was well aware of being under suspicion yet, in spite of the gathering storm-clouds, he still appeared unfazed, declaring himself perfectly willing to face trial and undergo the scrutiny of the law.

His last conversation with Lizzie Wilson took place in the late evening of Wednesday 22 March, precisely a week after the poisoning incident, by which time, of course, both of her parents had breathed their last. Riding home after a meeting with Campbell of Newfield - its substance unknown - Hay called in at Ploughland and presumably was somewhat taken aback to find the door barred against him. Knocking at a window, he persuaded Lizzie to approach and open the door. The conversation that then ensued was one of which Matthew Hay and Lizzie Wilson would later give substantially differing accounts. Still sick in bed, Lizzie's sister, Margaret, was outwith earshot.

According to Hay's version of events, he had informed Lizzie that night that, in the light of recent events, he no longer expected her to travel to Edinburgh in advance of the birth of her child. Lizzie, he claimed, was agreeable. He then went on to discuss with her the possibility of giving her baby away. When he learned that Lizzie and Margaret had no money in the house, Hay stated that, before leaving, he provided her with a sum of money.

Ploughland farm, Dundonald, today

Lizzie's recollection, by contrast, was rather different. She believed that Hay had left no room for doubt that the Edinburgh arrangement still stood and emphasised his insistence on secrecy concerning her child's paternity. He had gone on to propose a financial settlement whereby she would receive an immediate payment of £50, followed by annual payments of £4 for life - subject, of course, to her continuing discretion. Lizzie claimed that she had declined this offer. Hay had denied any involvement in the death of her parents and had said that he would return the following morning to discuss matters further.

As things turned out, however, it was a conversation that never took place. Matters came to a head the following day - Thursday 23 March - when Matthew Hay was arrested on suspicion of murder and consigned to the tolbooth of Ayr. For whatever reason, he was released almost immediately but his freedom was to prove short-lived. On 29 March a second warrant was issued and by the end of the month once again Hay found himself behind bars in Ayr where he had no option other than to exercise patience until his trial was due to be held in May.

Letters that Hay wrote during his time in jail offer an interesting insight into his state of mind. His wife, Ann, suffered from a nervous disorder which required constant attendance by a paid-companion, Peggy Dunlop, who was, it seems clear, a highly-regarded member of Hay's household. In letters to Peggy, Hay is candid in facing up to his shortcomings as a husband. 'The devil', he admits, 'my wicked heart has led astray.' On the face of it, his contrition appears equally sincere in connection with Lizzie Wilson's unborn child: 'I am ashamed of myself,' he writes - 'How can I look virtue in the face?' At no point, however, does he come close to admitting involvement in the Ploughland poisoning and insists that his conscience is clear. Responding to an appeal to confess his guilt, he declares 'I neither can nor will.' 'I have enough sin of my own,' he concedes, 'without taking any part of others' sins.'

As it turned out, Hay spent considerably longer on remand than was originally anticipated. Owing to the sudden illness of Lord Gardenstoun, the trial was delayed by several months before finally getting off the ground on 7 September. A total of 23 witnesses were called upon to testify, the greater number on behalf of the prosecution, including both Lizzie and Margaret Wilson - the latter too delicate to walk into court unassisted.

Expert witnesses included Dr Joseph Black, Professor of Chemistry at Edinburgh University, who confirmed the presence of arsenic in the Wilsons' cooking-pot. Perhaps surprisingly, one of the very few witnesses to speak up in Matthew Hay's defence was John Wilson who cited various instances of the accused's kindness towards his late father. (John's wife, Margaret, by contrast was called upon to give evidence on behalf of the prosecution.) Hay's defence relied largely on the notion that Lizzie Wilson had attempted to take her own life, along with the lives of her entire household, in preference to facing the ignominy of an illegitimate child.

At first glance the jury's composition might have boosted Hay's morale, given that several jurors were men with known smuggling connections. Any optimism, however, would prove short-lived. The entire court proceedings were completed within twenty-four hours and a short time later, the jury reached its verdict: 'by a great plurality of voices', Hay was found guilty. All that remained now was for Lords Kames and Braxfield, presiding, to pass sentence. Hay would be returned to the tolbooth, he was told, to be sustained by bread and water alone until Friday, 13 October - a month or so hence - when he would be 'taken furth of the said Tolbooth to the place of execution on the Common Muir of Ayr and there betwixt the hours of two and four in the afternoon [he would be] hanged by the neck […] until he be dead.' His body would then be cut down and delivered to George Charles, an Ayr surgeon, for the purposes of dissection.

Those present in court reported that the condemned man appeared visibly shaken but gathered himself sufficiently to address the judges, maintaining his innocence to the last and pointing an accusatory finger at Lizzie and Margaret Wilson. Lord Kames replied, reminding Hay that he had received a fair trial under Scots law and urging him to devote what time he had left in this world to prepare for his entry into the next. Not everyone, however, believed that all of the judge's comments were quite so well measured. A former opponent of Hay's across the chessboard, it has been claimed that, apprised of the guilty verdict, Lord Kames was heard to mutter - 'That's checkmate to you, Matthew.'

It might reasonably have been assumed that Hay's departure from this life at the hands of the reviled Glasgow hangman, John Sutherland, would bring matters to a decisive close. But no. A curious postscript requires to be added to his story, documented by the nineteenth century portrait painter,

John Kelso Hunter, in a volume of autobiographical sketches. It seems that the author was in attendance when, some three decades after Hay's execution, his grave in Dundonald kirkyard was opened up and, to the intense surprise of those present, the coffin was found to contain not the smuggler's last remains, as expected, but rather in their place a quantity of sea sand. Such was the man's enduring fame - notoriety, perhaps - that, when word of the find got out, local people turned out in numbers in the hope of verifying the strange phenomenon for themselves. The artist himself records that he acquired as a memento a small specimen of sand from the coffin. Intriguingly, the theory was aired that not only might Hay's burial have been a sham but also his execution. An ever-resourceful man with varied influential contacts, was there just a chink of possibility that he had somehow engineered his own survival? In any event, no explanation for the disappearance of the body has ever been forthcoming and its fate post-dissection remains to this day unknown.

A perennially divisive figure, during his lifetime Matthew Hay was widely acclaimed for his model husbandry at the Holms and romanticised in equal measure for his illicit activities by moonlight. But he was also a man with an indisputably dark streak - a ruthless self-seeker who endured spells behind bars, faced trial for murder and who finally ended his days, dangling ignominiously at the end of a hempen rope. Controversy and intrigue dogged Matthew Hay's footsteps throughout much of his lifetime, and it is entirely fitting that they should have continued to do so even after his death.

22 Robbery at Rosemount

In the late autumn of 1814, venturing on to the rural roads of Ayrshire appears to have been a fairly hazardous enterprise. A farmer on horseback, Mr Dick of Gateside, Craigie, was waylaid near his home by three unknown men, one of whom thrust a pistol in his face. The would-be robber got more than he bargained for, however, when the plucky farmer reached out and wrested the firearm from his grasp before riding off at speed, startled for sure but otherwise unscathed. He'd had a lucky escape: when he took the weapon to Kilmarnock the following day, it was examined by the town magistrates and found to be loaded and dangerous. A few days later a young man was similarly menaced at Spittal Hill, scarcely a mile from Gateside, by an assailant also brandishing a firearm.

Around the same time, a post rider near Maybole reported being intercepted by two men on foot who threatened his life if he refused to hand over the mailbags. Rejecting their demands, the postman recounted how he had struck one of his aggressors full in the face - with such force, he claimed, that the man fell instantly to the ground. When his accomplice attempted to discharge a pistol, by sheer good fortune the weapon loudly misfired, causing the postman's horse to bolt and thus preserving both its rider and the mails. When examined more closely, however, the postman's story began to fray until, questioned under oath, he finally confessed that, having picked up news of recent robberies in the local area, he had fabricated the whole episode in a fairly pathetic attempt to gain kudos for having thwarted a similar attempt. When the truth became known, it seems unlikely that the would-be hero would have reaped much glory from his attempted deception.

Despite debunking the postman's colourful fictions, the authorities remained jittery nonetheless concerning an undeniable upsurge in highway robbery, now a far more common event, it was noted, than in previous years. Chaired by Lord Eglinton, a committee of Justices of the Peace issued a proclamation during November 1814 which, in order to reach as broad an audience as possible, clergymen were instructed to read to their congregations. In their announcement, the JPs made reference to 'the very alarming state of the country' due to 'multiplied instances of Highway Robbery, aggravated, in many cases, by wanton and barbarous assaults.' A reward of twenty guineas (£21) was offered to any member of the public who might apprehend a person who was subsequently convicted of 'Murder, Highway Robbery, or Housebreaking.' In addition to the proclamation from the pulpit, the Justices also released a public notice, exhorting farmers and country people in particular to keep a close eye on 'all Vagrants and Suspicious Persons' and to carry out a citizen's arrest if deemed necessary. Innkeepers, the notice suggested, were 'more in the way of observing suspicious characters than any other class of people' and they were therefore urged to pass on any relevant information to Magistrates and Constables. Failure to do so, it was made clear, might result in the loss of a publican's licence to trade. But the JPs did more than simply pontificate. Based on the selection of a sub-committee, 'a very enterprising man', Angus Gunn, was appointed to the post of Head Constable for Ayrshire at the not inconsiderable salary of £80 per annum. Perhaps it was events of several weeks earlier which had served to focus the minds of the authorities. On Thursday, 27 October the half-yearly feeing fair known as 'Dudsday' had taken place in Kilmarnock, an occasion when the surrounding landward population flooded into the town - as intent on carousing, possibly, as on commerce - with the result that many travellers were late on the road.

During the late afternoon of Dudsday, the publican, James Ballantine's, wife got a bad feeling when four unknown men planted themselves in her husband's establishment in Monkton. Ballantine eyed his customers warily as they drank two gills of whisky and disposed of fourpence worth of bread - these were meagre times - their voices dropping any time his wife approached to serve them. They did not, she observed to her husband, have the look of men who were engaged in legitimate business. One of the four was a tall man, around six feet in height, dressed in a long, dark coat with yellow buttons and wide, grey trousers. The skin of his nose was disfigured by a conspicuous black blemish and his sallow complexion gave him an unhealthy look. It would later be said that he had something of the appearance of an old soldier.

Of his drinking companions, one was a much smaller man, a little over five feet perhaps, dressed in a brown coat and whose red hair and matching beard were accompanied by a notably florid complexion. The third drinker, by contrast, was dark with copious black whiskers about his face. About five feet six inches tall, he wore grey stockings and a blue coat with small yellow buttons. It did not escape the publican's notice that he had equipped himself with a stout stick. This dark-featured man was the only member of the party able subsequently to be identified. Strangely, nothing is known about the fourth drinker in Ballantine's hostelry. Perhaps his back was kept turned or maybe he was careful to remain in the shadows, outwith the feeble glow of candlelight.

At five o'clock, James Henry, a weaver living nearby, arrived on Ballantine's premises to buy candles from the small grocery store which the innkeeper operated alongside his public house. Indicating the four sinister characters who had come in earlier, the landlord mentioned to his neighbour on the quiet that the men had made his wife uneasy and he specifically asked Henry to take a close look at them. When they finally got up and departed, the landlord voiced his strong suspicion that, before the night was out, some of those returning from the Dudsday fair would have been relieved of their wallets.

As it turned out, the first was David Dickie, an apprentice to Kilmarnock upholsterer, William Lamont. Dickie had left the fair just after 5 p.m., making for Ayr on horseback, but his journey by moonlight did not go entirely to plan when his pony cast a shoe at Symington, obliging him to continue at a more leisurely pace. A short time later he was nearing the first belt of woodlands at Rosemount when he became aware of four men, travelling from the opposite direction, one of whom blocked his pony's progress by tightly gripping the reins. Dickie was left in no doubt about the man's intentions when he peremptorily demanded his wallet and, as if to dispel any doubt that he meant business, proceeded to strike him a violent blow to the head with his stick. The pony reared up at this but before it could break free was restrained by the highwayman's three companions, enabling Dickie's initial attacker to take hold of his right leg and thereby dislodge him from the saddle. The men then bundled their victim into a ditch where they proceeded to rifle through his clothing and pockets, searching even the tops of his boots, and taking from him some seven shillings in silver, a pair of gloves and his handkerchief as well as a second black, silk handkerchief that he had been wearing around his neck.

Not yet satisfied, however, Dickie's first attacker demanded that he hand over his pocket-book - or wallet - while at the same time compressing the apprentice's neck in order to ensure his silence. Meanwhile the robber's three accomplices continued to search his clothing in what proved a fruitless search for a pocket-watch. At one point Dickie attempted to break free and make a run for it, but his efforts were thwarted when the smallest of the men produced and threatened him with a pistol. His ordeal only came to an end when, suspecting that someone was approaching, his attackers released him and slipped away quietly into the darkness. Shocked and badly shaken, Dickie was forced to resume his journey on foot, making his way down the brae to Rosemount smithy where he was fortunate to find his pony waiting. The only detailed description that he was subsequently able to provide was of his initial attacker who was, he reported, a swarthy, dark-complexioned man with a long beard who had been wearing a medium-length blue coat with small yellow buttons. Interestingly, he felt it worth mentioning that, because the highwaymen had been careful to keep their voices lowered, he was unable to say whether any of them had spoken with an Irish accent.

David Dickie was not the only unsuspecting soul who fell among thieves that late October evening. The upholsterer was still recovering from his ordeal at Rosemount smithy when two more men arrived on the scene with similar reports of having fallen prey to the violent gang. Monkton farmers, James Ferguson of Newlands and Alexander Paterson of Aikenbrae, had left Kilmarnock Fair together, travelling on horseback, but by the time that Ferguson arrived at the sixth milestone from Ayr - somewhere in the vicinity of present-day Hansel Village - his companion had fallen some way behind. As he passed the Rosemount plantation, Ferguson was riding alone and the attack he suffered there was as merciless as it was unexpected. In a similar manner to David Dickie before him, the farmer's horse was seized by its bridle allowing him to be pulled to the ground. Despite being threatened with a pistol and beaten about the head with sticks, Ferguson refused to surrender his valuables without a struggle. Even as his pockets were being rifled, he managed to rise to his feet and drag his attackers across the road. Ultimately, however, force of numbers prevailed and he was overpowered and robbed of his possessions: a one pound note, some shillings and other small coins and (something he only became aware of the following morning) the keys to his desk. For all his cuts and bruises, perhaps the Newlands farmer got off relatively lightly: he was said to have been carrying a larger sum of money, secreted about his person, which the robbers failed to locate.

Following on behind, Alexander Paterson rode into an identical ambush. Hauled from his horse and brutally assaulted, his red leather pocket-book, containing the considerable sum of £19 in pound- and guinea-notes, was snatched from his pocket. In addition to cash, he also lost a silver pocket-watch, numbered 47,599. When finally released, Paterson struggled on and overtook James Ferguson and the two men made their way down to Rosemount smithy where they found the gang's earlier victim, David Dickie, still recovering from his ordeal.

It is hard to imagine that the publican, James Ballantine, and his neighbour, James Henry, were unduly surprised when word reached Monkton of the violent robberies that had taken place some two miles up the road. A posse of twenty or so men (including Henry) was quickly assembled who armed themselves with sticks and made their way directly to Rosemount, encountering Ferguson and Paterson along the way. In spite of their injuries, the two doughty farmers had retraced their steps in search of their attackers, having first taken the precaution of equipping themselves with the Rosemount blacksmith's poker. (David Dickie, by contrast, had clearly had enough by this time and was content to resume his journey to Ayr.) Arriving at Rosemount, the Monkton men combed the surrounding countryside but of the four highwaymen there was not a trace.

Perhaps what put the men of the Monkton posse off the scent was Alexander Paterson's impression that, in the aftermath of the ambush, his attackers had made off in the direction of Kilmarnock. For entirely understandable reasons, however, the bruised and battered farmer was mistaken. In reality the four highwaymen had veered east, following back-roads in the direction of the village of Craigie, where they carried out their fourth robbery of the evening - a crime too far, as it turned out. Around 7 p.m. they waylaid a third local farmer, Robert Guthrie of Townhead of Drumley, and, in a violent attack, dragged him from his horse and robbed him of his valuables. Unfortunately for one of his assailants, Guthrie recognised the man as a hawker who routinely travelled the local countryside, selling items out of a green pack. He named the man as Witheredge.

The name provided by Robert Guthrie wasn't too far off the mark. In fact the man was John Worthington, an itinerant pedlar who had at one time based his operations at Kilmarnock before later relocating to Glasgow. Around 8 p.m. on the evening of the Dudsday fair, Worthington and a single companion - by his speech an Irishman - turned up on the doorstep of Robert Hamilton, a Kilmarnock weaver with whom Worthington had lodged some three years earlier. Hamilton would later claim to have been uneasy at the hawker's unannounced arrival, knowing full well that he had previously been banished from Ayrshire as a consequence of his criminal activity, but he took him in nonetheless. The presence in Hamilton's home that evening of Worthington's young son and daughter, the latter having arrived from Glasgow earlier in the day, may put a different complexion on matters, giving the contrary impression that, despite the weaver's assertion, the arrival of his guests was not perhaps entirely unexpected. Once settled, Worthington produced a £1 note and sent his son out to buy a 'mutchkin' of whisky - something short of a modern-day pint - but when the twelve-year-old returned empty-handed, saying that no change was to be had, his father handed him instead the sum required - two shillings - in silver. During the course of his visit, Worthington revealed nothing to his host of his movements earlier that day, and when he and his companion finally got up to go he indicated his intention to carry on to Irvine. As he left, Worthington passed two shillings and sixpence to Robert Hamilton's wife to pay for a new shirt for his son. Margaret Hamilton would later state her suspicion that the pedlar might also have given his daughter a sum of money to provide for her return journey to Glasgow. At no point in the Hamiltons' account of events is there any reference to the children's mother.

Worthington did not go to Irvine. Reunited with all three of his companions, he appears instead to have made his way to Rose Fenwick, a small settlement on the site of present-day Laigh Fenwick, arriving there shortly after 10 p.m.. Though the landlord of the Black Bull Inn, David Taylor, had already shut up shop and was on the point of retiring for the night, in response to the men's knocking, his wife, Jean, unbolted the door and allowed them to enter. Although Jean Taylor did not know any of her visitors by name, their faces were familiar to her and Worthington in particular she had known for several years as a travelling salesman. Settling themselves in the kitchen of the public house, the four men talked for an hour or so, consuming as they did so two half-mutchkins of spirits, after which they approached the landlord's wife to request overnight accommodation. Supplying them with a candle and a third half-mutchkin of spirits, the landlord's wife showed her late-night guests to an upstairs room containing a bed. She would later recall overhearing John Worthington at this time saying that they still had business to be settled.

Jean Taylor's suspicions had been aroused. From the kitchen below, she could hear the chink of money being counted, so she tiptoed upstairs in her stocking soles and, peering one-eyed through a gap in the lathing, spied on her guests - something she would later insist that she was not in the habit of doing. Seen through the narrow cranny, banknotes had been laid out on a table, and, as the intrigued landlady continued to watch, she saw Worthington place a number of shillings on top of each. From the snatch of conversation that she overheard, Jean Taylor formed the impression that there was some disagreement over the division of the money. Having seen enough, she slipped quietly back downstairs and, not long after, the men descended, made their excuses and promptly vanished into the night. It would not be the last that Jean Taylor of the Black Bull would hear of her four shady guests.

In spite of his traumatic experience, Alexander Paterson, the farmer of Aikenbrae, was not one to let the grass grow under his feet. On Friday 28 October, the day after the Dudsday fair, he and James Henry travelled to Kilmarnock, hoping to spot the robbers in the streets, but without success. Continuing to Glasgow at the Sheriff-Depute's request, the two men drew a similar blank in the city. Some weeks later, however, Henry's luck turned. He travelled again to Glasgow and on this second occasion was able to identify John Worthington as one of the four drinkers that he had seen in Ballantine's public house on the afternoon of Kilmarnock Fair day. Whether he came face to face with Worthington by chance or, probably more likely, after the hawker had already been picked up by the authorities is not on record. Whatever the circumstances, the accused man was duly transferred to Ayr where witnesses, including James Ballantine and David Dickie, confirmed him as one of the four highway robbers.

During his spell in Ayr tolbooth we are provided with a rare glimpse of Worthington the man. It seems that throughout his time behind bars his spirits remained buoyant and, for whatever reason, he never doubted his impending acquittal. A joker of sorts, he is said to have indulged in various antics at his fellow inmates' expense, frequently donning an old bonnet in dark parody of the infamous black cap worn by a judge when passing the death sentence. In early December he was removed from Ayr and conveyed for trial to the High Court of Justiciary in Edinburgh, travelling, as it happened, in the company of John Anderson, a sailor on board the brig *Amity*, who was accused of murdering his wife by throwing her from the parapet of the Auld Brig in Ayr. Anderson was subsequently acquitted but, as things turned out, John Worthington's earlier optimism proved ill-founded. Despite his plea that on the day of Kilmarnock Fair he had been more than a hundred miles away, visiting Lochgilphead as part of a selling trip to the West Highlands, the Edinburgh jury remained unconvinced. The dismissal on a technicality of one of the charges - that relating to the attack on Robert Guthrie near Craigie - did nothing to save him. By a unanimous verdict, John Worthington was found guilty of three charges of highway robbery and was accordingly sentenced to death, the execution to be carried out two months later, on Friday, 17 February 1815.

In an Ayrshire context, what was unusual - probably unique - about the arrangements for John Worthington's execution was the court's stipulation that the sentence be carried out as close as possible to the scene of the highwayman's crimes. Consequently, on the appointed day - Candlemas Friday - a deputation of Ayrshire's great and good processed across the Fenwick Moor to Floak where, at the county boundary, the man at the centre of it all, John Worthington, was passed by the Renfrewshire authorities into their hands. Sheriff Eaton and Procurator Fiscal Murdoch formed part of the reception committee, as well as the recently appointed Head Constable, Angus Gunn, in whose charge the condemned man was placed. Travelling rather grandly in a horse-drawn coach, Worthington then proceeded to Kilmarnock, escorted all the while by a troop of the Second Regiment of the Queen's Cavalry, later augmented by twelve special constables on horseback from Wallacetown, Ayr, who had volunteered for the task. As the cavalcade wound its way down past Fenwick, we might wonder whether the landlady, Jean Taylor, watched it pass and thought back to the evening four months earlier when she had spied on Worthington and his partners in crime in an upstairs chamber of the Black Bull.

A little farther down the road, at Kilmarnock, the condemned man was obliged to trade his horse-drawn comfort for the ignominy of an open cart. He requested, and was granted, permission to see his young son, an apprentice shoemaker in the town, and it was reported that the boy's acute distress was evident to all present. Unsurprisingly Worthington too grew emotional but succeeded in composing himself before saying his final goodbye. The fateful caravan resumed once more, accompanied through Kilmarnock by the town magistrates plus a further one hundred and twenty special constables who escorted Worthington as far as the burgh boundary at Riccarton Bridge. From there, the condemned man had only a short distance to travel - five or so miles - before arriving at Symington Toll, the setting for his ordeal to come.

What must Worthington have thought when he came within sight of the vast multitude of men, women and children who had converged on this place to view his final torment? As he readied himself for death, the band of the Ayrshire Militia played to a holiday crowd while a detachment of the 91st Regiment, stationed at Ayr, remained on hand to maintain good order. The precise location of the whole morbid extravaganza is no longer certain, though it was said at the time that the Sheriff had made a point of positioning the gallows in a spot which ensured a clear and unobstructed view for all in attendance. One suggestion is that it was erected on the brow of Helenton Hill - a conspicuous, green knowe to the east of Jeanfield farm - and this may well have been the spot where the Glasgow hangman, Thomas Young, prepared for his first call to duty, anxiously testing and re-testing his rope-work and knots. When an inquisitive jackdaw landed on the crossbeam and promenaded back and forth, a flutter of speculation rippled through the crowd as to its significance. A carriage that pulled up from Ayr was found to contain Worthington's son-in-law, temporarily released from jail, it was said, in order to take his final farewell.

Amid the morbid razzmatazz, it may be that the condemned man was afforded at least some degree of solace by the two Catholic clergymen - Mr Paterson of Glasgow and Mr Scott of Paisley - who had accompanied him on his final journey and who prayed with him now at the foot of the gallows. In the moments immediately prior to his ascending the platform, Worthington happened to overhear a sympathetic onlooker who had referred to him as a 'poor man'. His response came instantaneously when he replied - 'I am not a poor man today.' His message seems clear and unambiguous. Even faced with imminent death, Worthington's spirit had not been entirely crushed. Though reviled and condemned and poised now on the brink of eternity, his defiant utterance was a final assertion of his pride and human dignity and it may well be that those were his last ever words. Once atop the platform, Worthington showed no inclination to address the crowd and wasted no time in signalling his readiness to die. At twenty minutes past three o'clock in the afternoon, Tam Young drew back the bolt and the highwayman, Worthington, was sent plummeting to his death. He expired quickly, it was said, and with no apparent struggle.

But, even as his body dangled at the end of a rope, the sorry tale of John Worthington was not yet quite at an end. After being left to hang for the best part of an hour, the body was then cut down, placed in a coffin and transported to Kilmarnock to be interred in the yard of the Laigh Kirk. Those of his friends who attended the burial were surprised at the shallowness of the grave and surmised that a deliberate attempt had been made to facilitate the work of resurrectionists who were known to be active at the time. In order to thwart the body-snatchers' macabre pursuits, two of Worthington's associates used a spade to prise open the coffin lid, after which they poured a large bottle of vitriol and a bucket of quicklime over the corpse with a view to accelerating the process of decomposition and thus rendering the body unsuitable for dissection. An eye-witness observed wryly that Worthington's grave was 'reekin' like a lime kiln.'

A strange sequel to events at Symington Toll involved William Evans, the Duke of Portland's overseer at Troon. Riding by on the day of Worthington's execution, Evans was asked by the elderly toll-keeper whether he intended to wait in order to view the forthcoming spectacle. 'I attend no such gatherings, sir,' came Evans's haughty reply before he galloped off at speed. Little more than a year later, however, the Duke's overseer made a notable exception when he was present in May 1816 at an execution in Ayr. The crime on that occasion was one of forgery and the man who was hanged was William Evans himself.

23 The Lion of Waterloo

In the early hours of the first day of April 1938 a team of workmen set about the task of unearthing human remains from an old cemetery in Salford, near Manchester. They had quite a job on their hands. For a good many years much of the cemetery had been paved over for a timber storage yard while another section had disappeared entirely beneath the buildings and machinery of a printing works. The men, however, persisted in their efforts until, several feet down, they were finally rewarded when a lettered stone confirmed the spot where they were digging as the final resting place of Ensign Charles Ewart who had passed away in March 1846 at the age of 77. Witnessing the exhumation was Ewart's only living relative in Salford, Miss Elsie Lomas, who must surely have felt a surge of pride in the knowledge that her illustrious forebear had been lionised in his time as a hero of the Napoleonic Wars.

Charles Ewart was not a native of Salford, hailing rather from north of the border where he was born at Waterside, Kilmarnock, sometime in the late 1760s. Not a great deal appears to be known about his background or early life but by one account he spent some time in the barbering trade. Towering well over six feet tall, it wasn't his ideal calling. 'The shaving didna suit me at a',' he is said to have commented in later life - 'I stood ower heigh aboon the folk's heads.' He was around twenty years old in 1789 when he signed up with Scotland's only cavalry regiment, the 2nd Royal North British Dragoons (widely known as the 'Scots Greys' on account of the soldiers' preference for grey horses, a nickname which stuck and eventually gained official status). Several years of hard campaigning followed as Ewart fought his way through the Netherlands during the French Revolutionary Wars of the 1790s, briefly made captive by French forces following the allied defeat at Fleurus. While there were many at this time who succumbed to cold, hunger and exhaustion Ewart made it through, undoubtedly aided by his exceptional strength and stamina. No doubt luck also played a part.

It was nearly twenty years before Napoleon's flight from exile on the island of Elba reignited his country's territorial ambitions and resulted in the Scots Greys' being called once again to the field. By now in his mid-forties, Ewart had lost none of his youthful vigour. During the intervening years he had been promoted to the rank of sergeant while his skills in swordsmanship had been recognised in being appointed as the Greys' Master of Fence'. Matters on the continent came to a head in June 1815 when two great armies faced one another across a broad Belgian plain: to one side the French, commanded by Napoleon Bonaparte; directly opposite, a coalition of nations under the joint command of the British Duke of Wellington and the Prussian, General von Blücher. Lying immediately to the north of the two opposing armies was the small Belgian town of Waterloo whose name would soon become a byword for utter, irreversible defeat. As hostilities commenced on 16 June Ewart and the Greys were among the coalition ranks.

Remarkably, Ewart's own account of his involvement in the battle has survived in the form of a letter that he sent to his brother afterwards. In it he records that in the early hours of 16 June he was among a group of Greys who were called upon to defend a band of British foot-soldiers who had been 'cut up most shockingly' by enemy cavalry. His comrades and he prepared themselves for battle, arriving on the field shortly before noon, but by then the enemy had pulled back into the safety of a wooded area where, for the time being at least, they stayed put. In the absence of any further action the Duke of Wellington called the following day for an infantry retreat and Ewart's Greys were part of a cavalry-force that provided the battalions of foot-soldiers with cover as they pulled back.

While the retreat was ongoing, the French cavalry chose the optimum moment to break from cover and they swarmed from the woods in considerable numbers. As a savage thunderstorm raged overhead, they surged forward, harrying the British so hard that the retreating forces were obliged to halt, form a line and set up cannon. This, according to Ewart, was the point where the tables turned. 'We gave them some of our British balls,' he gloated, 'which silenced them for that night - we lost but few that day [but] the enemy must have lost a great number'.

The main action of Waterloo (which Ewart never mentioned by name) took place the following day, Sunday 18 June. According to his account, early skirmishes seemed relatively minor but a sense gradually built up that there was something serious to be done'. It wasn't long before the premonition proved well-founded when the sound of 'tremendous firing' heralded a French assault on the British right, soon to be followed by an attack on the left 'where they were received by our brave Highlanders' ('Never men could behave better' was Ewart's approving observation.) The British responded by launching two powerful cavalry charges, during the course of which the highpoint of Ewart's military career arrived when he single-handedly captured one of the enemy's imperial standards. Based on a Roman model, this consisted of the figure of an eagle, mounted on top of a tall staff, which, carried into battle, was used by French forces as a rallying point. Known simply as an 'Eagle', it was a powerful symbol of French pride and prestige and - by Napoleon's command - was to be defended from the enemy at all costs. Ewart's version of events went as follows:

'It was in the first charge I took the Eagle from the enemy - the bearer and I had a very hard contest for it; he made a thrust for my groin; I parried it off, and cut him through the head; after which I was attacked by one of their lancers, who threw his lance at me, but missed the mark, by my throwing it off with my sword by my right side - then I cut him from the chin upwards, which cut went through his teeth. Afterwards I was attacked by a foot soldier, who, after firing at me, charged me with his bayonet, but he soon lost the combat, for I parried it, and cut him down through the head: so that finished the combat for the Eagle.' A tasty irony of the situation was that Ewart had captured the standard that was associated with the French 45th Regiment - the self-styled 'Invincibles'.

The matter-of-factness of Ewart's account comes across as strangely at odds with the gory reality as he overcame three enemy soldiers to secure possession of the Eagle. He was, of course, a seasoned, professional soldier as was amply demonstrated in the moments that followed while he continued fighting, 'Eagle and all', until ordered by a general to carry the trophy back to safety. 'I was obliged to obey', he wrote to his brother, 'but can assure you, with a great deal of reluctance.' Retreating to higher ground, Ewart spent the next hour monitoring the progress of the battle. 'I cannot express the sight I beheld', he wrote to his brother, 'to see so many of my brave comrades lying upon the field; the bodies were so thick, that is was scarcely possible to pass, and horses innumerable.' Whether or not the Greys put up a battle cry of 'Scotland for ever!' (if they did so, Ewart fails to mention it) the charges which they made were instrumental in breaking the French army and freeing Europe from the long drawn-out curse of Napoleon Bonaparte's ambition.

In spite of the horrors that he had come through, Ewart concluded the letter to his brother on a more upbeat note: 'I took the Eagle into Brussels', he recounted, 'amongst the acclamations of thousands of the spectators who saw it.' His relief at having survived must surely have been intense. As he knew full well, not all of his comrades had been so fortunate: nearly 100 fellow-Greys perished during the engagement, with almost as many wounded. A lighter moment, however, is said to have occurred in the aftermath of the battle when Ewart met up with his wife in Brussels. Overcome by emotion, Margaret Ewart threw her arms around his horse's neck, prompting her husband to exclaim - 'It seems, Maggie, that ye think mair o' the horse than ye do o' me.'

Returning to Britain, Ewart was accorded a hero's welcome. Soon after the battle he was promoted to Lieutenant and then sometime later once again, this time to Ensign when he received a commission with the 5th Royal Veterans Battalion. He was awarded the newly-minted Waterloo Medal, and such was his fame that the badge of his regiment, the Scots Greys (nicknamed in his honour 'The Birdcatchers') was redesigned to incorporate the effigy of a French Eagle. In 1816 he came to Edinburgh and attended a reception at Leith where he was rapturously received by those in attendance, his health toasted by no less a personage than Sir Walter Scott who paid tribute to his countryman's gallant conduct. Ever reticent, Ewart offered the briefest of replies, indicating that he 'would rather fight the Battle of Waterloo over again, than face so large an assemblage'. Around the same time he was accorded a similar honour in his hometown of Kilmarnock. When the 5th Royal veterans were disbanded in 1821, he retired from the army on full pay. Inevitably in time Ewart slipped from the limelight, settling for the last sixteen years of his life in a cottage at Davyhulme, Manchester (not far from his wife, Margaret's, childhood home) where he supplemented his income by teaching swordsmanship. Retaining his remarkable spirit into old age, he is said to have made a trip home each year to visit his relations in Ayrshire. Finally Charles Ewart passed away at Davyhulme on 23 March 1846 in the 78th year of his life. He was buried in the cemetery of the New Jerusalem Chapel, Bolton Street, Salford, a short distance from his home.

And there, after a full and eventful life, his bones lay undisturbed for the best part of a century until 1 April 1938 when his grave was opened up once again and his last remains removed to be carried that same day to Edinburgh. Late that evening they were reburied on the Castle Esplanade in a low-key ceremony attended by a handful of onlookers, one of whom, 80 year-old Alexander Boa, was an old soldier whose late wife had been a relative of Ewart and who had, until the age of ten, lodged with his widow, Margaret.

But the quiet re-interment of Charles Ewart's bones was by no means the end of the matter. An altogether grander affair took place a fortnight later as crowds lined the Edinburgh streets to watch a procession of Scots Grey veterans and representatives of the Gordon Highlanders march from St Giles to the Castle Esplanade to the accompaniment of a military band. Awaiting at their destination, guests and dignitaries had already gathered for the unveiling of a newly-erected granite monument in honour of the hero of Waterloo. In pride of place among the assembled audience was a small group of the Ensign's proud descendants: David Ewart had travelled for the event from Glasgow while his kinsman, Hugh, had made it south from Turriff in Aberdeenshire. A number of other family members had converged on Edinburgh from various corners of England.

When the parade came to a halt on the Castle Esplanade, the 12th Earl of Haddington - himself a former Captain of the Greys - was invited to carry out a ceremonial inspection of the marchers, including the splendidly-attired 32-man guard of honour whose swords, it was said, formed a magnificent spectacle as they glinted in the spring sunshine. Turning to the assembled crowd, the Earl voiced the sense of privilege that he felt at being granted the opportunity to pay tribute to a man whom he described as 'the greatest, most illustrious "Grey" in history'. And who could argue? As the Earl pointed out in conclusion, the heroism and courage that Charles Ewart displayed on the field of battle had made him no less than a living embodiment of the Greys' regimental motto, *Nullius Secundus* - unquestionably 'second to none'.

24 Daft Pate's Excursion

It appears that over the centuries the powers of darkness have resorted to a variety of means of locomotion. The legendary witch of Ayr, Maggie Osborne, used the power of flight to transport herself to Galloway where she indulged in nightly revels, though ultimately found herself unable to rise above the flaming pyre that spelled the end of her existence. When the reviled persecutor of the Covenanters, Sir Robert Grierson of Lag, died in 1733, the crew of a night-time fishing-vessel were startled when a coach, drawn by six black horses and manned by shadowy torch-bearing figures, cut across their path, powering its way across the moonlit waves. When hailed by the fishing-boat's incredulous skipper, the reply came back that the demonic ensemble was on a mission to retrieve Lag's soul and escort it to its eternal, fiery home. Just over a century later, in June 1842, a rumour went round that the Prince of Darkness himself was making his way through the Ayrshire countryside, travelling - if you please - by a revolutionary form of two-wheeled transport.

The question of who first developed the bicycle is not as straightforward as you might imagine. As far back as 1790 a French inventor, Comte Mede de Sivrac, had devised a fairly basic four-wheeled contraption, laboriously propelled by a seated rider who in order to maintain his impetus was obliged to press his feet repeatedly to the ground. In 1817 the German Baron von Drais reduced the number of wheels to two but the pedal-system normally associated with a modern bicycle did not appear until twenty or so years later when a twenty-six year old Dumfriesshire blacksmith, Kirkpatrick Macmillan, came up with a radical innovation.

Forever tinkering with devices and inventions which few believed would ever amount to much, 'Daft Pate', as he was known locally, had taken the opportunity to examine an example of an early bicycle - known at the time as a 'hobby-horse' - when it was brought to his smithy for repair. Following his investigations, he went on to develop a bicycle of his own whose system of pedals and levers avoided any need for the rider's feet to be in contact with the ground. The bicycle's gearing mechanism was apparently inspired by that of an early steamboat which had been tried out (some say with Robert Burns aboard) half a century earlier on nearby Dalswinton Loch. A hefty four stones in weight, Macmillan's muscular machine must have required considerable strength to operate on the bumpy unmade roads of rural Dumfriesshire.

A few years later Macmillan made plans to subject his invention - known at the time as a 'velocipede' - to an altogether more rigorous testing than it had hitherto faced on his jaunts around Thornhill. On Monday 6 June 1842, in fine, summery weather, Pate set out from his smithy at Courthill with the intention of paying a visit to his three older brothers, all resident in the city of Glasgow, the best part of 70 miles away. Shortly after leaving home, he would have cycled past Drumlanrig Castle - seat of his employer, the Duke of Buccleuch - before, following the wooded banks of the Nith, he came into the coal-country to the north-west, pedalling through the straggling mining villages of Sanquhar and Kirkconnel.

The next stage of Pate's route must have raised something of a challenge. West of Kirkconnel, the roadway rises and falls in a series of undulating switchbacks and we might imagine that even an athletic young blacksmith would have had no option but to dismount from time to time, wiping the sweat from his brow as he wheeled his bicycle uphill. Cresting each summit, of course, he would have been immediately rewarded with

Courthill Smithy, Keir Mill

the glorious sensation of freewheeling effortlessly down the opposing slope. The March Burn marked a significant milestone as he passed out of his native Dumfriesshire and moved on into Ayrshire. Overlooking the winding turns of the Nith and the shapely lines of Corsencon beyond, in a few more miles he reached New Cumnock where, for the first time in the journey, his route parted company with the river.

By the time he reached Cumnock, nearly halfway to his destination, the long daylight hours of June were finally fading. Local lore insists that, descending MacKinlay's Brae, Pate's novel contraption interrupted a lovers' tryst between a local shoemaker, James Kennedy, and his sweetheart, Jean Vallance, causing the startled pair to flee in panic. Thankfully, the couple's romance was quick to resume and three months later wedding bells rang out, the proclamation of marriage duly signed by one John MacKinnell, local schoolmaster, Session Clerk to the Parish Church and Pate's host, as it happened, during his overnight stay in Cumnock. MacKinnell had been an old university acquaintance of Pate's brothers and, despite the day's exertions, the two men are said to have burned the midnight oil, examining the velocipede, chewing over the journey so far and discussing possible road conditions ahead.

Much has been made of the notion that, such was Macmillan's impact on the local population during his ride to Glasgow, that he was routinely mistaken for some supernatural creature, even, as has been suggested, 'the verra De'il himsel'.' Mothers, we are told, would snatch their infants from the roadside and hustle them indoors at the sight of the sinister apparition - part-man, part-machine - which materialised out of nowhere and trundled inexorably past their homes. Yet, for all that, after his night at Cumnock, Macmillan was reported to have been given a cheery send-off by the inhabitants and, as he left the town and continued to the north and west, farm-labourers, it is said, abandoned their work in the fields to rush to the roadside to watch Daft Pate pass by. At Kilmarnock, word of his imminent arrival had preceded him and townsfolk gathered in the streets to gawp and stare. No doubt the sight of the burly blacksmith, lumbering past on his velocipede, was an entertaining novelty - possibly even a little alarming for some - but we might suspect that, for the most part, comparisons with His Satanic Majesty were decidedly tongue-in-cheek.

All had gone to plan during Pate's journey north through Dumfriesshire and Ayrshire but when he arrived in the city of Glasgow matters took a distinct turn for the worse. Passengers alighting from the Carlisle coach had reported seeing a strange figure, pedalling inexorably towards the city, and by the time that Pate had made his way through the south-side suburbs and into the Gorbals area, crowds of eager on-lookers had assembled to await his arrival, their numbers apparently augmented by a goggle-eyed band of Irish immigrants, recently discharged from the Belfast boat at the Broomielaw. So dense was the crush, we are told, that at one point Pate swerved to take evasive action - his bicycle being without brakes - and inadvertently grazed the leg of a five-year-old girl who had dashed at the last minute across his path.

Alerted to the disturbance, a number of burly Gorbals policemen shouldered their way through the crowd, apprehended the disconsolate cyclist and impounded his machine pending trial. Charged the following morning with 'having ridden along the pavement on a velocipede in the Barony of Gorbals [...] and with having, by so doing, thrown over a child', a contrite Pate was fined the sum of five shillings - the first ever road-user, as some would have it, to be prosecuted for speeding. Legal matters thus attended to, the presiding magistrate went on to express astonishment at the speed of Pate's journey from Cumnock - five hours apparently - and requested a private demonstration, admiring no doubt the fine carving of a horse's head which fronted the velocipede. The suggestion that he slipped Pate five shillings on the quiet is unable to be verified.

Presumably it was with a considerable sigh of relief that Pate said goodbye to his brothers, mounted his bicycle once again and, cheered by the Glasgow crowd, departed for the country - though his spirits, it transpires, had not been entirely crushed by his unfortunate brush with the law. On the outskirts of the city he encountered a stagecoach heading for Carlisle and undertook to race it the twenty or so miles to Kilmarnock. Without the need to pick up or drop off passengers, he had no trouble in showing the coach and its passengers a clean pair of wheels.

During the years that followed, Kirkpatrick Macmillan produced several more bicycles to be handed over as gifts to his friends and, when he presented one to his employer, the Duke of Buccleuch, he was delighted sometime later to receive an order for a second. Perhaps surprisingly,

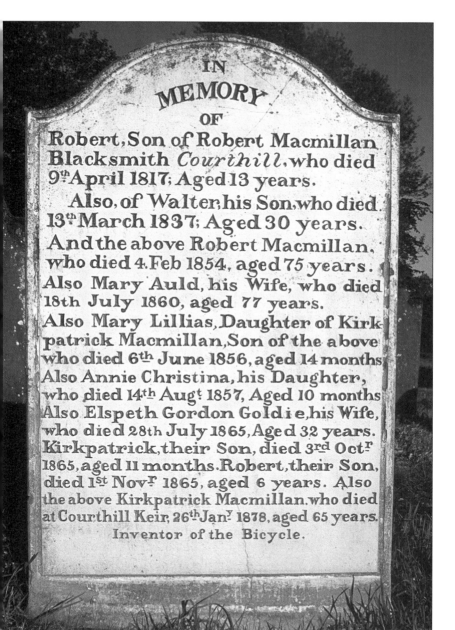

IN

MEMORY

OF

Robert, Son of Robert Macmillan Blacksmith *Courthill*, who died 9th April 1817; Aged 13 years.

Also, of Walter, his Son, who died 13th March 1837; Aged 30 years.

And the above Robert Macmillan, who died 4. Feb 1854, aged 75 years.

Also Mary Auld, his Wife, who died 18th July 1860, aged 77 years.

Also Mary Lillias, Daughter of Kirkpatrick Macmillan, Son of the above who died 6th June 1856, aged 14 months

Also Annie Christina, his Daughter, who died 14th Augt 1857, Aged 10 months

Also Elspeth Gordon Goldie, his Wife, who died 28th July 1865, Aged 32 years.

Kirkpatrick, their Son, died 3rd Octr 1865, aged 11 months. Robert, their Son, died 1st Novr 1865, aged 6 years. Also the above Kirkpatrick Macmillan, who died at Courthill Keir, 26th Jany 1878, aged 65 years.

Inventor of the Bicycle.

Kirkpatirck MacMillan's headstone, Keir Mill

Macmillan made no effort to benefit financially from his invention. Some years after his trip to Glasgow a letter arrived at the smithy, containing an offer of employment from the owner of a Glasgow foundry who had seen him cycle past in 1842. Accordingly he repeated the 70-mile journey by bicycle but we must assume that city life was not to his taste for, within a very short time, he was back at work at his forge at Courthill. Apparently content with the life of a country blacksmith, Daft Pate is reputed to have been a popular figure locally, playing the fiddle at weddings, regularly called upon to pull teeth for both humans and horses, and enjoying cycling along the quiet roads near his home. He is thought never to have returned to the city.

There were others, however, who possessed entrepreneurial instincts a good deal stronger than Pate's. During the 1860s, a Kilmarnock joiner and cartwright, Thomas McCall, was involved in the manufacture of bicycles at his premises in Langlands Street, later High Street. Based largely on Macmillan's design, McCall initiated various small improvements of his own and his bicycles, aimed principally for the Glasgow market, went on sale at a reported cost of £7 each. Coincidentally born at Penpont, a few short miles from Courthill Smithy, it is tempting to suspect that McCall, as a small child, might have witnessed Daft Pate's departure on his epic ride of 1842.

25 Man of the Outback

In 1871 the sand-dunes of the Ardeer peninsula provided Sir Alfred Nobel, the inventor of dynamite, with a secluded location for his new explosives plant – the British Dynamite Factory. Half a century earlier, the local parish minister and eminent naturalist, Rev. David Landsborough, had engaged in rather quieter pursuits along this stretch of north Ayrshire coastline as he introduced his young sons to the area's abundant animal and plant life. The learned clergyman could hardly have foreseen that, for one of his sons at least, those boyhood rambles would prove little more than a foretaste of far grander adventures, a world away from the breezy shoreline of Ardeer.

After completing his schooling at Irvine, Rev. Landsborough's third son, William, left home, aged sixteen, to join his two elder brothers down under. Arriving in New South Wales in 1841, he followed his brothers into the cattle business until, lured by the prospect of more rapid wealth, he changed direction and embarked on a career as a gold-miner. This new venture, we may assume, must have paid off handsomely since before long he was in a position to set himself up as proprietor of a large outback sheep station. Things did not go entirely to plan, however, when, faced with the difficulties associated with a dry climate, coupled with the hostility of the land's rightful aboriginal owners, he found himself obliged to sell up and move on.

As things turned out, his departure from sheep farming was possibly a blessing in disguise, an event which prompted him to discover his true forte. Making his way north, Landsborough became one of the first Europeans to explore vast areas of little-known country, much of which he considered ideally suited for the pasturing of livestock. When the outback explorers, Burke and Wills, went missing in 1861, there was a national outcry and William Landsborough's skills in bushcraft were quickly called upon. Appointed leader of one of the four search parties that were organised for the intended relief of the vanished men, the plan was to transport Landsborough and his team by ship to the Gulf of Carpentaria on Australia's northern coast from where they would strike south in the hope of locating the lost explorers.

Before the expedition managed to get off the ground, an unfortunate mishap occurred when the supply-ship, *Firefly*, foundered on a reef during a two-day gale in the Torres Straits, resulting in the loss of food and other important supplies. Fortunately the horses upon which the expedition would depend succeeded in swimming to the safety of a neighbouring islet with a single unfortunate exception which was badly trampled during the panic. Once the situation was brought under control, Landsborough and his men continued to the mainland where they established a base some miles inland on the banks of the Albert River. The next few weeks were spent scouring the surrounding country while the horses steadily recovered from their ordeal at sea. Wildlife and game, Landsborough observed, were locally abundant - in his journal he lists a variety of creatures from crocodiles to cockatoos - and the local aboriginal population appeared inquisitive and unthreatening, though cordial relations were inhibited by a language barrier that was insurmountable even to his aboriginal members of staff. True to form for the tropics, the weather was hot and humid.

By mid-November 1861 preparations for the attempted rescue mission were complete and Landsborough and his men set out from their Albert River base, heading south-west into what at the time was a blank on the map. Following the course of an unknown river, which he named the Gregory, his eight companions - four of them indigenous Australians - were accompanied by a team of more than twenty pack-horses. The men did their best to live off the land where possible, something that Landsborough appeared to find no hardship. The native cabbage palm, he noted, 'tasted like asparagus' but, when lime juice was added, reminded one more of rhubarb. Meat came in the form of birds as varied as ducks, cranes and rose-cockatoos. Wild marjoram could be made into 'a pleasant drink', and 'nice little figs' could be used to create an acceptable dessert. Truly his father's son, Landsborough's journals reveal him as a keen observer of natural phenomena as he lists the many tree varieties which he encountered along the way. 'With the pandanus [palm],' he records wryly, 'I got too intimately acquainted.' Struggling to control an unruly horse, he fell to the ground and 'got its thorns into all parts of [his] body.' The mosquitoes, predictably, he found 'troublesome.'

A week or so out, the level landscape showed signs of changing when a long line of hills came into view, rising above the dried-out grass of the plains. Landsborough and an aboriginal companion, Fisherman, peeled away from the main party to scale one of the rocky summits from where they were rewarded with extensive views of yet more hill-ranges, receding into the distance. Back on the riverbank, a small group of aborigines - three women and six children - initially appeared terrified at the appearance of Landsborough's men but they quickly mastered their fear to the extent that one of the women had to be dissuaded from tagging along behind the explorers when they left.

When it came to water, the problem appears to have varied between feast and famine. Crossing the main stream of the Gregory River presented problems periodically, and one morning an old black horse belonging to the expedition (curiously named 'Ginger') was found to have drowned overnight. A second mare was lost at Camp 29 despite the men's efforts to save her. Away from the river, by contrast, Landsborough records the lengths to which he and his men were obliged to go in order to locate water, though they soon caught on to the fact that smoke rising from an aboriginal encampment would normally indicate its near-presence. The dry conditions, however, appeared to present no difficulties for the local fauna and Landsborough notes that in certain areas 'kangaroos are numerous'. Unsurprisingly his aboriginal companions were adept at providing for the cooking-pot, coming up on occasion with a fat emu or a wild turkey or finding and recovering wild honeycomb. Landsborough himself experienced a close encounter with the local wildlife which he would have preferred to avoid. Stung by some creature - probably, he speculates, a scorpion - he writes with commendable restraint that 'the pain that it gave was sufficient to make me uncomfortable during the night.' The incident is never mentioned again.

Given Landsborough's tendency to underplay hardship, events occurring in early December must surely have been gruelling in the extreme. With his second-in-command, Mr Campbell, under the weather and his horses suffering from intense heat and lack of water, Landsborough realised that moving on to a new camp that day was not a possibility so, accompanied by one of his aboriginal companions - Jemmy - he set out to scour the surrounding country for any possible source of water. By early afternoon the men's quest had not yet born fruit when Jemmy's horse became unfit to be ridden, obliging him to transfer to their accompanying

Ship of the desert

pack-horse. Landsborough relates how he felt taunted at this time by the area's prolific birdlife whose ceaseless cries he interpreted thus: 'We know where there is water, but you foolish fellows cannot find it.' By late afternoon his thirst had grown to such proportions that, highly untypically, he no longer felt able to jot down times and distances to be transcribed later to his journal.

Relief came at last when, picking their way along a dried-out riverbed, the two men were excited to spot an area of ground that showed distinct signs of dampness. Digging with a sharp stick, they were able to obtain a small quantity of water with which both they and their horses, careless of its muddy appearance, quenched their thirst. Their spirits thus boosted, the men resumed their search on foot, their efforts rewarded sometime later when they came across a depression in the creek-bed which contained a few more gallons of water. It was three o'clock in the morning before they had retrieved their horses and brought them to the creek to be watered. Landsborough notes in his journal that by then they had spent 'twenty-two consecutive hours, more or less' in their search for water, generously adding that 'Jemmy never showed any signs of fatigue, or unwillingness to proceed.'

Mercifully things took a turn for the better. Late the next morning they located a sizeable pool of water, and when they returned to camp during the afternoon Landsborough was further heartened to learn that 'Mr Campbell [...] had quite recovered.'

Thankfully there were lighter moments. When it came to his dealings with the native people, Landsborough's stated policy was to impinge as little as possible on their lives. Frequently, however, he disregarded his own rule, taking obvious pleasure in the delighted reaction of the locals when presented with various small gifts. A curious incident occurred on Christmas Day 1861 which Landsborough had opted to spend in the vicinity of a pleasant waterhole which he had christened Mary Lake. During the course of an afternoon ramble, Jemmy and he stumbled across an elderly aboriginal couple whose startled reaction was fairly dramatic. Apparently concerned for the safety of her four dogs, the old lady gripped one of the creatures tightly in her arms until, finally losing her nerve, she abandoned it to its fate and retreated from the riverbank to the safety of mid-stream. Meantime, the white-haired old gentleman, had shinned up a nearby tree, prompting his spouse to emerge from the water and follow suit. Jemmy attempted to make conversation through the branches but to no avail. He could make nothing of the elderly couple's language. Fortunately there is nothing to suggest that they were any the worse for their unsettling experience and we might wonder whether Landsborough was the first white man that they had ever set eyes on.

After two punishing months spent scouring previously unknown territory, Landsborough and his team of men and horses wearily retraced their steps down the banks of the Gregory River, arriving back at their base on 19 January 1862. During the course of their expedition, they had not succeeded in unearthing any trace of Burke and his men. But if Landsborough anticipated a spell of relaxation now, then it was not to be. Hearing that tracks, believed to be those of Burke and Wills, had been discovered on the Flinders River, far to the south, he opted to forego a leisurely sea-voyage home in favour of embarking on a second arduous overland journey. His depute, Campbell, would be replaced on this expedition by George Bourne, and the two men would be joined by a cook, Gleeson, plus three aboriginal staff, two of whom - Jemmy and Fisherman - were veterans of the previous journey.

This time Landsborough and his party headed south-east, trekking for twelve days in relatively cool and showery conditions before reaching the Flinders River, along whose banks Burke and Wills were thought to have passed. Here one of Landsborough's mares produced a foal, duly named 'Flinders', which, he notes with pleasure, proved capable of keeping up with its mother from the day of its birth. As previously, Landsborough's journal continues to express admiration for the hunting and tracking skills of his aboriginal companions: during one of their 'rest' days Jackey and Fisherman captured five live opossums; a few days later Jemmy and Jackey's quarry consisted of two snakes which, despite Jackey's being bitten, they proceeded to serve up for dinner. On another occasion their meal consisted of 'a great number of rats.' For all the gravity and hardship of the men's mission, spirits were undoubtedly high. When an unexpected shower drenched Fisherman and Jackey's clothes and bedding, the situation was viewed not as a disaster but rather 'a subject for merriment'. His aboriginal partners knew full well that their leader was not a man to let them sleep in wet, uncomfortable conditions.

During this stretch of his journey, human inhabitants appeared thin on the ground: the first sighting recorded in Landsborough's diary was a solitary aborigine, spotted more than three weeks out from the Albert River. The situation changed a fortnight or so later when Landsborough and his party encountered a large group of women and children who had been hunting for small animals on a grassy plain beside the Flinders River.

Overcoming an initial shyness, the aboriginals made unmistakably friendly overtures and Landsborough records in his journal, with perhaps a trace of Victorian condescension, that the younger women had 'fine eyes, white teeth and good expression.' Their children, he adds, 'looked particularly lively and intelligent.'

Several weeks later relations grew a little more strained. Landsborough's men had been travelling through a lightly-wooded area, dotted with conical hills, when Jackey and he fell a little behind the main group. When they finally straggled into camp, they found a tense situation in progress. A band of heavily-armed locals - in Landsborough's words, 'fine, tall, powerful fellows' - had evidently approached a little too close for comfort and, feeling under threat, his second-in-command, Bourne, had fired off warning shots above the head of one particularly precocious aborigine, a powerfully-built warrior whose height Landsborough estimated at six feet. Refusing to be intimidated, however, the man in question had gestured as if to launch a boomerang in Bourne's direction.

There may well have been misunderstanding on both sides but thankfully Landsborough's arrival had the effect of defusing the tension. Received in a warm and friendly manner, he was presented with gifts of spears and boomerangs, in exchange for which he handed over a hatchet. Questioned by Jemmy, the aborigines were cooperative in passing on information to the effect that no explorers with carts and camels had passed that way. Over the following few days Landsborough and his men received periodic visits from members of the local population who were, it seems, happy now to act as guides and to supply geographical information about the surrounding countryside. In an area not too far off, they indicated, the aboriginal people possessed iron tomahawks and were in the habit of wearing clothes, raising in Landsborough's mind the possibility that country settled by Europeans might not now be too far away. He in turn distributed small presents such as a comb, a needle and thread and unwanted items of clothing and treated the local children to pony-rides while Jackey and Fisherman performed a corroboree dance, streaking their bodies white 'like skeletons'. He notes in his diary that his aboriginal guests 'did not steal.'

If only relations could have remained this cordial but Landsborough must surely have smelt a rat when one of his short-term guides, Wittin, slipped away quietly one morning, believing, it emerged, that were he to continue any farther his life would be in danger from hostile tribes. A short week later, on the Barcoo River, Landsborough was left in no doubt that the guide's caution had been amply justified. He records in his journal that late one night catastrophe was only averted thanks to the vigilance of Jemmy who urgently roused his sleeping comrades to alert them to the prospect of imminent attack. Shocked into wakefulness, the men fired off their guns in the darkness before igniting two flares in an effort to intimidate hostile tribesmen who had crept to within yards of the campfire. The first rocket proved a damp squib, eliciting ridicule rather than fear, but the second was more successful and had the effect of making the aborigines pull back.

Landsborough's subsequent handling of the situation may well have been influenced by his knowledge of events that had taken place six months earlier at an isolated sheep station in central Queensland. A group of white settlers had been crossing the plains - complete with horses, bullock-carts and ten thousand sheep in tow - with a view to taking up residence on an expanse of grazing land called Cullin-la-Ringo when they were attacked by a group of local aboriginal people. Out of a total of 25 settlers, no fewer than nineteen men, women and children lost their lives in the ensuing massacre. When news of the outrage became known, it was greeted with horror and recriminations against aboriginal people were swift, savage and disproportionate. Facing hostilities on the Barcoo River, Landsborough had a suspicion that some of his adversaries might have been involved in the slaughter at Cullin-la-Ringo and have witnessed the consequences first-hand.

Overnight the tension did not ease. Despite being urged by Jemmy to pull back, a group of warriors, heavily armed with clubs and throwing-sticks, advanced at breakfast-time to within a hundred yards or so of Landsborough's camp. Feeling himself under threat, he gave his men the order to fire with the result that one of the aborigines went down injured while the rest drew back. Why Landsborough's men advanced towards them at this stage is not entirely clear - possibly to ensure the safety of their horses - but, as they did so, they opened fire once again, wounding another aboriginal man. With reference to the first casualty, Landsborough states rather bluntly that his men caught up with the unfortunate man and 'shot' him a second time, presumably thereby putting an end to him. Certainly it was enough to see off the rest of the war-party but, viewed from a modern-day perspective, events on the Barcoo River were regrettable, to say the least.

Thinking things over, it seems likely that, when Landsborough's party loomed on the horizon, the people of the Barcoo River had foreseen the shape of things to come. News might already have reached them of aboriginal waterholes elsewhere poisoned by white settlers, and the people themselves harried, persecuted and shot. Evictions to make way for sheep and cattle were already widespread and, living in closer proximity to lands already settled by white Australians than, say, the friendly natives of Carpentaria, the chances are that the Barcoo River people knew exactly how much was at stake. As far as Landsborough was concerned, his expedition diary makes his vision for the country crystal clear, and throughout its pages references abound to 'good sheep country', 'well-grassed land' and 'fine pastoral country'. Where he imagined that the land's ancient guardians, the aboriginal people, might fit into the picture is never made clear. In many ways a decent, principled man, Landsborough's personal failings in this regard were no more than a reflection of the shortcomings of his age.

For all that, it is clear that the Barcoo River episode lay heavily on his conscience and, in a letter written sometime after, Landsborough confides his regrets about the fatal altercation. Thankfully the expedition faced no further serious conflict with the aboriginal population but the hardships that his men were obliged to endure were not by any means at an end. In early May temperatures plummeted and the men found ice which had formed in their tin containers overnight. Sleeping too close to the campfire, Jemmy's clothing caught light and he suffered burns so severe that he could not bear for the wounds to be bandaged. Such was his discomfort that he even begged his companions to go on and leave him behind. In spite of the intense cold, water was still hard to come by and on one occasion Landsborough's men were forced to travel virtually non-stop for more than 72 hours in order to reach a serviceable waterhole.

Shortage of provisions presented an ever-growing problem, and it is doubtful if the search-party would have survived without food taken from the wild by its aboriginal members. Landsborough discovered that the boiled egg of an emu, shared with his second-in-command, Bourne, had 'as delicate a flavour as a hen's egg.' The remaining members of the crew combined three more emus' eggs to bake pancakes which they consumed enthusiastically despite the absence of any form of seasoning. Things on the food front looked grave indeed and the prospect loomed of slaughtering one of the horses to eat when Jackey saved the day by returning to camp with the carcase of an emu. When the unfamiliar sight of grazing domestic cattle panicked the pack-horses on 20 May, it is likely that the weary band of famished men who accompanied them experienced an altogether different emotion.

The following day, Wednesday, 21 May 1862, Landsborough and his men arrived at a sheep station on the Warrego River and, after more than six months of rough living, we might imagine that their relief was intense. Yet, although Landsborough records his appreciation for the 'hospitable reception' he was accorded by the station owner, Mr Williams, the entry in his journal is surprisingly brief, his mood perhaps subdued by hearing from the farmer that both Burke and Wills were dead. Almost certainly the thought must have occurred to him that, in its primary objective at least, his expedition had failed. But, based on the rousing reception that awaited him when his epic trek finally terminated at Melbourne, there were others who gauged the success of the venture rather more positively.

After leaving Warrego River, 800 miles still had to be covered before Landsborough reached his final destination, mostly through more populated districts where relatively few problems cropped up, other than the difficulties associated with rounding up and controlling a stray camel - of which there were relatively few in Australia at the time - which had mysteriously materialised on the Darling River. Ultimately the exercise proved a futile one when the beast took it into its head to go walkabout once again, the blame for its loss placed squarely on the carelessness of poor Jackey who, we might suppose, can hardly have relished being given responsibility for handling such a notoriously intractable creature.

In contrast to the wayward camel, Flinders, the foal born six months earlier, made it all the way to Melbourne where a tumultuous reception awaited Landsborough's party as the first explorers to cross Australia from north to south. Accompanied by Fisherman and Jemmy, Landsborough attended a meeting of the Royal Society of Victoria where a gold watch, awarded by the Royal Geographical Society, was presented to John King, the sole survivor of Burke's ill-fated expedition. Attention then turned to Landsborough's recent achievements which were hailed by Sir Henry Barkly, Governor of Victoria, as 'among the most brilliant exploits which grace the history of Australian exploration.' The following month a public meeting was held in the Exhibition Building in honour of Landsborough and fellow-Scot, John McKinlay, who had led the equivalent South Australian search party. Again the evening was graced with the poignant presence of John King, and the hall in which the meeting took place was packed out by an estimated 3,000 enthusiastic members of the public. Following a further series of glowing tributes, the gallant explorers were accorded three hearty cheers before the meeting adjourned.

Jackey wasn't present in Melbourne. Similar to the unruly camel in his care, he had become inclined to stray without permission and was thus dismissed from Landsborough's service, though he quickly found new employment with a farmer on the Darling River. Never having visited a city before, Fisherman and Jemmy appeared surprisingly unimpressed by the attractions of Melbourne where they stayed for a month before boarding a steamer for Brisbane and home. A stalwart of the expedition, perhaps it had all become too much for poor Fisherman when he became a little unhinged during his time in the city. His constitution being generally sound, it was hoped that his wits would soon be restored once settled again among the familiar scenes of home.

A few months after his grand reception in Melbourne, Landsborough and his new wife, Caroline, departed from Australia on a trip to Britain where he was honoured with a gold watch by the Royal Geographical Society of London. During the course of his stay in Britain, he is believed to have renewed his acquaintance with some of his relatives though whether he returned to Scotland to do so is not clear. Back in Australia, William Landsborough's life brought him a succession of joys and sorrows; striking successes offset periodically by fairly serious setbacks. Ending his life, aged 61, at his home at Golden Beach, Queensland, the story is told that he asked to be lifted from his deathbed to view for one last time the ocean and mountains beyond. During those final few moments, we can only wonder whether Landsborough's mind drifted fleetingly back perhaps to a shoreline on the far side of the globe where he had wandered as a child among the dunes and sandy hollows of Ardeer.

26 Henry Reid the Piper

The chances are that most passers-by would have put it down to the effects of drink. With every public house brimming full, he wouldn't have been the only man not to make it home from Ayr Races, languishing instead in the lee of a hedge. Hurrying by in the darkness, no-one, it seems, noticed the tell-tale stain of blood though, in response to the man's pitiful entreaties, at least one good Samaritan stopped off to offer a helping hand. Robert McCroskie spoke to the injured man in the early hours of Saturday morning and attempted unsuccessfully to help him to his feet. When the man cried out 'Oh, chappie! Let me doon again!', naturally the Tarbolton miner attributed his delicate condition to the excesses of the day and continued on his way without a further thought. Only later did McCroskie's wife point out that his coat had been smeared with blood.

When John McCracken stumbled across the same man shortly after 6am, he was barely alive. Making for a day's harvesting in the fields, McCracken and his wife and daughter had been walking from their home in George Street, Ayr, along the Cumnock road when they came across the injured man, some 250 yards east of Holmston Toll, with his coat and hat lying not far off. In an effort to make him more comfortable, McCracken slackened the man's tie a little and tried to help him to his feet but gave up in the attempt when he noticed blood oozing from beneath his waistcoat, prompting McCracken to remark that it looked as though he had been stabbed. Clearly in a befuddled state, the injured man showed no recollection of any such event but managed to gasp out that he had been in Ayr the previous day and had become separated from his friends during the evening. 'I doubt you are dying,' McCracken told the man bluntly who replied, 'Do you think so?' before quietly repeating to himself the words of the Lord's Prayer.

McCracken retraced his steps to Holmston Toll where he alerted the toll-keeper, John Montgomery, to what he had just discovered. The two men then returned to where the injured man was lying and gave him a little water to drink but all to no avail as, within a few minutes, he took his last breath.

McCracken asked two passers-by to notify the authorities and, following a visit by Superintendent Clarke of Ayr police, the man's body was taken in a barrow to the Fever Hospital in Ayr where medical examination revealed a gaping chest-wound, two inches deep and almost an inch across, caused, it was surmised, by a sharp object such as the blade of a knife. The resulting blood-loss was such that the surrounding clothing had become entirely saturated. A subsequent post-mortem, carried out by three local doctors, confirmed as cause of death a stab-wound to the left ventricle which had penetrated the wall of the heart. A letter found in the dead man's pocket solved the mystery of his identity.

It fell to Margaret McCallum of Rutherglen Road, Glasgow, to identify the body of her 22 year-old son, William, an engineer in the city who had been spending a month's holiday at the home of a friend, Jane Hillhouse, a widow residing at Shaw farm, Coalhall. It transpired that in the morning of Friday 20 September 1872 McCallum had travelled with a cart-load of race-goers into Ayr where he had gone on to spend the day. Much the worse for wear, he had left Wattie Miller's hostelry in the High Street during the late evening in the company of a farmer's son from Potterhill, William Thom, but the pair had parted company when McCallum struck up a conversation with a miner named Bannerman in Kyle Street and the two men decided to prolong their evening's entertainment in Graham's public house. (Bannerman was subsequently cleared by police of any involvement in McCallum's killing.) Around 10 p.m. a policeman on duty near the railway station, Sergeant Irvine, recalled being accosted by an inebriated man resembling McCallum who had invited him to arrest another individual with whom he had become involved in a quarrel. As the drunk man had seemed the more boisterous of the two and the matter appeared relatively trivial, the sergeant had declined to take any action.

Based on his known movements, police estimated that the attack on McCallum was likely to have taken place sometime shortly before midnight. Evidence of a scuffle was apparent in the form of trampled grass and footprints but it appeared that robbery could be ruled out as a motive since the dead man's pockets were found to contain some eight shillings (40p) in change. As police inquiries got underway, the crime scene was visited during the late forenoon by Sheriff Anderson, Procurator Fiscal Murdoch and the Chief Constable of Police, Captain Young.

It didn't take long for a suspect to emerge. When interviewed by police, a gypsy couple - John Mackenzie and Dorothy McCallum - revealed that they had been settled the previous night in a wood beside the River Ayr when, around 2 a.m., a disorientated young man had turned up in their camp, claiming to have been robbed and seeking their permission to bed down alongside. His dishevelled clothes, he had explained, were the result of his having become lost and having had to scramble through thorn bushes and hedges. After resting for a few hours, the overnight visitor had slipped away quietly around daybreak. Hopes of an imminent arrest were raised but in the event it turned out to be a false alarm. The man in question, John Hughes, was traced the following day to near Cumnock and his suspicious behaviour explained when he confessed under questioning to being a deserter from the 11th Regiment, at present stationed in Ayr.

The gypsy couple, however, provided a second, more positive lead. The two children in their care, they divulged, were not their own but had been left with them the previous day - Friday - by their father, a close associate of Mackenzie's, who had undertaken to pick them up later in the evening but had failed to do so. The children's father, Henry Reid, was a 41 year-old native of Perthshire who earned his living as a travelling piper and maker of horn spoons. A native speaker of Gaelic, he was described as being of medium height and with rather a stout build and dark features. When last seen he had been dressed fairly modestly in patched tweed trousers, a grey home-made waistcoat and a home-made tweed coat, though his red flannel shirt, black neckerchief and Balmoral bonnet must surely have cut a bit of a dash. Henry's partner, Betsy Townsley, was considerably younger than himself - perhaps just over twenty years old - and was not the mother of his children. She was a small woman, just over five feet in height, with a slim build, blue eyes, reddish hair and a fair complexion. Dressed in a red-striped petticoat, a checked shawl of shepherd's plaid, a woollen cap and lacing boots, Betsy's clothing was described as well-worn and possibly in need of a wash.

As police inquiries progressed, an outline emerged of the couple's movements during the evening of Friday 20 September and over the days that followed. Late on Friday night, William Thom recalled an encounter with Henry and Betsy as he made his way home to Potterhill and he reported that they had asked him for directions to Cumnock. At Holmston, the toll-keeper's wife recounted how Betsy was 'crying very sore' as the couple went by and that she had paused to cadge a few matches in order to light her pipe. Asked where they were aiming for, Betsy had pointed vaguely in the direction of John Mackenzie's overnight camp. A change of plan, however, must have occurred soon after because, little more than an hour later, the toll-keeper's wife noticed the couple hurrying back and turning up a minor road that led towards Castlehill. As they appeared fairly agitated, her curiosity was piqued. Peering through the moonlight, she saw Henry make a sudden, quick movement but failed to realise at the time that what she had witnessed was most probably a throwing action.

By Betsy's (later) account, Henry and she spent what was left of the night in the shelter of a haystack, their first priority at daybreak to reunite themselves with Henry's children. At Friarland, the ploughman's wife, Sarah Adams, recalled that the couple had stopped off around 7 a.m. to make inquiries. Henry went back into Ayr where he scouted around for a time but, failing to locate his children, it seems likely that he felt the need to put some space between himself and the crime scene, probably fairly secure in the knowledge that he would meet up again before long with John Mackenzie who was a regular travelling companion. By early evening Henry and Betsy were at Ochiltree where Betsy made a purchase of tea from Annie McLean's shop while Henry remained outside and struck up a tune on the bagpipes - a surprising course of action, you might think, for a man supposedly intent on maintaining a low profile. The need to turn a penny or two was perhaps second nature. For Betsy's part, she must surely have been taken aback when Annie McLean asked whether she had heard rumours of a man found dead at Holmston Toll. Henry and Betsy hurried on that night through the Cumnock district before arriving sometime later at the isolated moorland settlement of Dalblair. Thought to be holing up in the woods by day and travelling largely after dark, the supposition is that they slipped quietly into Lanarkshire, following the lonely track that climbs into the hills above the Glenmuir Water.

Back at Holmston Toll, a significant development had occurred when John Montgomery recovered from the vicinity of the crime scene a piece of green twine, a yard or so in length - just such a cord, it was suggested, as a piper might use to tie up the drones of his instrument. It wasn't the only piece of evidence linking Henry with the crime. Two observant police officers, Sergeant Moodie and Constable Gilliland, found a woollen rosette closeby, the kind that might normally be found attached to a Balmoral bonnet. Sometime later, a teenage girl was harvesting mangold wurzels - a beetroot-like crop - when she came across a rusty knife, hidden from view among the shaws and which she suspected might have been thrown from the Castlehill road. Realising its possible significance, Agnes Hannah took the knife the following day to the County Buildings in Ayr where she handed it over to Sergeant McMath of the local police.

It took no more than a week for Henry Reid and Betsy Townsley to be traced. Henry was already known to Sergeant James Anderson of the Perthshire Constabulary though he had never previously been in any trouble with the law. On receiving word that Henry was wanted by police in Ayrshire, Anderson made a few local inquiries which led him directly to Strathallan Wood where he found Henry and Betsy's camp. Sergeant Anderson made a point of mentioning that, at the time of Henry's arrest, no rosette was to be seen on his Balmoral bonnet.

Arriving under escort back in Ayr, Henry Reid found himself charged with the murder of William McCallum, engineer, on 20 or 21 September 1872 but he was obliged to wait for another six months before his case was heard. When he appeared in the dock in April 1873, Henry was described as shabbily dressed with a weather-beaten complexion and ragged hair and whiskers but, despite his dishevelled appearance, he was said to have responded with a firm 'not guilty' when the charge of murder was read out. Perhaps he felt he had reason to be confident. The evidence stacked against him was entirely circumstantial - a length of green cord, lying by the roadside; a rosette detached from a bonnet; and a knife recovered from a nearby field. If there had ever been any trace of blood on the blade, the elements had soon put paid to that.

Henry's strategy, it seems, was to deny everything. 'I assaulted no-one and no-one assaulted me,' he stated in a written declaration to the court. He claimed not to recognise the knife that had been found in the mangold field, though he admitted to having lost his own knife while at Ayr. The first he had heard of the death of William McCallum, he insisted, was at the time of his arrest in Perthshire. There was, of course, the small matter of a witness to Henry's actions on the day of Ayr Races whose testimony was likely to be critical. But before Betsy Townsley could be called to on to give evidence, there was a matter which required to be cleared up. Married in line with traditional gypsy practice, she could not be compelled to testify against her husband unless the marriage contract was deemed by the court to be unfounded in law. In an effort to shed light on the situation, Betsy was asked to supply details of what form her wedding ceremony had taken.

When Betsy took the stand, it quickly became obvious that all was not well between her and Henry. 'I have known the prisoner, Reid, as long as I have known myself,' Betsy stated at the outset and went on to describe how two years previously their marriage ceremony had taken place in a barn in the presence of her parents. She recalled how Henry and she had sworn on the Bible to be man and wife and their agreement had been solemnised by the taking of drink. It was not, she added, her people's custom to be married by a minister. She recounted for the court how she had sworn loyalty to Henry 'as long as he did not ill-use me', and, if she is to be believed, then her reservations were well founded. She described how Henry 'swore on the blessed Bible that he would be true and loyal to me as his wife - but he did not do it'. Marital tensions apart, however, there was no doubt in Betsy's mind that she and Henry had undergone a bona fide marriage ceremony. 'My people and those who knew us, I suppose, considered us man and wife,' she stated in conclusion. Gypsy traditions, however, cut little ice with the learned judges, Lord Cowan and the Lord Justice Clerk, who were disposed to take a different view. Lord Cowan stated his belief that Betsy Townsley 'was not a wife, but a woman who lived and cohabited with [Henry Reid] as a wife'. The Lord Justice Clerk, Baron Moncreiff, expressed himself in agreement, stating that a gypsy wedding 'could not imply marriage in the eye of the law'. By this decision, the law lords swept aside any impediment to Betsy Townsley taking the stand.

As the court listened agog, Betsy recounted in her evidence how Henry and she had spent the day of 20 September at Ayr Races and had left the track around 6 p.m. to go into the town where Henry had spent the evening playing his pipes and visiting public houses. In spite of his alcoholic intake, Henry's mood had soured somewhat by the time that he and Betsy headed out of Ayr in the direction of Holmston Toll. 'I was greeting on coming forward to the toll,' Betsy said - 'Reid had given me two or three severe blows on the breast.' Possibly, even at this stage, Henry was venting frustration at the tricky prospect that was looming of locating Mackenzie's camp in the dark. As far as the court was concerned, the nub of the matter lay in what might have taken place during the next hour or so, after the couple had left Holmston Toll (where it will be remembered that Betsy received matches from the toll-keeper's wife) and before their hurried return in the moonlight. According to Betsy, much of the hour had been spent in a fruitless hunt for Mackenzie's camp before they gave it up as a bad job and headed back towards Holmston. For reasons already stated, the atmosphere between the two was cool and Betsy was walking a short distance ahead of Henry.

Somewhere just east of the toll Betsy passed a man who was travelling in the opposite direction but no conversation was exchanged. Immediately afterwards, she told the court, she became aware of the sound of raised voices as a skirmish broke out behind her. Several times she called out to Henry to come away but he replied that he couldn't as 'the man was striking him'. Perhaps hoping for assistance, Betsy continued in the direction of the toll but Henry soon caught up with her. What, she asked him, had given rise to the dispute? Henry's reply didn't provide an answer to her question but it certainly created a stir in court. 'I stabbed the man!' he is supposed to have blurted out. 'My heart trembled with fear,' Betsy told the packed courtroom, 'and I said he would suffer for that.'

The couple went on to spend what must surely have been an uneasy night under a haystack near the Castlehill road, rising at around sunrise for a final search for Henry's children. According to Betsy, Henry appeared nervous when they observed a huddle of people on the site of his previous night's confrontation. He coached her in the story she must stick to and threatened to implicate her in the crime if she failed to comply. As far as locating his children was concerned, once again they drew a blank and abandoned the search to make tracks inland, away from the scene of the crime. According to Betsy, they deliberately avoided the busier thoroughfares - 'going through fields and over dykes and hedges on the way'. Following her conversation with Annie McLean at Ochiltree, Betsy confessed to Henry that '[her] heart was afeared' but he retorted 'For God's sake, come on and I will bring you to where your people are.' Avoiding towns and villages where possible, they arrived back in their home country in Perthshire within a week - a distance not much short of 100 miles on foot. If Betsy's testimony wasn't sufficiently damning already, she went on to identify the knife found in the mangold field as Henry's property and the length of green cord as one which he had used to tie up the drones of his bagpipes.

When Betsy Townsley stepped down from the witness stand, it must surely have been obvious to everyone present that a bombshell had just been dropped. In what looked very much like damage limitation, Henry's solicitor, Mr Jameson, made great play of the 'animus' which Betsy had exhibited towards his client and went on to remind the jury of how drunk William McCallum had been on race-night. In his encounter with Sergeant Irvine near the railway station he had already shown himself to be in a quarrelsome mood. Henry Reid, by contrast, was viewed by his local police back in Perthshire as 'a peaceful, honest man'. McCallum and he had never met before. The crime could not have been premeditated and no possible motive had ever come to light. Therefore, Jameson argued, culpable homicide rather than murder would be the appropriate verdict. He went so far as to suggest the rather far-fetched possibility that William McCallum had fallen by accident on to Henry's knife.

There is little doubt that the defence was faced with an uphill struggle. When Betsy Townsley's testimony was taken in conjunction with the weight of circumstantial evidence, the case against Henry Reid was virtually unanswerable. In relation to the charge of murder it took the jury little more than twenty minutes to return a guilty verdict but it did so with a strong recommendation attached that the convicted man be referred to the mercy of the court. The Lord Justice Clerk, however, reminded the jury that in cases of murder the law permitted him no discretion. After assuming the customary black cap, he went on to sentence Henry Reid to 'the last doom of the law', informing him that in little more than a fortnight, on 30 April 1873, he would pay for the death of William McCallum with his own life.

Not surprisingly, Henry took it badly. Confined to his cell, he rarely rose from his bed though sleep proved constantly elusive. Refusing solid food for more than a week, he subsisted on liquids alone and it was reported that he showed great distress at being separated from his children. For all his signs of depression, however, Henry was a biddable prisoner who listened attentively to visiting clergymen, of whose Christian message, it was noted, he appeared well-nigh ignorant. All, however, was not yet lost. While Henry awaited his fate, a petition was got up on his behalf which appealed for clemency and a commutation of his death sentence on the basis that it was impossible to determine which of the two men who had clashed near Holmston Toll had been the aggressor. Lodged in banks and other local business premises throughout Ayr, it soon attracted some 800 signatures and was then forwarded to London for the consideration of the Home Secretary.

Perhaps the truth had leaked out - or what might have been the truth - as Henry was being escorted back to prison following his conviction. Sentenced to die within days, presumably he felt that he had nothing to lose now by opening up to his accompanying constables and the account he gave went as follows. When Betsy and he crossed paths with William McCallum on the night of Ayr Races, he said, Betsy had asked the stranger if he could spare any matches. For whatever reason, McCallum had appeared offended and had sworn at Betsy, prompting her to respond in a similar vein. McCallum became angry at this and struck out at her and, when Henry intervened, a tussle had developed during which he had been thrown to the ground. As Betsy moved away, Henry struggled once more to his feet, only to be knocked down a second time and at this he reached snapping point and, drawing his knife, stabbed the stranger through the heart. Undoubtedly Henry's belated revelations made for a dramatic tale but it possibly raised more questions than it answered. Why, we might ask, had Henry not come clean from the outset? If his defence had been able to argue that he was the victim, not the aggressor, and that his actions had been motivated by self-defence, then the outcome of his trial might have been radically different. At the end of the day who was in a position to contest his version of events? By her own account, Betsy had been too far off to know what triggered the altercation and if she ever subsequently found out her testimony gave no indication of it. Perhaps the greatest puzzle associated with Henry Reid's case is why he never entered a plea of self-defence.

Languishing in Ayr prison, Henry's agony was finally relieved when a telegram arrived from London on Friday 25 April 1873 indicating that his reprieve was to be placed in the post that night. Advised of the development, Henry was reported as expressing his heartfelt gratitude to all who had taken an interest in saving his life. The following day he was informed that the death penalty imposed on him had been commuted to a sentence of life imprisonment with hard labour. And with that, Henry Reid vanished into the workings of Britain's prison system where almost certainly he spent the rest of his days. Betsy Townsley, by contrast, was free to put events at Holmston Toll behind her and resume the wandering life once again with the tinker folk of Perthshire. Who can say whether she ever gave a thought to her old companion and the part she played in his conviction? As to what really happened on 20 September 1872 when two drunk strangers clashed in the night, we might suspect that Henry carried that with him to the grave.

27 Parcel in the Post

On Monday, 19 November 1906 an elderly gentleman, William Lennox of Woodside Cottage, Cumnock, received an unexpected parcel in the post. When the brown paper wrappings were removed, it was found to contain the gift of a tin of shortbread which had been topped with icing sugar and was accompanied by a card which read – 'With happy greetings from an old friend'. The anonymous present must surely have created a flutter of speculation at Woodside before it was set to one side to be kept for a suitably special occasion.

A 77 year-old widower, William Lennox had sometime earlier retired from farming at Whitehill, New Cumnock, to settle in a cottage built to his own specification in Glaisnock Road, Cumnock. In spite of his age, Lennox was said to enjoy robust health, his only bugbear being the problem of chronic deafness. Living with him at Woodside Cottage were his 56 year-old unmarried niece, Grace McKerrow, who had moved to Cumnock from Prestwick Road, Ayr, in order to nurse her late Aunt Grizzel through her final illness before staying on to act as housekeeper when her uncle was eventually widowed. Grace was assisted in this task by the third member of the household, a fourteen year-old housemaid named Elizabeth Thorburn.

A few days after the delivery of the package - on Friday 23 November - William Lennox received a visit from a nearby friend, Mrs Bain, and when the company sat down to tea around 8 p.m. the mysterious shortbread was on the table. First to taste it was Grace McKerrow who commented immediately on its unusual bitterness but this was not sufficient to deter her from returning to the plate a second time. William Lennox and his guest, Mrs Bain, also sampled the shortbread but it wasn't long before all three experienced unpleasant symptoms. Worst affected was Grace who lay down on a couch, exclaiming 'We're poisoned!' By the time that Elizabeth Thorburn was able to summon a doctor, Grace was in dire straits, her symptoms - such as rigidity of the limbs - all tending to confirm her initial suspicions. In the event, there was nothing to be done for poor Grace who died in great discomfort an hour and a quarter after she had first tasted the shortbread. Her two companions, however, were more fortunate and were able to be saved when Doctor Robertson managed to eradicate the poison from their systems; likewise the maid, Elizabeth Thorburn, whose symptoms were comparatively minor, having taken no more than a tiny piece of the offending shortbread. She had, nonetheless, to be helped back to Woodside after accompanying Mrs Bain to her neighbouring home. Naturally highly suspicious, Doctor Robertson took the precaution of sealing the shortbread tin with a view to having its contents subsequently analysed. Then he made contact with the local police.

Within the Cumnock community William Lennox was a highly-respected figure and, when events of 23 November became known, the possibility that he could have even a single enemy was a notion that generated a degree of consternation. His niece, Grace McKerrow, was held in similar high regard and, faced with her suspected murder, the forces of the law wasted no time in swinging into action. The Procurator Fiscal for Ayrshire, Peter Fraser Mackenna, spent several hours conducting inquiries at Cumnock while Police Superintendent Cunningham got down to the business of attempting to identify whoever it might have been who had sent the parcel. According to the postmark, it had been posted in Kilmarnock earlier on the same day that it was delivered to Woodside.

On Monday 26 November a post-mortem examination was carried out on Grace McKerrow's body and strychnine poisoning was confirmed as the cause of death. Her funeral took place the following afternoon. Given the tragic circumstances relating to the case and the wide publicity it had received within the local area, it was hardly surprising when townspeople, friends and relations turned out in large numbers to accompany the funeral procession through Cumnock where many of the shops remained closed and local people kept their blinds drawn as a mark of respect. At the close of her final journey, Grace McKerrow was laid to rest in the churchyard at Auchinleck.

Of course, it had still to be verified that the poisoning had been a deliberate act. In theory at least the possibility couldn't be ruled out at this stage that the shortbread had been sent in good faith, perhaps as an early Christmas present. Two things, however, worked against this: first, the festive season was still some weeks hence; and, secondly, the sender's concealment of his or her identity looked undeniably suspicious. When local bakers failed to recognise the shortbread, or the tin in which it was sent, it was concluded that it was most likely to have been homemade – though this was an assumption that would later require to be revised. None of Lennox's relatives and friends admitted to recognising the handwriting on the accompanying card which was duplicated by police and distributed widely throughout the local community in the form of leaflets. Written in pencil, the lettering was initially suspected of being a 'disguised female hand', so faint and indistinct that those of a more lurid persuasion were disposed to interpret its message as – 'Happy greetings from a fiend!'

With little more to go on than a Kilmarnock postmark, it came as something of a surprise when the dramatic news broke the day after Grace's funeral that police had made an arrest. It soon became known that, during the course of their inquiries at New Cumnock, Captain Hardy McHardy and Superintendent Cunningham of the Ayrshire Constabulary accompanied by Procurator Fiscal Mackenna and a local policeman, had hired a carriage at the Castle Inn and driven the short distance to Ardnith House where they took into custody the householder, Thomas Mathieson Brown, a parish councillor, member of the local school board and former managing director of the Lanemark Coal Company. Brown's connection with Woodside was clear. His wife, Isabella, was a much-loved niece of William Lennox who had, since Grace McKerrow's death, been nursing her uncle back to health. Brown himself was a regular visitor at Woodside and had been present among the mourners at Grace's funeral.

Escorted by Hardy McHardy and two other police officers, the arrested man was taken that afternoon from New Cumnock to Ayr by train. News of his arrest had spread with remarkable rapidity and a crowd of onlookers had gathered to await his arrival at Mauchline Station, eager to catch a glimpse of the alleged poisoner. What they saw as they peered through the carriage windows was a small, bearded man in his 40s, dressed in a tweed suit and a long, waterproof coat who reportedly stared directly ahead of him, pale-faced and sullen. Conditions being showery, he kept his cap pulled low over his brows as he and his accompanying officers made their way across the platform to change trains. At Ayr, he made a declaration before the Sheriff-Substitute, John Campbell Shairp, in which he denied the murder of Grace McKerrow and of endangering three other lives. He was then remanded in custody pending further inquiries. What remained of the shortbread was forwarded to Edinburgh to be analysed by the eminent forensic scientist, Sir Harvey Littlejohn.

Back at New Cumnock, crowds stood in the rain outside newsagents' premises, eager for updated news when the evening papers arrived by train. As it happened, the great majority of those waiting were to be disappointed when no more than half a dozen copies of the late edition came in and it was a similar story the following morning when daily newspapers were sold out by 8 a.m. Thursday was the local market day and naturally the case formed the chief topic of conversation. So deaf was William Lennox, however, that news of the arrest of his niece's husband had to be communicated to him in writing and, hardly surprisingly, his reaction was one of shock.

On the face of it an affluent and upstanding member of the local community, there was, however, another side to Thomas Mathieson Brown which was at best a poorly-kept local secret. Widely viewed as eccentric, he was subject periodically to epileptic seizures for which he had been receiving medical attention for more than twenty years. While most of the attacks lasted no more than a few minutes, their after-effects lingered a good deal longer, perhaps a number of hours or even, in extreme cases, days. Those he came in contact with at such times recognised his tendency to fixate on certain recurring themes - the size and importance of the New Cumnock coalfield was a particular favourite - and to make exaggerated claims of his own importance. No other man, he would boast, was as capable in business as himself. Morbidly suspicious, he experienced a persistent feeling of persecution and would regularly confide in his listeners that he had the power to have various local businessmen jailed, or even sent to the gallows, for their corrupt practices.

As time went on the frequency and severity of his attacks increased and he suffered from excruciating headaches. Even worse, he fell victim to bizarre fantasies during which he claimed, for example, that half of the town of Airdrie was his own personal property or that the directors of the local railway company had all got down on to their knees before him. To the astonishment of his colleagues at the Lanemark colliery, on one occasion he had removed all of his clothing and knelt to pray, apparently under the impression that he was about to go to bed. On other occasions he wrongfooted those around him when he behaved with disarming equanimity, calmly discussing the weather or other local topics. Inevitably,

Brown's illness affected his ability to carry out his professional duties and, unreliable for some time, he finally stepped down as colliery manager in May 1905, a post he had held for some fifteen to twenty years. But even relieved of the pressure of work, his condition continued to worsen as his eighteen year-old house servant at Ardnith, Violet Lambie, was in a position to confirm. She recounted how she had watched while he chased and captured some of his wife's hens and, with no explanation given, incarcerated them in a box. (The compassionate maid released the terrified birds as soon as his back was turned.) In addition she he had known him, for no obvious reason, to uproot and cast aside newly-planted flowers from his garden. Despite never having shown signs of being physically threatening, Brown's eccentric behaviour quickly made him a suspect in relation to Grace McKerrow's death.

On being informed of the poisoning incident by telegram, Brown and his wife, Isabella, had travelled to Woodside the following day by pony and trap. Also visiting at that time was William Lennox's next door neighbour, David Murray, a draper in Cumnock, who subsequently reported having been discomfited by what he viewed as Brown's odd and inappropriate behaviour. Never at any stage did Brown sit down but, constantly pacing the floor, he sounded forth on a variety of topics ranging from the mineral wealth of New Cumnock (again!) to his thoughts on the rearing of children. Never once did he allude to the tragedy that had occurred, his inexplicable omission prompting David Murray to exclaim - 'Mr Brown, death by strychnine is a hell of a death.' This interjection, Murray would later state, appeared to have no effect whatsoever on Brown who went on to suggest that William Lennox would now be likely to move from Woodside Cottage to Ardnith. He went on to add that his wife, Isabella, was the old man's 'favourite niece' and that inevitably she would benefit from the terms of her uncle's will. (Lennox would later deny that Thomas Brown could have had any knowledge whatsoever of arrangements he had made in connection with the will.)

According to Murray, the conversation grew increasingly bizarre when Brown informed him - apparently in all seriousness - that nothing whatsoever could upset him, that he had the ability to endure the pain of pins inserted throughout his entire body, and - topping it all - that he had three bullets lodged inside his body, the result of being shot at by North

American Indians. At this point, David Murray made his excuses and exited. For anyone unfamiliar with Brown's condition, the two men's conversation was likely to have been a distinctly uncomfortable one and Murray was sufficiently disturbed by what he had heard that he approached Doctor Robertson immediately afterwards, going so far as to voice his suspicions that Brown might possibly be the person responsible for sending the deadly parcel.

When chemical analysis of the shortbread was completed in Edinburgh, it confirmed the presence of strychnine, not in the shortbread itself, but rather in the icing with which it had been topped. The records of Glasgow chemists, Frazer and Green of Buchanan Street, revealed that some six months earlier Thomas Brown had purchased a bottle containing an ounce - more than 400 grains - of the deadly poison for the stated purpose of eradicating rats in the vicinity of his home. A single grain was generally reckoned to be sufficient for a deadly dose. Admittedly the chemists' grains were not an exact match for those detected in the shortbread icing, but it was suggested that a grinding process could quite easily have accounted for the discrepancy. The circumstantial case against Brown appeared strong and it became even more compelling when police investigations placed him in Kilmarnock during the forenoon of 19 November, the date on which the parcel was posted.

That morning, it transpired, Brown had set out bright and early, walking from Ardnith House to New Cumnock railway station where he caught a train for Glasgow. Travelling first class, he arrived in the city shortly after 8 a.m. and presented himself at the Conservative Club, of which he was a member. Handing over a shilling to the hall porter, David Laidlaw, he was provided in return with the key of a room containing washing facilities where he proposed taking a bath, apparently having found it too cold to do so at home the night before. Staff at the club would later report that Brown appeared to be in a thoughtful mood but no-one noticed that he was carrying a parcel of any kind. A little over an hour later he arrived at Coopers' grocery store in Howard Street, half a mile or so from the club, where he spent the next half-hour making various purchases and arranging for them to be sent on to St Enoch Station to be placed on the 11.10 a.m. train for New Cumnock. The manager at Cooper's, Henry Dougal, noticed nothing unusual about Brown's behaviour and the two men held a fairly normal conversation during which Brown talked about New Cumnock' low crime-rate which he attributed to the high quality of the town': education system. Dougal was able to confirm that Brown had no purchased any shortbread from Cooper's store.

From there, Brown went on to St Enoch Station where, by prio arrangement, he met up with his wife's sister, Jessie McCutcheon o Creetown, and the two travelled together by the 11 a.m. express to Kilmarnock where Brown said goodbye to his sister-in-law when he alighted in order to change trains. Other than his waterproof, Jessie would later recall that her brother-in-law was carrying nothing larger than a poke of sweeties. The journey from Glasgow had taken exactly 35 minutes which left Brown with just under half an hour to spare before he needed to catch his onward connection for New Cumnock. At Kilmarnock the secretary o the Ayrshire Coal Owners' Association, James Borland, met him walking in a leisurely manner along John Finnie Street, close to where the post office was located. Brown grumbled that he had been travelling since 1 a.m. something Borland understood to be a joke - before taking his leave and making his way back to the railway station where a short time later he lef Kilmarnock on the 11.57 a.m. service to New Cumnock.

Ardnith House, New Cumnock (Dane Love Collection)

So, through the testimony of witnesses, police had successfully placed Thomas Brown in the vicinity of Kilmarnock post office at the time when the poisoned shortbread was believed to have been posted. Well, not quite. A problem soon emerged when it was noted that the parcel's address label had been endorsed by a post office teller whose stamp narrowed the time of posting to between 10.30 a.m. and 11.30 a.m., at least five minutes adrift of Brown's arrival in Kilmarnock. For a time it looked as though the police case had crumbled but more detailed investigation revealed that labels were sometimes stamped in advance of their being used which might possibly have accounted for the time discrepancy. Furthermore, it was not unknown for delays to occur in updating the stamp during busy times - such as was said to have been the case between 11 a.m. and 12 a.m. on the morning in question. Ultimately, though, questions relating to the counter clerk's stamp proved an unproductive line of inquiry which succeeded only in muddying the waters and leaving behind a niggling aftertaste of doubt.

Scarcely more productive was the outcome of continued police investigations into the origin of the poisonous shortbread. Given a sample to examine, George Skinner, the managing director of Skinner and Sons Ltd., concluded that it was very likely to have been produced by his bakery firm in Glasgow, though he was in no doubt whatsoever that the icing had been added at a later point 'by an unskilled hand'. But the company's foreman baker, James Moir, held a different opinion, pointing out that the edging - known as 'nipping' - was in a style unfamiliar to him and also that the poisoned shortbread was nearly a quarter-inch thicker than that which the company was in the habit of producing. He went on to point out that Skinner's invariably sold their shortbread in a tin containing, not one, but two rounds. True, the company's shop in Argyle Street was on the direct route that a pedestrian might take who was travelling between St Enoch Station and the Conservative Club and yet, despite this, the manageress, Euphemia Glass, was unable to summon up any recollection of Thomas Brown's having visited the premises on 19 November. The appropriate till roll indicated that no single purchase had been made that morning which tallied exactly with the cost of a tin of shortbread - two shillings and threepence (11p).

There was another vital area in which agreement proved elusive. When Brown's case came to court in Edinburgh in March 1907, the Crown produced two expert witnesses - an engraver and a lithographer - who were in agreement that the man on trial had been the author both of the parcel's address label and also the greetings card, though in the case of the latter they believed that an attempt had been made to disguise his handwriting. On the other hand, when Dr Birch, a handwriting expert of many years standing at the British Museum in London, was called by the defence, he expressed a different opinion, intimating that he could not be certain that the two documents had been written by one and the same person. After studying samples of Thomas Brown's handwriting, Birch concluded that it was impossible to be certain of his involvement.

When all was said and done, the case against Brown was anything but watertight. No-one had seen him buy any shortbread, and no-one had seen him post it. None of those whom he met during the forenoon of 19 November recollected that he had been in possession of a parcel - not even his sister-in-law, Jessie McCutcheon, who spent half an hour in his company. The suggestion that a man who was known to be 'helpless in the kitchen' had succeeded in icing the shortbread, ostensibly while 'bathing' at the Conservative Club, seemed at best rather dubious. The icing in any case would have taken a considerable length of time to dry without running - at least two hours according to Andrew Rolland, an Edinburgh confectioner whose expert opinion was sought by the court. Although it couldn't be denied that Brown (like innumerable others) had previously acquired quantities of strychnine in order to eradicate vermin, not a trace of the poison was detected when Ardnith House underwent a thorough police search in the aftermath of his arrest. Proof of the involvement of an accomplice might have helped to iron out some of these anomalies but, strangely enough, such a possibility never seems to have occurred to the authorities.

When charged with the murder of Grace McKerrow, Brown had strenuously denied the accusation, a stance that he maintained consistently during the four months that he spent in prison awaiting trial. During his time in court, however, he was given no opportunity to clear his name when - most unusually - prosecutors acting on behalf of the Crown argued that on the grounds of his insanity, Brown should not be allowed to plead. Evidence from Dr Carsewell of Glasgow - a man claimed to be in the habit of examining around 1,000 cases of insanity each year! - suggested that the accused was incapable 'of understanding the gravity and the nature of the charge against him' or of 'giving intelligent instructions for his defence'. Based on his conversations with Brown while on remand, Carsewell expressed his view - in the unfeeling language of the time - that he could reasonably be deemed a 'certifiable lunatic', an opinion supported by Dr Donald Fraser, medical superintendent of Paisley Asylum, who had also visited the prisoner in jail. Just what effect the two doctors' testimony had on Brown or on his poor wife, Bella, listening in the courtroom, we can scarcely imagine. The defence argued conversely that his client was perfectly sane and should 'thole his assize'. Instructed by the Solicitor General, members of the jury were advised that, if convinced by the two experts' medical opinions, then they were then under no obligation to come to any conclusion regarding Brown's innocence or guilt. In the event, by a majority of eleven to four the jury took a mere 45 minutes to return its considered verdict that the accused man, Thomas Mathieson Brown, was indeed insane. Lord Dunedin, in charge, ordered that the prisoner be detained during His Majesty's pleasure and at this point in proceedings Brown was duly led from the court, never again to be a free man.

Placed initially with the Criminal Lunatic Department at Perth, Brown was transferred a short time later, in May 1907, to the Crichton Royal Institution in Dumfries. He was subsequently moved on once again, this time nearer home, to the Ayr District Asylum, the forerunner of today's Ailsa Hospital, where finally he passed away, aged 56, in November 1915. It is hardly likely now that we can ever know for sure whether Thomas Brown was the innocent victim of an unfortunate combination of circumstances or rather a man at the mercy of a disordered mind whose actions in the aftermath of an epileptic attack were quite beyond his control. Whatever the truth of the matter, it may well be the case that, when Thomas Mathieson Brown was dismissed from the court in Edinburgh, any chance of the facts emerging disappeared for ever behind the forbidding walls of institutions for the insane.

28 A Life Well-Lived

Commemorated in fading gold lettering on the walls of Kilmarnock's 'old Academy' are the names of the school's most accomplished scholars over the years, the majority of whom and their modest academic successes are now long forgotten. Listed on one board is the *Dux Mathematicae* for each year - the pupil most adept with numbers - while a second bears the names of those nominated *Dux Litterarum* for their distinction in humanities. As the Victorian era drew to a close, the first *Dux Litterarum* at the dawn of a new century was John Kellie.

John was the son of Robert Muir Kellie, a Kilmarnock bailie - or magistrate - and the proprietor of the 'Boot Warehouse' situated in Waterloo Street, overlooking the Kilmarnock Water. It seems safe to assume that Bailie Kellie and his wife, Janet, would have felt a considerable degree of pride in their son's scholastic achievement - though his dux medal from the Academy turned out to be no more than the first step in what became a distinguished academic career.

After leaving school, John went on to study at both Glasgow and Edinburgh universities, graduating Master of Arts in 1904, followed by Bachelor of Divinity three years later. During the course of his studies in divinity, he came top of his class each year and, amongst various other awards and accomplishments, he won an important scholarship under whose terms he was enabled to continue his studies overseas at the German universities of Marburg, Heidelberg and Berlin. In 1909 he gained the degree of Doctor of Philosophy from the University of Erlangen in Bavaria. Even now his published doctoral thesis - *Alexander Campbell Fraser: A Sketch of His Life and Philosophical Position* - is still to be found on sale.

Given the cosmopolitan nature of his university education, it might come as something of a surprise that John chose to return home to Scotland where, following a short spell as assistant minister at Cathcart, Glasgow, he succeeded Rev. Henry Fairlie in March 1910 and settled down as parish minister of the quiet Ayrshire village of Kirkmichael. His move to the country becomes more understandable, however, when his enthusiasm for the great outdoors is taken into account. No desk-bound scholar, John was known as a keen golfer and lover of the open air. Nor was he the kind of academic, so deeply absorbed in his specialism that he lacked the human touch - as would soon be amply demonstrated under the most challenging of conditions.

By all accounts, Saturday, 25 June 1910 got off to a cheerful start as Kirkmichael Parish Church geared up for its annual children's picnic. A combined group of day-school and Sunday School pupils was to be accompanied on a trip to the seaside by Rev. Dr Kellie who would be assisted in the task of supervision by a number of parents as well as the local schoolmistress, Mrs Baird, and the minister's friend, John Anderson of Mount Florida, Glasgow, who was currently on a weekend visit to Kirkmichael. A jolly crowd of some two hundred souls left the village in horse-drawn carts to make the nine-mile journey to Croy Shore, a popular and picturesque picnic spot approximately midway between Dunure and Culzean Castle. For children for whom an outing was a rare treat, it must surely have been a happy and exciting occasion and it seems likely that Rev. Kellie - in post now a mere four months - would have relished the prospect of cementing bonds with his parishioners in a relaxed and holiday atmosphere.

Following the group's arrival at Croy, things ran smoothly enough for a time at least. But difficulties began at the time when the majority of the picnickers were enjoying refreshments on a flat, grassy area adjacent to the beach, and a small group of eleven peeled away to investigate the hulk of an abandoned yacht which was resting by the water's edge. The boat's presence there on the beach had a fairly strange story attached. Originally the property of William Lee, a bank clerk from Clydebank, it had been brought to Croy Shore from Greenock during the previous autumn, shortly before its owner was convicted of embezzlement and sentenced to a term of imprisonment with hard labour. Following his incarceration, Lee's yacht lay neglected, so the story goes, until a group of his relatives arrived on the scene with a view to reviving its fortunes. Their efforts, however, proved unavailing when it was found to be leaking badly and once again the vessel was abandoned immediately above the high water mark, its sail and oars reportedly taken for safekeeping to a house nearby. And there, it seems, the yacht had remained until a month or so prior to the day of the Kirkmichael picnic when a group of young men, presumably for a lark, had moved it to its current location.

Well aware of its dangerous condition, a local man, Hugh Watson of Balchriston, noticed the holidaymakers examining the dilapidated boat and made a point of approaching them to warn them against any attempt to re-float it. Why, then, the visitors - two adults among them - would have risked taking to the water, contrary to Watson's advice, is hard to fathom. There seems to be no doubt that the hazards were clear to see - a good many of the vessel's planks had become loose with daylight visible between.

Perhaps it all started out as a bit of harmless fun. It is perfectly possible that when they stepped aboard the boat's eleven passengers had no real intention of putting out to sea. The joke, if it was one, quickly turned sour however, when, prompted by the ebbing tide and assisted by a strong off-shore breeze, the old yacht stirred, awakened and headed out to sea. Sensing that events were spiralling out of control, two of the boat's passengers jumped ship in sufficient time to enable them to wade back to safety. Alerted to what was happening, Rev. Kellie is said to have rushed to the water's edge, calling out to the boat's remaining occupants and urging them to follow suit. A twenty year-old postal worker, David Findlay, leapt into the water and attempted to manhandle the boat back towards the shore but

Croy Shore

it quickly became obvious that the task was quite beyond him. When the boat was a hundred yards or so from land, to the horror of all those watching, the bow began to rise into the air and the stern to slip beneath the surface in turn. As she disappeared from sight, witnesses estimated that the yacht's final, fateful voyage had lasted no longer than five minutes.

For Rev. Kellie there was no question of hesitation. Pulling off his outer garments, he struck out from the shore and intercepted David Findlay who was floundering by this stage through exhaustion. Gripping the younger man tightly, the minister succeeded in bringing him safely to dry land. During this time John Fitzsimmons, a Kirkmichael ploughman, had made his way out and, by swimming on his back, had been able to keep three of the beleaguered children above water. Sadly, in the act of passing one child to John Anderson - the minister's friend from Glasgow - Fitzsimmons relaxed his grip on another who was subsequently lost to the waves. Meanwhile Rev. Kellie embarked on a second rescue mission, succeeding this time in saving the life of an eleven year-old boy, Alexander Clowes, whom he managed to escort to safety. The three rescuers were assisted in their efforts by various adult members of the party ashore who took into their care the rescued individuals. It was reported that Mrs Baird, the schoolmistress, had waded as far out into the water as she could. Finally the exhausted rescuers were obliged to admit that they were fit to do no more, though they must surely have been tortured by the heartrending sight of eight-year-old Mary Caldwell as she slipped from view beneath the waves.

Back ashore, artificial respiration was used to revive those fortunate souls who had been pulled from the sea with their lives still hanging by a thread. Details of the tragedy were communicated to the local policeman, Constable Morris at Dunure, as well as to officers at Maybole. Prompted by PC Morris, a number of Dunure fishermen directed their vessels to Croy Bay where they used grappling irons to trawl the seabed in an effort to locate the missing. It did not take long for their efforts to bear fruit but Dr Walker, who had arrived on the scene from Maybole, concluded that there was no prospect of any of the recovered bodies being successfully resuscitated. The waters of Croy Bay had claimed a total of five victims who varied in age from James Caldwell, a ploughman in his thirties, to Mary, his eight year-old daughter, and John Kennedy, aged seven - the son of a local joiner. Also drowned were Thomas Kennedy, fourteen, and a telegraph messenger James Anderson, who was sixteen years old at the time. All of the victims were resident in Kirkmichael and it was suggested at the time that all five were in some way related. In marked contrast to the high spirits of earlier that day, the mood of the picnickers as they made their way home was sombre and subdued.

For Rev. Kellie the prospect of mounting the pulpit the following morning must surely have been a daunting one but he did so courageously and in his sermon faced up to the catastrophe before a congregation whose wounds must have been raw in the extreme. And if, during the weeks and months to come, Dr Kellie agonised over his role in the affair and whether the deaths might have been prevented, it would be entirely natural, but to an impartial observer the part he played in the rescue was that of a hero, a fact acknowledged by the Royal Humane Society sometime later when along with John Anderson and John Fitzsimmons, all three men were honoured with the award of the organisation's Bronze Medal.

Sadly the disaster at Croy Shore wasn't the last incident of its kind in the locality that summer. Less than a month later, on a Sunday School trip to Blairquhan - a popular choice for similar outings - William Hill of High Row, Patna, left the picnic area in the company of a few friends with the intention of visiting the nearby village of Straiton. Somewhere along the way, however, the boys changed their plan and opted instead to take a dip in the Water of Girvan. Within a few moments of entering the water William was heard to cry out for help and he vanished from sight soon after. When word of the calamity reached the Straiton minister, Rev. Wellwood Landale, he broke off from conducting a funeral service in a determined effort to assist in the rescue but, despite a desperate attempt, the nineteen year-old's lifeless body was recovered from the river some twenty minutes later and the disconsolate clergyman trooped back to resume his funereal duties in dripping clothes. It didn't take long for news of William Hill's death to travel the short distance downstream to Kirkmichael where naturally it struck a particular chord. The following morning, Dr Kellie took the opportunity from the pulpit to extend his congregation's heartfelt condolences to their grieving neighbours at Patna.

Time, of course, would have lessened the pain as both communities came to terms with their respective losses - albeit on different scales - and gradually things returned to something approaching normality. In August 1913 - three years after the tragedy at Croy Shore - John Kellie married Margaret Ramsay, daughter of the Provost of Maybole, and sixteen months later the couple were blessed with the birth of a baby daughter, Jean. Inevitably, however, their domestic happiness must have been tempered by dark clouds looming on the horizon. Four months earlier war had erupted in central Europe and since 4 August 1914 Great Britain had officially been at war with Germany.

For a man whose courage was beyond question, it possibly came as no surprise when Rev. John Kellie enlisted in 1915 with the 6th Battalion of the Queen's Own Cameron Highlanders. For the two years that he served as military chaplain in France, the minister was said to have willingly endured every hardship faced by his men as they fought their way through many major conflicts, and such was his bravery and dedication to duty that his name was put forward on no fewer than three occasions for the Military Cross and he was in addition mentioned in despatches. Details are lacking of the end when it came when, true to form, Rev. Kellie had accompanied his troops over the top at Ypres on the last day of July 1917. The irony is palpable that a gifted man, educated in German universities in the scholarly European tradition and who was presumably fluent in the German language, should have lost his life at the hands of his former friends. Who can say what John Kellie might have gone on to achieve, what good he might have been capable of, had he been permitted to live out his allotted human span? Killed in action at the age of 34, his life was well-lived, if all too short.

The minister's death was not by any means the only blow to be sustained by the Kirkmichael community during the years of the Great War. On the village war memorial there are more than twenty names inscribed, including that of Private Robert Caldwell of the Royal Scots Fusiliers whose father, James, and younger sister, Mary, had numbered among the victims of the ill-fated outing to Croy Shore. Robert himself had been snatched from the waves, only to lose his life seven years later in the mighty conflagration of the First World War.

29 Son of the Old Horse

Matthew Anderson made no claims to great art. In the introduction to his *Poems of a Policeman* he freely admitted that he was 'neither Shakespere [*sic*] nor Burns', a sentiment that he would reiterate more than once during the course of his writings. Be that as it may, what is undeniable is that the verses contained within Anderson's seven published collections, appearing at intervals stretching over half a century, as well as his numerous poems which found a place in a variety of newspapers and magazines, found an appreciative audience among readers both locally and beyond.

Matthew Anderson was born on 7 June 1864 at Truffhill Row Waterside, near Dalmellington, the seventh of nine children born to William Anderson, an Irish coalminer, and his wife, Margaret McDonald. Matthew's father was nicknamed locally 'The Old Horse', a reference we might guess to his endurance and strength underground, and Margaret and he had been married in the village of Crosshill in October 1850. Sadly Margaret died in 1872, possibly the result of complications during childbirth, at a time when her youngest living child, Jane, was six years old and Matthew himself only eight. The children didn't have long to wait for a stepmother, however, when their father remarried the following year. A little light is shed on Matthew Anderson's early life by the brief autobiographical sketch which he placed in preface to his second collection of poems, published in 1898.

At the age of five, the poet tells us, he survived a near-tragedy when he fell into the River Doon, an episode which led, he was certain, to three years subsequent ill-health - presumably the reason why he failed to attend school until age eight. As well as belated, his education proved short-lived when he was removed from school a year later to take up farm work at the tender age of nine. In his later poetry Anderson would portray this phase of his life in surprisingly rose-tinted terms as the time when he experienced *'my first, my purest joy / At Muckleholm when herdin' kye / 'Mang broomy knowes sae bonnie, O.'* The Meikle [*sic*] Holm is a broad, riverside meadow, a mile or so north-west of Waterside, where a burn of the same name empties into the Doon.

At the age of twelve Anderson's enjoyment of the fresh air and open spaces of the countryside came to an abrupt end when he followed his father underground. The subsequent six years which he spent as a coal-miner instilled in him an empathy and respect for his fellow-colliers which he would never forget and which later found expression in a number of his poems. At the age of eighteen, Anderson left Scotland for South Wales where he soon enlisted as a gunner in the Royal Marine Artillery, a position that he occupied for the following three years. Invalided out as a result of an accident, he returned to Ayrshire in 1887 - the year of Queen Victoria's Golden Jubilee - where he joined the County Constabulary as a new recruit, based initially at Muirkirk. Subsequently posted to various towns and villages throughout Ayrshire, Matthew Anderson would serve the local public for the next 36 years as a trusted and efficient police officer.

And busy times they must surely have been. In March 1890 while stationed at Muirkirk, Constable Anderson, aged 25, was married to Nancy Blyth, a local woman some three years his junior. In the years that followed the couple went on to produce no fewer than thirteen children, born variously in Stevenston, Beith, Coylton, Dunlop and Symington, according to where their father happened to be stationed at the time. In addition to supporting Nancy in bringing up their large family, Anderson is said to have consistently carried out his professional duties in a exemplary manner as well as playing an active part in the campaign for improved police pay and conditions - a possible reason, it has been suggested, why he was destined to remain throughout his career on the bottom rung of the promotion ladder.

All the more remarkable, then, that he found time to craft his thoughts and feelings in verse. At a time when his baby son, William, was less than a year old, Anderson's first collection, *Poems and Songs*, appeared in 1891, followed seven years later by *Poems of a Policeman*. A third collection titled simply *Poems* was published in 1912 with a nine-year gap before *A Poetical Souvenir* followed on in 1921. *The Poetical Works of Matthew Anderson* came out in 1928, followed a decade later by *A Wee Bouquet frae Bonnie Scotland*. The poet's final collection, *John and Jean*, a blend of poetry and 'hamely cracks', was published in 1945, by which time Anderson had passed his eightieth birthday. And if all that wasn't enough, over the years he also made regular contributions to *The Kilmarnock Standard, Ayrshire Post* and

Ardrossan and Saltcoats Herald, while his work gained national exposure in the popular *Sunday Post* and in the *Police Review*, a magazine for police officers across Scotland.

For all his prolific output, few if any, I suspect, would place Matthew Anderson among the literary greats. He reaches too readily for the conventional - some might say, stilted - poetic phrase: a Dalmellington hill burn is 'a diamond-sparkled rill', while Symington, we are assured, is blessed with 'fairy bowers.' Similarly, there's no getting away from a narrow parochialism which surfaces from time to time in his work. In a short tribute to the villages of Symington and Craigie, Anderson declares that rivers such as the Thames, Rhine and Seine pale in comparison with 'the wee Pow Burn' which, in the poet's stated estimation, 'fair beats them a'.' Most likely the point he was making was - at least partly - tongue-in-cheek.

Matthew Anderson in 1898
(Donald L. Reid Collection)

For all his limitations as a poet, there is no denying, however, that Anderson was skilled in identifying and capturing the poignant or otherwise memorable moment. 'The Old Vagrant' is a sensitive response to the death of an elderly tramp, his identity never ascertained, who had been killed in a road accident at the foot of Rosemount Brae, near Monkton, in March 1912 - surely a fate uncommon enough in the early days of motoring. 'The Real Scots Girls', by contrast, was prompted by a heart-warming scene.

witnessed by Anderson during wartime, when a group of local girls assembled to cheer and wave to delighted American soldiers aboard a troop train that had made a brief halt at Hurlford railway station. In his best work, Anderson rejects artificial, stylised language and lets his own voice speak out, as in the authentic Scots of 'Jamie Todd - A True Tale'; or the simple unaffected English of 'My Son - Charles Blyth '- a moving poem to mark the death of Anderson's son in which the author's suffering is no less palpable for being understated.

Anderson's style was not one to dazzle. He spoke principally to a home-grown audience, many living in the towns and villages in which he served and where he himself was part of the community. For hard-working folk in the late nineteenth and early twentieth centuries, many of whose education had been curtailed in their early teens and who faced daily hardship in providing for themselves and their families, the homely sentiments and resolute faith of Anderson's verses probably struck a reassuring chord. For his part, if the evidence of his poems is anything to go by, Matthew Anderson's warmth and human sympathy remained entirely untarnished by his long years of service with Ayrshire County Constabulary.

30 Flight of No Return

On Tuesday 31 July 1928 George Dent was strolling along the foreshore at Flint, North Wales, when he happened to pick up a bottle which had been washed up by the tide. He noticed a scrap of paper inside and, finding the bottle tightly corked, he smashed it against a rock. Unsullied by its time at sea, the message inside was legible and clear: 'Goodbye all. Elsie Mackay and Captain Hinchcliffe [*sic*]. Down in fog and storm.' Thus, with Dent's chance discovery, the mystery surrounding the fate of two missing aviators that had preoccupied the nation and the media for the preceding three months appeared finally to have been cleared up.

Alas, no. The solution to the mystery that Dent's bottle seemed to offer quickly unravelled when it became clear that the handwriting failed to match either of the lost pilots and, in any case, the captain's surname had been misspelt by the addition of a superfluous 'c'. As a hoax, the bottle was neither sophisticated nor convincing, but before the year was out a more persuasive relic of the aviators' abortive mission would be released by the waves of the North Atlantic.

Of course, it was inevitable that the disappearance in dramatic circumstances of one of Britain's wealthiest women would generate enormous public interest. Born in the Indian hill-station of Simla, the Honourable Elsie Mackay was the third (allegedly favourite) daughter of shipping magnate and P&O chairman, Lord Inchcape. A modern and liberated young woman, Elsie was still in her teens when she succeeded in establishing herself as an actress in London's West End, and by age twenty she held the position of the theatre district's youngest leading lady for the part she played in the popular stage-play, *Grumpy*. On the occasion of her 21st birthday, she was reputed to have received a cool £1,000,000 from her doting father, an indescribable fortune at the time.

When war broke out in 1914, however, another facet of Elsie's personality came to the fore as she put her theatre career on hold to take up nursing in a London hospital which had been established by her mother. In the face of fierce opposition from her father, she eloped during 1917 with one of her patients, a South African soldier of the Wiltshire Regiment named Dennis Wyndham, and the couple were duly married in Glasgow. When Elsie's acting career resumed after the war - in film now, rather than theatre - her roles were credited under her new stage-name of Poppy Wyndham.

During 1919 and 1920 Elsie appeared in a total of eight film productions but, despite her success on the silver screen, major changes were afoot. By 1922 she had left the movie world behind, annulled her marriage to Wyndham and reverted once again to her maiden name. Reconciled with her father, she took up employment with P&O as an interior designer, working on the state rooms and opulent apartments on the company's luxury liners. On the family's Glenapp estate, just south of Ballantrae, 'Miss Elsie', as she was known, was a popular figure, well respected for her acts of kindness such as visiting the sick and elderly and organising activities for local children. It would be a mistake, however, to imagine that Elsie had settled down to a life of level-headed industry.

Whether galloping on horseback over the fields at Glenapp or alternatively behind the wheel of her personal Rolls Royce, Elsie was known for her enjoyment of high speed but her thrill-seeking soon climbed literally to new heights. In 1923 she graduated from the De Havilland Flying School, thereby obtaining her pilot's licence, and, notwithstanding at least one unnerving experience in the air, went on to acquire her own plane which soon became a familiar sight in the skies above Glenapp Castle. She made no secret of her ambition to become the first woman to fly the Atlantic - the venture, if successful, a double-first as no crossing had yet been made from east to west against the force of the prevailing winds. Once again Lord Inchcape's disapproval did nothing to deter his wilful daughter and, unbeknown to her father, Elsie established contact with an eminent pilot of the day, Captain Walter George Raymond Hinchliffe, in order to talk over her plans during lunch at the Ritz Hotel.

On the face of it Hinchliffe made an obvious choice of partner. Now in his early thirties, he was a man with an illustrious First World War record, having shot down several enemy aircraft during perilous dog-fights, and in recognition of his bravery had been awarded the Distinguished Flying Cross. On returning to civilian life, his wartime injuries - including the loss of an eye - did not prevent Hinchliffe from becoming a successful commercial pilot and in 1922 he was appointed Chief Pilot for the Dutch airline, KLM. For all that, however, it appears that Walter Hinchliffe was something of a dark horse.

Facing a charge of theft back in 1915, he had no option but to resign his army commission and, though never convicted, a reputation for dishonesty had dogged his subsequent service with the Royal Naval Air Service and later the Royal Air Force. Though his prowess in aerial combat was beyond question, Hinchliffe's own account of the incident which led to the loss of his left eye was rather more colourful than the official version of events. While he claimed that the injury had come about as the result of a dangerous solo-mission under cover of darkness during which he fell victim to Manfred von Richthofen, the infamous Red Baron, official accounts indicated rather that his plane had merely flipped over in an unfortunate accident during take-off. Hinchliffe's past may have had one or two murky corners, but by the time that he and Elsie met for lunch at the Ritz the present was generating its own share of difficulties.

Still working as a professional pilot, Hinchliffe was acutely conscious of his deteriorating eyesight and, in a climate of tightening regulation, was fearful for the loss of his commercial licence. With a dependant wife and baby daughter, and a second child on the way, he found himself perennially short of cash in spite of his current salary from Imperial Airways, a forerunner of British Airways. How much Elsie knew of Hinchliffe's chequered past is impossible to say but, in any case, there is no evidence that it had any bearing on events that followed.

By the time he rose after lunch at the Ritz, Hinchliffe's financial circumstances had eased considerably. In return for a salary of £80 per month, he had agreed to act as co-pilot during Elsie's forthcoming transatlantic bid and had been given responsibility for preparing a suitable aircraft beforehand. It had been further agreed that any prize money accruing from a successful crossing would be due to him alone. Finally, Elsie had undertaken to insure Hinchliffe's life to the tune of £10,000 to provide for his family in the event of his non-return.

As a figure very much in the public gaze, it was crucial for Elsie to shield her scheme from the prying eyes of the media, no less her own father. Hinchliffe, therefore, took the lead in organising the import of a dual-controlled monoplane, a Stinson Detroiter, which was duly shipped in parts from the USA to be reassembled on arrival in Britain. In preparation for its epic flight to come, the black-bodied, gold-winged *Endeavour* proceeded to undergo a series of tests and modifications, including the addition of an extra fuel tank which would substantially increase capacity and thereby provide a valuable extension to its normal range. For double assurance, full petrol cans would also be placed on board. Fearful of rival expeditions that might be waiting in the wings, Hinchliffe put it about that the Detroiter would take off from the airfield at RAF Cranwell, Lincolnshire, during March 1928, bound for Karachi in present-day Pakistan in a bid to create a new world record for non-stop flight, and that he would be accompanied on the trip by his co-pilot, Captain Gordon Sinclair. Meanwhile Elsie and a friend, known to us only as Miss Ries, had ensconced themselves as guests in the nearby George Hotel at Leadenham where Elsie made efforts to remain incognito.

The press, however, were not to be so easily duped. As Hinchliffe made a series of test flights, word got out that his co-pilot was not in fact Captain Sinclair, as had been intimated, but was instead the renowned heiress and former film-star, Poppy Wyndham, thus forcing Elsie into making a public denial and threatening the press with legal action. Conveniently remote from the scene of the action, Lord Inchcape, on holiday in Egypt, was one man whom her denial did not convince and he promptly sent his daughter what we must assume was a strongly-worded cable from Cairo as well as taking the additional precaution of dispatching her brother to Lincolnshire post-haste. But, as it turned out, all to no avail.

The weather forecast for Tuesday 13 March appeared favourable, signalling a possible break in the icy conditions that had recently held Lincolnshire in their grip. At the George Hotel, Elsie organised a wake-up call for 4 a.m., having previously ordered from the kitchen a supply of sandwiches and various flasks of soup, tea and coffee, sufficient to sustain two people over several days. Checking out of the hotel, she travelled in full flying gear to the town of Grantham where, by prior arrangement with a local priest, she took holy communion alone in the dimly-lit church. Having received the priest, Father Arenzen's, blessing, she departed Grantham for RAF Cranwell, some fifteen miles away, where she arrived shortly after 8 a.m. and promptly ensured that her photograph was taken alongside Walter Hinchliffe - proof, should such be necessary, that she had not joined the flight belatedly at St John's, Newfoundland, the first intended North American landfall before the *Endeavour* continued to New York and its ultimate destination at Philadelphia. Finally, after Elsie had exchanged places with Captain Sinclair as arranged, the Detroiter set off down the snow-covered runway, picking up speed as it went and rising into the air shortly after 8.30 a.m. As things turned out, neither of its two occupants would ever be seen again.

Around midday the *Endeavour* was seen, fighting a headwind in snow-laden skies above County Waterford on Ireland's southern coast, and then again, sometime later, the plane was spotted by a lighthouse keeper at Mizen Head on the country's extreme south-western tip. Contrary to the forecast, Atlantic weather conditions had deteriorated fairly seriously and the aircraft's final sighting was recorded by the crew of a French steamer, the SS *Josiah Macy*, some 170 miles west of the Irish coast, as, apparently undeterred by stormy weather, she gallantly held her course toward the west. Thereafter - nothing. The reputed crowd of 5,000 that gathered at Mitchell Fields, Long Island, to witness the making of history, awaited the arrival of the *Endeavour* in vain. In a forlorn but ultimately futile gesture the airfield lights were kept burning all night.

The loss of two such illustrious aviators made headline news on both sides of the Atlantic and, in the weeks and months that followed, a succession of rumours and theories circulated in the absence of hard facts. Various sightings were reported, mostly along the eastern seaboard of Canada and the USA, all ultimately proving false. In the aftermath of his daughter's disappearance, Elsie's grieving father, Lord Inchcape, devoted himself to dealing with her considerable estate, negotiating with the then Chancellor of the Exchequer, Winston Churchill, for a sum of £500,000 to be used for the reduction of Britain's national debt. In marked contrast to his wealthy employer, Walter Hinchliffe's estate totalled an altogether more modest £32. It emerged that payment of his monthly wage had fallen into arrears and, on top of that, that no valid life insurance had been taken out on his behalf as arranged - the result, ironically, of Elsie's cheque having bounced. When these omissions came to light, Lord Inchcape was prompted by a press campaign into making a gratuitous payment of £10,000 to Hinchliffe's Dutch-born widow, Emilie, in Purley, south London.

One of the most bizarre spin-offs arising from the loss of the *Endeavour* involved the Sherlock Holmes novelist and committed spiritualist, Sir Arthur Conan Doyle. A month or so after the plane's disappearance, Emilie Hinchliffe was contacted by the famous author, as a result of which she agreed to attend various séances where, through the offices of an eminent clairvoyant, Eileen Garrett, she received what purported to be messages from her late husband. Based on the information thus obtained, in 1930 Hinchliffe's widow went on to publish a book, *The Return of Captain W. G. R. Hinchliffe*, in which she relayed her late husband's psychic communications and presented for the reading public his account of the afterlife. Eventually remarried (and given away, as it happened, by a certain Captain Gordon Sinclair), Emilie and her new husband emigrated overseas, disappearing out of the limelight and into the obscurity of Australia. Meanwhile, back in Lincolnshire, stories grew up of a tall, ghostly figure, dressed in a flying-suit and sporting a left eye-patch, which was to be seen on certain moonlit nights, striding purposefully across the yard of the George Hotel.

In the aftermath of the *Endeavour's* disappearance, one thing at least became clear. Hinchliffe's insistence on the need for urgency was shown to have been well founded for, within just a few short weeks, the crew of a German Junkers W33, the Bremen, succeeded where the Endeavour had failed by flying west from Baldonnel Airfield, Dublin, to make landfall on Greenly Island, off the Quebec coast - a place so isolated that a Canadian nurse, Gretta May Ferris, had to travel fifteen miles by dogsled to give the three exhausted aviators a medical once-over. More than 1,000 miles adrift of its destination at New York, the Bremen had nonetheless undeniably completed the first successful east-west transatlantic crossing.

Two months later, in June 1928, an amateur American pilot, Amelia Earhart, became the first woman to cross the Atlantic by air, travelling in this instance as a passenger from Trepassey Harbour, Newfoundland, to Burry Port in South Wales. Four years later, the pioneering aviatrix topped the achievement by piloting her own aircraft during a solo Atlantic crossing, a feat which earned her the USA's first ever Distinguished Flying Cross to be awarded to a woman. Sadly Earhart's success was not to last. In 1937, during a tricky leg of an ambitious attempt to span the globe, her Lockheed Electra vanished without trace, somewhere close, it was thought, to the

Pacific international dateline. Thus, lost in the vastness of the ocean, the renowned American flier echoed the fate of her predecessor, Elsie Mackay, some nine years earlier.

In December 1928, nine months after the loss of the *Endeavour*, a tangle of aircraft landing-gear was discovered, washed ashore on the rugged coastline of the Rosguill Peninsula of County Donegal, north-west Ireland. By sheer good fortune a tyre which formed part of the wreckage still had a legible serial number attached - 76168547 - which was subsequently identified by the Goodrich Rubber Company of Akron, Ohio, as being that of a tyre supplied to the Stinson Aircraft Company of Detroit. The aircraft manufacturer was able to confirm in turn that this particular tyre had been used to equip a monoplane which the company had despatched to England in January of that year - the very machine, in fact, which Walter Hinchliffe and Elsie Mackay had used on their ill-starred venture. At long last matters appeared to be settled. Following the sea's revelations at Rosguill, there could have been few who retained any doubts concerning the fate of the lost aviators.

Glenapp Church

For the location of a memorial to his precious Elsie, Lord Inchcape turned to the quiet seclusion of his Scottish country estate. Tucked away in the unspoiled vale of Glen App, there was a tiny country church, a haven of peace, watched over, both front and rear, by steep, heathery hills. It was here that Lord Inchcape commissioned Dr Douglas Strachan to design in his daughter's memory a three-light stained glass window, to be installed on the church's east gable. The middle light of Strachan's resulting creation is a portrayal of Jesus Christ, risen and crowned in glory, while in the right-hand light a likeness of Elsie Mackay is to be seen, pointing upwards to the place above the clouds, perhaps, where her destiny awaited. Lord Inchcape arranged in addition for rhododendrons to be planted on a hillside opposite the church, positioned so as to spell out the letters E-L-S-I-E. The best part of a century on, the shrubs have now sprawled and multiplied and, though the banking is still flushed with purple in season, Elsie's name is no longer discernible.

Her father, it was said, never truly recovered from the shock of his tragic loss. Precisely at the time when Amelia Earhart was celebrating her own solo transatlantic flight in London, the elderly lord passed away aboard his yacht at Monaco, a little more than four years after his daughter's hopes and dreams disappeared beneath the merciless North Atlantic waves. Lord Inchcape's remains - and those in due course of Elsie's mother, Jean, who survived her husband by a further five years - were laid to rest within the tranquil precincts of Glenapp Church, a few short steps from the monument he had erected to the memory of a brave, beautiful, wayward and theatrical daughter.

31 Bridging the Gulf

Of the walking-sticks in my hallstand, there is one in particular which is rather precious to me whose history, as a boy, I heard recounted many times. The stick dates back to the 1930s - the time when my father first arrived in Kilmarnock, a young man fresh from the country and newly recruited to the burgh police force. One evening a complaint came in - by telephone, I am guessing - to the effect that travelling people - at the time, *tinkers* - had been spotted, setting up camp on the banks of the River Irvine, just within the burgh boundary. The owner of the land in question, Captain Cuninghame of Caprington Castle, insisted that they be removed forthwith.

Quite possibly my father was the most junior officer on duty. Dispatched to deal with the complaint, he made his way down to the riverbank, a mile or so away, where a short distance from Bridge Lodge he had no difficulty in spotting the travellers' wagon, parked on a patch of vacant ground with a tethered horse grazing alongside. A thread of smoke could be seen, rising from a low campfire where a young man on his hunkers was tending a blackened pot which had been suspended over the flames. A girl - in her late teens perhaps - was seated on the doorstep of the caravan, a shawl drawn around her shoulders against the evening chill. There appeared to be no-one else around. A scene of such harmony and quiet domesticity served only to intensify my father's unease about the task that now faced him.

He was received politely. When he explained the reason for his visit, however, the young man's face fell. Some hours earlier, he explained, his wife had given birth to the couple's first child, a baby daughter, and he was concerned that she had not yet recovered sufficient strength to pack up now and move on in darkness. Glancing across, my father noticed for the first time a tiny, sleeping baby, cradled within her mother's shawl. He faced a quandary. It was clear that the travellers were doing no harm and to force their eviction at such a delicate time seemed inhumane. Yet there was no question that they had settled for the night on what was indisputably private land, and back in the 1930s having 'Captain' in front of your name and

'Castle' as part of your address carried considerable weight - more perhaps than it might today. My father by contrast was young and a very junior police officer. He couldn't afford to disregard instructions.

Having grown up in an isolated, rural backwater, my father felt an affinity with country people. Raised by a struggling war widow, he was well aware of how it felt to occupy a lowly rung on the social ladder. The solution that he came up with involved a compromise of sorts. If the travellers undertook to move on before first light, he told them, he would be prepared to report back to the landowner that his concerns had been dealt with and the problem satisfactorily resolved. It was a risk, he was aware, but he could think of no better solution. Hearing his proposal, the young couple eagerly assented and, relieved at what looked like a reasonable outcome, my father made to leave but before he could do so the young man insisted on

Walking Stick

pressing upon him the gift of a walking-stick. Whether he had made it himself, I don't remember my father saying. Perhaps he never knew.

No workaday, functional item, the stick is something more akin to an *objet d'art*, honed and crafted to showcase the prodigious skill of the woodworker. Topped with a spherical knob, a little bigger than a golf ball perhaps, the shank tapers elegantly from head to toe, the upper third or so carved so as to resemble a neatly-plaited cord. The surface of the wood - possibly beech - has a rich, glossy sheen but, remarkably, when the stick is rotated through 180° its reverse side is revealed as much darker in colour - a deep, chocolaty brown. How the walking-stick's split-personality was achieved I have never been able to tell, but even today its dual-colouring shows no sign of fading.

The travellers kept their word. Sunrise found them gone, their campsite deserted and the only indication of their passing a few faint wheel ruts where the ground was softest and the scant remains of a carefully-smoored campfire. In his subsequent thirty years' service with Kilmarnock Burgh, my father was never again to cross paths with the travelling couple or their child.

Eighty-odd years have come and gone. My father's generation has passed away now and, if the daughter of the travelling couple is still to the fore, then even she must be well advanced into old age. The walking-stick alone remains unchanged, a precious memento of my father with a curious tale attached. But it is more than that. In its simple elegance, the walking-stick is an eloquent reminder that for the gulf of unfamiliarity and suspicion to be bridged all it need take is for goodwill and common humanity to prevail.

Index